Laughter is the Best Therapy

Compiled and Edited by Dr. Surendra Singh Singhvi

Sushila S. Singhvi and Sunit K. Jain

Design, Illustrations, and printing by:

Prium Graphics

Wellesley, MA

Email: priumgraphics@comcast.net

www.priumgraphics.com

LAUGHTER IS THE BEST THERAPY

Dedicated in memory of the following relatives and friends, all of whom have contributed jokes:
Mr. C.R. Singhvi, my brother, who died at the age of 70 in 2002.

Dr. Gyan Chandra, a friend, professor of accounting at Miami University, Oxford, Ohio, who died at the age of 64 in 2005.

Mr. Chandra Prakash Khurana, my friend's father-in-law, who died at the age of 84 in 1999.

Mr. Ike Beediwala, a friend and singer, who died at the age of 66 in 1999.

This book is also dedicated to my grandchildren (my monkeys):
Miss Sarina Jain
Master Sahil Jain
Miss Diya Singhvi
Miss Sanjana Jain
Master Vayd Singhvi

My grandchildren were my cheerleaders during my recovery. Whenever they came to see me at the hospital, Kettering Medical Center, Miami Valley Hospital and Drake Medical Center, they cheered me up and made other patients laugh.

JOKES ORGANIZED BY THE TOPIC/SUBJECT

ACKNOWLEDGEMENT OF THE INDIVIDUALS

I would like to thank the following individuals who have contributed three or more jokes to inspire me to make this project successful:

Gyan & Sadhna Agarwal (Chicago)
Vinod Anand (St. Louis)
Ravi & Manju Bafana (Dayton)
Jai Chand & Santosh Baid (Ajmer, India)
Rahul & Lavina Baldota (Mumbai, India)
Dilip & Subhagini Ballal (Dayton)
Nanda & Hema Balwally (Dayton)
Ike & Mumtaj Beediwala (Dayton)
Narpat & Chandra Bhandari (San Jose)
Pradeep & Sushma Bhanot (Chicago)
Anant & Shami Bhati (Cincinnati)
Kapoor & Sarita Choudhary (Jodhpur, India)
Bal & Padma Dubey (Detroit)
Gautam & Chandrakala Galada (Madras, India)
Rakesh & Manju Gupta (Dayton)
Anish Jain (New York)
Karamchand & Sunita Jain (Bangalore, India)
Ramesh & Kanta Jain (New York)
Sunit & Seema Jain (Chicago)
Krishan & Vicky Joshi (Dayton)
Sheela Karia (London)
Robert & Paula Lambrix (Baltimore, Maryland)
Mahesh & Shanti Mathur (Corning, New York)
Harvey & Suman Mediratta (Dayton)
Paul & Indra Mediratta (Dayton)
Arun & Geeta Meehan (Cincinnati)
Kailash & Saroj Mehta (Dayton)
Rakesh & Rachita Mehta (Mumbai, India)
Navneet & Anamika Patni (Bangalore, India)
Surendra & Anita Saini (Dayton)
Ashok & Nirmala Sancheti (New York)
Surendra Sharma (Hariyana, India)
Virendra & Rekha Sharma (Salisbury, Maryland)
Jagdish & Madhu Sheth (Atlanta)
Srinivas & Padma Shukla (Pune, India)
Jagjit & Chitra Singh (Mumbai, India)
Rajendra & Rita Singhvi (Pune, India)
Sandeep & Shraddha Singhvi (Dayton)
Virendra & Reena Singhvi (New Jersey)
Mahendra & Sangeeta Vora (Cincinnati)
Ritu and Rajeev Singhvi (Bombay)
Mahendra & Usha Mahajan (Dayton)

PREFACE

I, Surendra Singhvi suffered a stroke in May 2002 and went through many therapies: 1.) Physical Therapy (P.T.) i.e., Pain and Torture; 2.) Occupational Therapy; 3.) Speech Therapy; 4.) Recreational Therapy; 5.) Hydro Therapy; 6.) Laughter Therapy; and 7.) Grandkids Therapy.

My speech therapist encouraged me to tell her jokes every day to make her laugh, which forced me to dig deep into my memory, organize my thoughts and communicate in a way so that she did not get offended and, at the same time, translate in a cultural context. Each joke made her laugh, and in reaction, I laughed, which helped me come out of depression.

Researchers at a famous U.S. university have found that "laughing is not only an excellent way to lift your mood, but it's actually a mini-workout for the body. Even mild laughter is good exercise, a kind of stationary jogging. When you laugh, your chest, thorax and abdominal muscles, as well as your diaphragm, heart, lungs, and possibly your liver, contract. A belly laugh can make your systolic blood pressure rise and can double your pulse rate. Laughing is said to pump extra adrenaline into your bloodstream, and it may stimulate a rush of endorphins — the body's natural painkillers — to the brain. After a good laugh, all systems return to normal or even a little below normal, resulting in less stress, less hypertension and fewer muscle tension headaches, as well as an all-around good feeling not only for you but for those around you" (published in a company newsletter for employees of Armco Steel Corporation in the mid-1900s).

So I decided to write a book entitled "Laughter is the Best Therapy" (no pain or medicine required). These jokes are modified for all audiences.

Most of these jokes I collected from social parties. I would tell a joke, and others would share a joke. Some jokes also appeared over the years in Reader's Digest (Laughter is the Best Medicine section) and from Rotarian magazine, a monthly publication of Rotary International. We have edited these jokes for the purpose of consistency and style.

There are no "dirty" jokes. They are dirty only to the extent a reader's mind is dirty. There are many jokes that came to me from friends and the Internet. Once a young girl came to me and said, "Uncle, do you want to hear a dirty joke?" I was shocked at this but I replied, "Yes." She said, "A man fell down in the mud." Then she told me a clean joke. "The man, who fell down, took a shower."

Collecting jokes has been my hobby since 1957 when I graduated from high school. Since I am not a singer or dancer, I enjoy telling jokes and making people laugh. One good friend enjoys my jokes so much that one day while listening and laughing at my joke, he fell down from his chair.

One friend of mine laughed three times for every joke I told. The first time he laughed because everyone else was laughing. The second time he laughed because he finally understood the joke. The third time he laughed because he realized how stupid he was to laugh the first time when he didn't understand the joke.

You will enjoy this book only if you read it with the intent that you want to laugh and relax your mind and body. Throughout the world, there are many laughter clubs where people get together and laugh without any inhibition and/or worrying about other people's reactions.

I have used my middle name, Singh (lion), as the person who becomes a laughing stock. The purpose of this book is not to offend anyone but if there is any resemblance to any person or group, it is a mere coincidence and I assume no liability if someone feels offended.

I have separately acknowledged the individuals who have contributed three or more jokes, and I am very thankful to them. I am very grateful to my wife, Sushila Singhvi, who acted as my censor board at parties and encouraged me to tell jokes in different situations: wedding receptions, parties and many occasions when I was a master of ceremony for different events. I am very appreciative of my son-in-law and my co-editor of this book, Sunit Jain, for his technical and moral support and encouragement in completing this project and for spending countless hours helping me. I am equally appreciative of my caring and loving daughter, Seema Jain, for helping me to complete the book and regularly making suggestions to improve the quality and contents of the book. I am also thankful to Dr. Manoj Jain of Memphis, TN, who provided guidance on the publishing process, and to Ms. Preeti Jain of Boston, MA, for helping us complete the design and publishing process.

I have told jokes in my business classes and management seminars to break the ice and put students at ease to make a dry subject like accounting, finance or statistics more lively and interesting.

After you have read the book, if you have any suggestions or additional jokes, please feel free to forward them to the below email address:

Surendra Singhvi
ssinghvi@yahoo.com

BIBLIOTHERAPY

By Kevin Helliker, Wall Street Journal, July 31, 2007

Below is a summary of a recent Wall Street Journal article in the Health section by Kevin Helliker about the concept of bibliotherapy.

A growing number of therapists are recommending something for depression and anxiety patients. The treatment is called bibliotherapy and it is getting support from recent research showing that some self-help books can significantly improve mental health.

The national health system in Britain this year is prescribing self-help books for thousands of patients seeking medical attention for depression. Revenue this year in the U.S. for these kinds of books will exceed $600 million, says Simba Information, a market research firm in Stamford, Connecticut.

Mental health professionals in the UK, U.S. and elsewhere are determined to distinguish the most proven self-help books. The aim is to recommend books that have been shown to be successful in published trials conducted by reputable, independent researchers, such as: "Feeling Good: The New Mood Therapy," by David Burns; "Mind Over Mood," by Dennis Greenberger and Christine A. Padesky; and "Control Your Depression," by Peter Lesinsohn.

Trials are conducted by notable researchers comparing a patient's depression symptoms before and after the treatment. Numerous clinical trials have shown that "Feeling Good" and "Mood Therapy" reduced depression symptoms in a large number of patients.

In the UK, where the wait for traditional treatment can stretch six months or more, the National Health System has embraced bibliotherapy as the first line of treatment for non-emergency cases.

In the U.S. no official list of bibliotherapy exists, but a lot of mental health professionals have contributed to self-help manuals that Dr. Norcross, co-author himself of a self-help book, "Changing For Good," has been updating since 2000. "The Authoritative Guide To Self-Help Resources in Mental Health," available from many bookstores and libraries, ranks more than 1,000 self-help books according to their effectiveness, based on clinical trials and on the clinical experience of professionals.

Bibliotherapy works best on patients with mild to moderate symptoms and is not regarded as a replacement for traditional treatment. A 2004 article in the Journal of Clinical Psychology reviewed the published research on bibliotherapy and concluded that it could successfully treat depression, mild alcohol abuse and anxiety disorders, but was less effective with smoking addiction and severe alcohol abuse.

Most research suggests that bibliotherapy is most effective when used in conjunction with conventional therapy or while waiting for conventional therapy to begin.

SMILING IMPROVES OVERALL HEALTH
"Hello, Everybody," Joe Kita, Reader's Digest (December, 2008), p. 108-111

It has been clinically proven that smiling lowers blood pressure, boosts immunity, and releases internal painkillers (endorphins), each of which lowers stress, boosts happiness and improves health.

Canadian research has found that call center employees who played a five minute smile hunting game before work in which they repeatedly picked the smiling face from a photo assortment had 17% less of the stress hormone cortisol after their shift.

JOKES, THE WORLD'S BEST MEDICINE TO REDUCE STRESS
By Boyd Troublerr, MD

What were the last jokes that made you roll around on the floor because you were laughing so hard? Did it involve a doctor, a priest and a lawyer? Was it on a TV show, or part of a stand-up comedy routine, or part of a recent lecture? In any event, do you remember how it made you feel?

More likely than not you can remember the last time, and if you took a minute, you could probably tell me the joke, and it probably made your day. It either gave you relief from the stress of taking yourself or what you were doing so seriously, or it took your mind off of something that was causing you grief, or it just livened up an otherwise boring talk. Probably and, most importantly, it allowed you to laugh, which as we all know is "the world's best medicine."

But have you ever thought more about why this was so? Is there actually something about jokes and the resulting laughter that can change our health in a beneficial way? What is it about laughter that we love so much? Why are comedies so popular? Why is there such a thing as comic relief and why is it so effective — even in the most serious of plays or dramas? Well, you shouldn't be surprised to find out that scientists have been studying it, but you may be surprised to find out that there is actually something about laughter that affects us more profoundly than we think.

Basically there is good evidence now that laughter produced by jokes can change the chemical milieu that courses through our body on a second to second basis, and in a profound degree. Laughter releases natural endorphins that act on the same receptors as morphine that produce the feelings of relaxation and heightened mood. Levels of dopamine, serotonin, and norepinephrine are altered, as well as those that produce an endogenous anti-depressant effect.

Researchers then wondered about what action in particular was producing these changes — was it smiling, or the physical changes that take place in rate of breathing, in blood pressure, increased heart rate, etc.? What they found was (as usual) that it most likely was a combination of physical changes in the body that occur with laughter. Each one of these changes by itself produced small effects, but together were synergistic in producing these stress-relieving and mood-improving results. It was interesting to note that spontaneous laughter was better than self-produced laughs, but not by as large a difference as you might think. Also, merely smiling produced significant changes in blood chemistry. So, basically, tell someone jokes, smile more, and laugh even if you have to fake it — it does the body good!

1   There were three brains for sale: a lawyer's, a doctor's and Mr. Singh's. Mr. Singh's brain was the most expensive because you have to kill a thousand of them to find one brain.

2   Mr. Singh decides to use a decision-tree technique to determine whether or not to join the military. "If I work in the back, I can cook and feed fellow soldiers. If I work on the front lines, I may die, my body will be brought back to my country and I may get a medal of honor. Or my body may stay in enemy territory. It may be thrown in a field and I may become food for birds, or the body may dissolve and become fertilizer used for agriculture. If grains are grown, I will feel satisfied that I made a contribution to agriculture and helped hungry people. If my body fertilizer is used where bamboos are grown, it could be used to make huts for homeless people or pulp for paper. If it is used for writing paper, I will feel that I made a contribution in education. Or, the pulp could be used to make tissue paper – facial or toilet tissue, which could be used in men's or women's bathrooms. If it is used in the women's bathroom, I will feel embarrassed, so I don't want to join the military."

3   A blue collar worker is wondering why there is a big difference in his salary from his boss's. He asks his boss and the boss explains, "It's based on intelligence and I will explain by playing a game." He says, "I'll put my hand on this table and you try to hit it. Let's see who is faster." The man misses and hits the table several times and now understands the difference in salary. Then the worker goes to his friend and says, "The boss taught me a new game that involves two hands and a table. Since there is no table here, I will hold my hand in front of my face."

4   A young salesperson, who is not very creative, did not offer alternative items requested by a customer. One day, his boss came to him and suggested, "If we don't have an item requested by a customer you should suggest an alternative. For example, if a customer asks for Coke, and there is no Coke in the store, say 'Sorry, we don't have Coke, but we have Pepsi.'" One day, an old lady asked for toilet paper. The young sales clerk responded, "Sorry, we don't have toilet paper, but we do have sandpaper."

5   Three people, an engineer, an architect and an economist, go on a picnic. They forget to bring a can opener. The engineer tries to find a stone to open the can. The architect draws a blueprint of a can and someone punching the can to make a hole. Finally, the economist says, "Let's assume we have a can opener."

6   A villager goes to a barbershop and asks how much it costs for a haircut. The barber tells him that it ranges from $1 to $10. The villager tells the barber, "Give me the $1 haircut. If I don't like it, I'll try the more expensive one." The barber then proceeds to shave his entire head. The villager looks in the mirror and is not happy. "OK. Now give me the $10 haircut."

7   One day, a student asked her teacher, "What should the length of our speech be?" The teacher replied, "It should be like the length of a mini-skirt: long enough to cover the subject, but short enough to keep the interest."

8   There once was a tailor shop that closed and the tailor ran away. Some of the customers gathered at the shop and started complaining about their lost items. "He took my jacket and then ran off," said one customer. Another customer turned to him and exclaimed, "And he took my measurements!"

9   A customer was stuck in a liquor store accidentally after it closed for the night. The customer called the shopkeeper and asked, "Hey, what time do you open?"

10   There once was this clerk who liked to make bets at work. One day, this new boss was hired and was informed that there was a clerk who loved to make bets. The boss said that he would take care of it. As the boss approached the clerk, the clerk said, "I'll bet you $500 that you aren't wearing any underwear. But in order to prove it, you have to drop your pants." The boss thought, "This is the easiest $500 I've ever made," and then dropped his pants, revealing a set of boxers. At that point the clerk lost his bet and gave the boss $500. The boss was confused and asked him, "Why do you make bets like this; you lost so much money?" The clerk replied, "See those 100 people that are watching from the window? They bet me $10 each that I couldn't get the boss to pull down his pants on the first day. Thanks for the $500, chief!"

11   A small company's CEO was invited to speak at an international conference in Paris. He was very worried about flying. He asked his economist to find out what the probability is of having a bomb on the flight from JFK to Paris. After some research, the economist told him there is a one in a thousand chance that his flight would have a bomb. The CEO said that it was too high of a chance, and he asked if his economist could reduce the chance of having a bomb on the flight. The economist went to his office and came back with a small package. He gave it to his CEO and said, "If you carry this package the probability of having a bomb is reduced from one in a thousand to one in a million." At this point the CEO asked, "What is in this package?" The economist said, "This package contains a small bomb, and the probability of having two bombs on one flight is much smaller than having one bomb on the flight."

12   Mr. Singh went to the shoe store and was trying and trying to find a pair of shoes that fit. He wasn't having any luck. Suddenly, the electricity went out and Mr. Singh shouted, "I found shoes that fit me!" When the light came on, the salesman replied, "Sir, your foot is in the shoe box."

13　Three engineers were scheduled to be executed. On the day of the execution, the electric chair didn't work for the first two engineers. The third engineer exclaimed, "The electric chair did not work for the first two engineers. I know how to fix it." He died.

14　An interviewee asked the potential new employer, "Why do you pay so little in fringe benefits compared to my previous employer? My previous employer offered many more benefits." The employer said, "Why did you leave the company that was paying such good benefits?" The interviewee replied, "Because they went out of business."

15　A turtle asked a consultant what he should do to be able to fly. The consultant told him, "Grow a pair of wings. The turtle asked, "How do I do that?" The consultant said, "My job is to give strategic advice. Execution is your job."

16　A lazy man asks his boss, "Can I get a raise if I work hard for the next two days?" The boss replies, "Can you raise the room temperature if you hold the thermostat in your hand for the next two hours?" The lazy man says, "That is not practical."

17　There is a brothel with three floors. The first floor is staffed by housewives who always complain that they have a headache. The second floor is staffed by hair stylists who always complain about getting their hair messed up. The third floor is staffed by teachers who say, "Do it right the first time, otherwise we will have do it again and again until you get it right."

18　A beggar said, "I do not accept credit cards or check donations. Too many people default on their donations, and I have a lot of difficulty collecting the money in today's economy and I end up having to use a collection agency."

19　A beggar tells a donor, "I do not accept less than $10. After all, I am a *professional* beggar."

20　Two friends are interviewing for the same job and go for a job interview. The second friend isn't very bright, so the first friend says, "Let me go first for the interview and I will tell you the questions asked." The first friend goes to the interview and is asked three questions for the interview. 1.) First question: "Who is the greatest leader in India?" Reply: "I cannot tell one name because that will put other leaders down." 2.) Second question: "When did India get her freedom?" The friend replies, "The Freedom movement began in 1942 and freedom came in 1947." 3.) Third question: "What did India do to solve the energy shortage?" The friend responds, "Research is going on and the results are not out yet." The second friend goes in for the interview and he is asked three questions. 1.) "What is your father's name?" Reply: "I can't tell because if I tell one father's name then I will put down other fathers." 2.) "When were you born?" He replies, "I was conceived in 1942 but delivered in 1947." The interviewer, getting frustrated, asks, 3.) "Do you think I am an idiot?" The second interviewee replies, "The research is going on and the results are not out yet."

21   An honorarium of $200 was given to a speaker at Rotary Club, who donated the money back to the club. When asked for suggestions on how to use the money, someone shouted, "Put this money into the speaker fund so that we can get better speakers."

22   Mr. Singh asked his boss to increase his salary because his mother was sick, wife was pregnant, sister was dying of cancer and son had a drug problem. The boss said, "You're fired! How can you function at work properly with a sick mother, pregnant wife, cancer-stricken sister, and a kid with a drug problem?"

23   A man gave a loan of $10,000 to his relative who refused to acknowledge it in writing. When it was time to collect, the man wrote to his relative, "Please repay my loan of the $20,000 you borrowed from me." The relative replied, "You are mistaken, I borrowed only $10,000 from you."

24   Mr. Singh walks into an antique shop and asks, "What's new?"

25   A secretary tells her boss, "Your wife is calling and wants to give you a kiss." The boss says, "Take a message and give it to me later."

26   A candidate tells the interviewer that his ability is second to none. The interviewer then asks, "Name one of your weaknesses." He says, "Exaggeration."

27   A plane crashed and four teams of two managers and one secretary survived on an island. The U.S. team decided that the managers would share the secretary, even and odd days. The Kenya team shot one manager so the other manager could have the secretary for himself. The Polish team shot the secretary so there was no conflict. And the Indian team was still waiting for instructions from Delhi.

28   A friend's wife asks, "You are not going to screw my husband if he becomes your business partner, are you?" The man replies, "No, I only screw their wives."

29   One barber always told scary stories to his customers while shaving their beards so that their hair would stand up with fear and he could shave it more easily.

30   A young man on a Bombay train was selling handheld fans: two for 10 rupees with a 5-year guarantee. A man bought two fans and the moment he walked away, one of the fans broke. The man yelled and called at the lad, who replied, "You do not know how to use it. You're supposed to move your head, not the fan."

31   A city boy, Kenny, moved to the country and bought a donkey from an old farmer for $100. The farmer agreed to deliver the donkey the next day. The next day the farmer drove up and said, "Sorry son, but I have some bad news, the donkey died." Kenny replied, "Well then, just give me my money back."
The farmer said, "Can't do that. I went and spent it already."
Kenny said, "OK then, at least give me the donkey."
The farmer asked, "What are you gonna do with him?"
Kenny said, "I'm going to raffle him off."
The farmer said, "You can't raffle off a dead donkey!"
Kenny said, "Sure I can. Watch me. I just won't tell anybody he is dead."
A month later the farmer met up with Kenny and asked, "Whatever happened with that dead donkey?"
Kenny said, "I raffled him off. I sold 500 tickets at 2 dollars apiece and made a profit of $898."
The farmer said, "Didn't anyone complain?"
Kenny said, "Just the guy who won. So I gave him his 2 dollars back."
Kenny grew up and eventually became the chairman of Enron.

32   Behind every successful man there is a woman, because women do not like to go after unsuccessful men.

33   God asks a businessman, "Where do you want to go – heaven or hell?" The businessman replies, "Depends. Where can I make more money?"

34   There are three ways to become rich: 1.) inherit, 2.) earn and 3.) sue.

35   An astrologer predicted that Mr. Singh will remain poor for 40 years and then he will get used to it.

36   There was this man who didn't want to go to heaven. You see, because his business went to hell and he wanted to follow it.

37   The good lawyers are not available in hell. They've all been promoted to judges.

38   There once was an aggressive salesman who sold lawn equipment. He always up sold his customers. He once sold a lawn mower, a hose and a gas container to someone that wasn't even looking for those items. He ran into a young lady who was in desperate need of a tampon. He said he obviously didn't have one, but asked her if she would like to buy a lawn mower, since she couldn't do anything such as swim or ride horses.

39   What's the difference between a prostitute and a defense supplier? One charges higher for a screw.

40   A customer wants to buy a shirt and the shopkeeper says, "That costs $50." The customer says, "Your competition is selling it for $10. Why do you charge $50?" The shopkeeper says, "Why don't you buy from the competition?" The customer answers, "He is out of stock." The shopkeeper says, "When I am out of stock, I will sell for $5."

41   A beggar with a hat in his hand tells his friend, "Business is very good, so I decided to open a branch."

42   To reduce construction cost for an office, the lady's rest room was combined with the gentlemen's rest room. Result – the smell improved due to the ladies use of powder. And now the sign says, "Only one person at a time."

43   A customer asks a sales lady, "Do you have Elizabeth Taylor's Passion?" The sales lady replies, "No, why would I work here if I had passion like Elizabeth Taylor?"

44   A lawyer tells his high-profile client, "Good news! Your wife found a photograph that's worth $7 million dollars. The bad news is that it's a photograph of you and your secretary in bed."

45   Mr. Singh is not allowed to enter an appliance store. He asks for a refrigerator and points to a washing machine. The next day Mr. Singh removes his beard and turban and asks the same question. This time he dresses like a woman so he is not denied any purchases from the store.

46   A doctor, a priest and a lawyer's plane crashed and landed in an ocean. The doctor and the priest did not want to swim to reach the nearby island because they were scared of sharks. The lawyer said, "I'll swim. I am going to swim and know that sharks won't hurt me because of professional courtesy."

47   If Federal Express and UPS merged, the new name of the combined company would be Fed UP.

48   The last wish of three different nationals: The American wants a hot dog, the Russian wants vodka and the Indian wants to lecture.

49   A beggar asks a man for money in Las Vegas for food and promises that he will not spend it on gambling. "Why should I believe you?" The man asks. "Because the money I made gambling is in my savings account."

50 A prostitute is filling out her Census form and struggles on what to put for profession because there is no category for prostitutes. "I know!" She exclaims. "Poultry farming sounds about right. After all, I do raise cocks."

51 Three friends decide to make a film. The first one says, "I'll finance it." The second one says, "I'll market it. Mr. Singh says, "I'll watch it."

52 Certain professions make surgery easier for doctors. Surgeons like patients who are:
1.) C.P.A. accountants, because all their body parts are numbered,
2.) Engineers, because all their body parts are color coded,
3.) Librarians, because all their body parts are alphabetically arranged, and
4.) Lawyers, because their heads and assholes are interchangeable.

53 Mr. Singh likes to have a warranty for everything. One day, he goes to buy underwear and asks the clerk for a written warranty for some underpants. The warranty clerk writes, "This underwear is guaranteed to outlive your butt."

54 A judge asks a defendant to answer all questions yes or no. The defendant tells the judge, "Not every question can be answered yes or no. For example, how would you reply if I asked you, "Judge, have you stopped beating your wife?"

55 Which profession is the oldest? 1.) Doctors were created by God to get Adam out of Eve which required a surgical procedure, 2.) Engineers created order out of chaos, 3.) Lawyers created the chaos.

56 A boss says to his secretary, "Who told you to neglect the office work just because I kissed you at the Christmas party?" Reply: "My attorney."

57 An employer asks a job applicant, "We are looking for a responsible person." The applicant responds, "That works out well, because in my previous job I was always held responsible for anything that went wrong, like fire, theft, rape, etc."

58 Four salesmen were bragging about their sons' achievements. The first says, "My son is a car salesman, and he did so well that he gave a car to his friend on his birthday." The second says, "My son is a stock broker, and he did so well that he gave 100 shares of Google to his friend on his birthday." The third says, "My son is a real estate broker, and he did so well that he gave a condo to his friend on his birthday." The fourth salesman was in the rest room and when he came out, his friends asked him what his son did. He said, "My son is just a barber but he is very good in interpersonal relations. On his birthday his friends gave him a car, a condo and 100 shares of Google stock."

59 A lawyer who makes $100 an hour got two notes of $100 bills, each from an old lady for preparing her will. He is faced with an ethical dilemma: should he return the $100 to his client or tell his partner that he received an additional $100 by mistake?

60 Advice for giving a speech: 1.) stand up to be seen, 2.) speak up to be heard and 3.) sit down to be appreciated.

61 A man goes to a call girl, and after having sex, sends 50% of the agreed upon compensation with a letter stating that her condo rent is too high since it was previously used, too large and had no heat. The call girl replies, "Good condos do not remain vacant, it is not too large if you bring proper furniture and there is heat if you know how to turn it on."

62 Women like four types of men: Doctors who say, "Take off your clothes"; dentists who say, "Open your mouth wide"; milkmen who say, "Where do you want delivery — front or back?" and bankers who say, "Early withdrawal will cause you to lose interest."

63 A beautiful young girl goes shopping with her grandpa. The salesman says, "The price of cloth is one kiss per yard." She agrees and asks for several yards of cloth. The salesman is very happy and starts to pucker up, but the young girl starts to walk out of the shop. The salesman stops the young girl, who says, "My grandpa pays for everything."

64 Mr. Singh goes to Paris to explore the furniture market. He does not know English or French. He meets a French lady who smiles at Mr. Singh and draws a picture of a restaurant. Mr. Singh understands that she wants to eat. Then she draws a picture of a liquor bottle and Mr. Singh takes her to a bar. Then she draws a picture of a bed and Mr. Singh thinks to himself, "How does she know I'm in the furniture business?"

65 Two ladies buy a used car and are sitting in the parking lot. A police officer comes up to them and asks, "Are you trying to steal a car?" The ladies reply, "Of course not, officer." The officer says, "Then why don't you drive away?" The ladies exclaim, "We don't have a driver's license but our friends told us that if we bought a used car, we'd get screwed."

66 A speaker wanted to say, "I would like to welcome the Governor of the Virgin Islands," but by mistake he said, "I would like to welcome the virgin of Governor's Island."

67 At the end of his speech the speaker says, "I would like to thank you from the bottom of my heart." His wife, sitting next to him, asks, "What about me?" The speaker says, "I want to thank you all from my wife's bottom too."

68 Three friends go to a dance club and watch a beautiful girl dance. The engineer says, "The dancer has a perfect figure: 36-24-36." The architect says, "Her body's built and the muscles are perfect." The planner says, "Everything is OK, but the recreation center and the garbage disposal are too close."

69 An interviewer asked applicants, "If my farm is 100' long and 200' wide, then what is my age?" Many of the applicants were confused, but one answered, "You are 68 years old." The interviewer was impressed and asked, "How did you know?" He replied, "My uncle is 34 years old and he is half crazy. Judging by your question, you seem to me you are 100% crazy."

70 A temporary employee asked her old boss, who was hard of hearing, if she could be made a permanent employee. Her boss said, "Before I retire I will make you pregnant."

71 Mr. Singh went to a bar and asked the bartender the price of a beer. He responded, "One penny." He asked, "What about a bottle of wine?" "That will cost you 10 cents." Mr. Singh commented, "I don't understand your pricing strategy. Let me talk to the owner." The bartender replied, "He is upstairs with your wife." Mr. Singh asked, "What is he doing?" The bartender replied, "Same thing I'm doing right now. Screwing with a customer."

72 "Today I had the second best introduction of myself," a man said. Friends asked, "When was your best introduction?" Reply: "When I went to a conference and the person who was to introduce me did not show up so I was asked to introduce myself."

73 One problem with being punctual is that everybody thinks you never have anything to do.

74 What's the difference between a gossip, a bore and a brilliant conversationalist? A gossip talks about others, a bore talks about himself, and a brilliant conversationalist talks about you.

75 "My boy," said the store owner to his new employee, "Wisdom and integrity are essential to the retail business. By integrity I mean if you promise a customer something, you've got to keep that promise – even if it means we lose money. "And what," asked the new man, "is wisdom?" "That," said the boss, "is not making stupid promises."

76 In a barber's shop a customer was twice nicked by the razor. The customer said, "Hey barber, please give me a glass of water." The barber said, "What's wrong? Hair in your mouth?" "No, I want to see if my neck leaks."

77 A foreman asked his absent-prone worker, "Why do you only show up to work four days a week?" "Gee, boss," was the reply, "Well, I can't make a living on three!"

78 Philip: "Is your brother a good salesman?" Lisa: "Good? He is the best. On his very first day he got two firm orders – one to get out and the other to stay out."

79 The president of a famous corporation entered his large limousine and noticed that there was a new driver.
"Ah, a new driver," he said. "What is your name?"
"Charles, Sir."
"Sorry, but I never call my employees by their first names," said the executive.
"What is your surname?"
"It's Darling, sir."
"Well…drive on, Charles."

80 A man in Louisiana rented three stores side-by-side in his new shopping plaza to three competitors. Observers waited for mayhem (chaos) to ensue. The retailer on the right put up a huge sign saying, "Gigantic Sale! – Super Bargains!" The retailer on the left responded with an even bigger sign that proclaimed, "All Prices Slashed 25%! Fantastic Discounts!" The store owner in the middle then prepared his own large sign: a large plain sign which simply stated, "ENTRANCE."

81 After the same bank teller had been robbed five times by the same crook, the FBI man asked if he noticed anything special about the thief. "Yes," recalled the victim, "Every time I see him, he's wearing better clothes."

82 A crowded Air India flight was canceled. A single agent was re booking the long line of inconvenienced travelers. Suddenly, an angry passenger pushed his way to the desk. He slapped his ticket on the counter and said, "I HAVE to be on this flight and it has to be FIRST CLASS."
The agent replied, "I am sorry, sir. I'll be happy to try to help you but I have got to help these folks first, and I'm sure we'll be able to work something out."
The passenger was unimpressed. He asked loudly so that the passengers behind could hear, "DO YOU HAVE ANY IDEA WHO I AM?"
Without hesitating, the agent smiled and grabbed her public microphone, "May I have your attention please," her voice said clearly throughout the terminal, "We have a passenger here at Gate 14 who does not know who he is. If anyone can help him find his identity please come to Gate 14". With the folks behind him in line laughing hysterically, the man glared at the Air India agent, gritted his teeth and swore "F... you!"
Without flinching, she smiled and said, "I'm sorry sir, you will have to get in line for that too!"

83   Four insurance companies are in competition.
One comes up with the slogan "Coverage from the cradle to the grave."
The second tries to improve on that with "Coverage from the womb to the tomb."
Not to be outdone, the third comes up with "From sperm to the worm."
The fourth insurance company really thought hard, and almost gave up, but, finally came up with "From the erection to the resurrection."

84   North American Corp: You have two cows. You sell one, and force the other to produce the milk of four cows.
French: You have two cows. You go on strike because you want three.
Japanese: You have two cows. You redesign them to 1/10 the size of ordinary cows, producing 20 times the milk. You then create clever cow cartons called "Cowmilkon" and market them worldwide.
German: You have two cows, re engineered so they'll live for 100 years, eat once a month and milk themselves.
British: You have two cows. Both are mad.
Russian: You have two cows. You count them and learn you have five cows. You count them again and you learn you have 42. You count them again and learn you have 12. You stop counting cows and open another bottle of vodka.
Swiss: You have 5,000 cows. None belong to you. You charge others for storing them.
Hindu: You have two cows. You worship them.
Chinese: You have two cows and 300 people milking them. You claim full employment, high bovine productivity and arrest the newsman who questions the numbers.

85   Mr. Singh walks into a bank in New York City and asks for the loan officer. He says he is going to Europe on business for two weeks and needs to borrow $5,000. The bank officer says the bank will need some kind of security for such a loan, so the man hands over the keys to a new Rolls Royce parked on the street in front of the bank.
Everything checks out fine, and the bank accepts the car as collateral for the loan. An employee drives the Rolls into the bank's underground garage and parks it there. Two weeks later, the man returns, repays the $5,000 and the interest, which comes to $15.41. The loan officer says, "We are happy to have had your business, and this transaction worked out very nicely, but we are puzzled. While you were away we checked out and found that you are a multimillionaire. What puzzles us is why would you bother to borrow $5,000?" Mr. Singh replied, "Where else in New York can I park my car for two weeks for 15 bucks?"

86   A prostitute goes to deposit a $100 bill in a bank. The teller says, "Sorry, madam, the note is fake." "Oh, no!" exclaimed the prostitute, "I have been raped."

87   A secretary said publicly about her boss, "You have a small penis, would you comment on this?" The truth is that she has a big mouth.

88   Smart boss + Smart employee = profit
Smart boss + dumb employee = production
Dumb boss + Smart employee = promotion
Dumb boss + dumb employee = overtime

89   Two economists were on an airplane flying from New York to London. About halfway across the Atlantic, they heard the captain's voice:
"Ladies and gentlemen, I must report to you that one of our four engines has malfunctioned. There is no cause for alarm, but it does mean that we will be a little late. The flight will reach its destination at 6:00 a.m. instead of 5:30 a.m. I am sorry for any inconvenience."
Ten minutes later, the captain was heard again, reporting the loss of a second engine.
"Nothing to worry about," he assured them, "but our arrival at Heathrow will be further delayed until 6:30 a.m."
Ten minutes later the captain announced that a third engine was not working, but said that the fourth engine would be adequate to land safely, at 7 a.m. Finally the captain said, his voice shaking, "Ladies and gentlemen, I regret to inform you that the fourth engine is no longer functioning."
One economist turned to the other one and said, "by my extrapolation theory, that means we will land at 7:30 a.m.!"

90   It has been said that Christopher Columbus must have been the first economist, because he didn't know where he was going; when he got there, he didn't know where he was; when he left he didn't know where he had been; and he did it all on borrowed money.

91   Old accountants never die —— they just lose their balance.

92   A recruiter was interviewing three job applicants.
He asked the same question to each one, "How much is two and two?"
The finance major said, "Four."
The marketing major said, "Do you mean two plus two? Two times two? Two to the second power?"
Finally the accounting major faced the question, thought for a moment and said, "How much do you want it to be?"

93   An economist is someone who sees something work in practice and wonders whether it works in theory.

94 When Albert Einstein got to heaven, he was told he would be sharing a room with three other souls of eternity. When he introduced himself to his roommates, he inquired politely about their I.Q.s.

The first roommate said he had an I.Q. of 180.

"Wonderful," said Dr. Einstein. "We can discuss Quantum theory and the shape of the universe."

The second roommate said he had an I.Q. of 140.

"Fine," said Dr. Einstein. "We can discuss art, and music and literature."

The third roommate said he had an I.Q. of 80

"So tell me," Einstein said, "What's been happening in the stock market?"

95 A business executive told this story. He said, "Our sales force ran a contest. The prize was a safari in Africa. When the contest was over, we evaluated the sales team's results, picked the winner, and she packed her bags and took off to Africa. She joined the safari and they started through the jungle. One day, they came across a clearing which contained a very unusual kind of institution. It was a cannibal supermarket. Well, clearly the saleswoman had never seen anything like this before and was curious. So she started looking around and over in the corner she found some baskets. They contained legs. Over in another corner, she saw some more baskets and they contained arms. Over in a third corner, she saw some baskets and the first one had a little tag on it that said, "Salesperson's brains - $.50 a pound." She looked at the next one and it said, "Engineer's brains - $.60 a pound." She looked at the next one and it said, "Surgeon's brains- $.80 a pound." And then finally, there was a fourth very small basket and it had a tag that said, "Lawyer's brains- $5.00 a pound." The saleswoman thought, "I know lawyers are smarter than salespeople but not that much smarter." So she called an attendant and asked, "Tell me, why is there so much difference between a salesperson's brain and a lawyer's brain?" The attendant drew himself up very straight and said, "Have you ever thought of how many lawyers we have to catch to get a pound of brains?"

96 Corporate Life Cycle Tree: A part of the corporate ladder

Part 1

The Organization is like a tree full of monkeys, all on different levels, some climbing up. The monkeys on top look down and see a tree full of smiling faces. The monkeys on the bottom look up and see nothing but assholes.

Part 2

All of the time the monkeys on the top always will get fruit first, and most of the time they will produce shit for all the monkeys below. And all the time, that is what monkeys below will get.

Part 3

During times of great difficulties and hardship, the monkeys on the top may fall a few branches down and hit the monkeys below. The monkeys below will be fallen upon and eventually some will fall off the tree. As compensation, these monkeys that fell off get to keep the fruits that were shaken off the tree during the commotion. The tree becomes lighter and life slowly returns to normal. And that is what we call a corporate life cycle.

97 Prison vs. Work

In prison, you spend the majority of your time in an 8x10 cell.

At work, you spend most of your time in a 6x8 cubicle.

In prison, you get three meals per day.

At work, you get one meal and you have to pay for it.

In prison, you get time off for good behavior.

At work, you get rewarded with more work for good behavior.

In prison, a guard unlocks all the doors for you.

At work, you have to carry around a security card and unlock and open all the doors yourself.

In prison, you can watch TV and play games.

At work, you will get fired for doing this.

In prison, you are ball and chained when you go somewhere.

At work, you are just ball and chained.

In prison, your family and friends can visit.

At work, you cannot even speak to these folks without a fuss.

In prison, all expenses are paid by taxpayers, with no work required.

At work, you get to pay all the expenses to get there, and then they deduct taxes from your salary to pay for prisoners.

In prison, you spend most of your life looking through bars from the inside, wanting to get out. At work, you spend most of your time wanting to get out and go inside the bars.

98 Once upon a time, there was a non-conforming sparrow who decided not to fly south for the winter.

However, soon the weather turned so cold that she reluctantly started to fly south. In a short time, ice began to form on his her wings and she fell to earth in a barnyard, almost frozen.

A cow passed by and crapped on the little sparrow. The sparrow thought it was the end, but the manure warmed her up and defrosted her wings. Warm and happy, able to breathe, she started to sing. Just then a large cat came by and hearing the chirping, investigated the sounds.

The cat cleared away the manure and found the chirping bird and immediately ate her.

The moral of the story: Everyone who shits on you is not necessarily your enemy.

Everyone who gets you out of the shit is not necessarily your friend.

And if you are warm and happy in a pile of shit, keep your mouth shut.

99 In a department store: "God helps those who help themselves. We prosecute."

100 In a men's shop: "Close-out sale on famous brand pajamas for men with tiny flaws."

101   A businessman had a reputation for never throwing anything away, especially correspondence that dated back years.

One day his assistant, cramped for filing space, asked if they could dispose of some of the older, less useful material.

The boss was reluctant, but finally said, "Well alright, but be sure you make a copy of everything before throwing it out."

102   Two thugs were holding up a bank. After tying and gagging the manager, they led the rest of the employees into the vault. They had filled their sacks and were ready to leave when they heard the manager thrashing around on the floor and mumbling through his gag.

One of the robbers lowered the gag and asked, "What do you want? Make it quick."

"Please," whispered the manager, "Take the books too. I am $15,000 short!"

103   A clerk was dismissed from his job at a department store because of his lack of courtesy to customers.

A month later, the store sales manager spotted him walking about in a police uniform.

"I see you've joined the force, Bill," said the sales manager.

"Yes," replied Bill. "And I've never been happier. On this job, the customer is always wrong."

104   An employee with an already heavy workload was handed yet another task by his boss.

"But you know I am overloaded as it is," protested the stressed worker. "I cannot see when I'll have time to handle this."

The manager suggested that employee work during lunch hour.

"But I already work through my lunch," he replied.'"

"Well," said the boss, "then take a longer lunch."

105   A man walked into an appliance store and asked the salesman if he had a cheap refrigerator in stock.

"You are in luck," the salesman replied. "Today we have a big sale. If you buy this refrigerator now, you can save half your money"

"Great!" said the customer. "I'll take two of them and save all my money!"

106   Mr. Singh was sitting on a tree branch and his wife told her friends that her husband works in a world renowned city bank as a branch manager.

107   Two women were walking in the woods when a frog hopped out in front of them. "Kiss me! Kiss me!" said the frog, "and I'll turn into your very own personal financial advisor. You will be rich!"

One woman reached down, grabbed the frog, and put it in her backpack.

"Why did you do that?" asked her friend.

"I can make more money with a talking frog than I can with a personal financial advisor."

108   Several weeks after a young man had been hired; he was called into the HR office. "What is the meaning of this?" the director asked. "When you applied for the job, you told us you had five years of experience. Now we discovered this is the first job you've ever held." "Well," the young man replied, "in your advertisement you said you wanted somebody with imagination."

109   New Company Rules:

SICK DAYS: We will no longer accept a doctor statement as proof of sickness; If you are able to go to the doctor, you are able to come to work.

SURGERY: Operations are now banned. As long as you are an employee here, you need all your organs. You should not consider removing anything. We hired you intact. To have something removed constitutes a breach of employment.

PERSONAL DAYS: Each employee will receive 104 personal days a year. They are called Saturday and Sunday.

VACATION DAYS: All employees will take their vacation at the same time every year. The vacation days are as follows: January 1, July 4 and December 25.

BEREAVEMENT LEAVE: This is no excuse for missing work. There is nothing you can do for dead friends, relatives or coworkers. Every effort should be made to have non-employees attend to the arrangements. In rare cases where employee involvement is necessary, the funeral should be scheduled in the late afternoon. We will be glad to allow you to work through your lunch hour and subsequently leave one hour early, provided your share of the work is done.

OUT FROM YOUR OWN DEATH: This will be accepted as an excuse. However, we require at least two weeks' notice as it is your duty to train your own replacement.

REST ROOM USE: Entirely too much time is being spent in the rest room. In the future, we will follow the practice of going in alphabetical order. For instance, all employees whose names begin with "A" will go from 8:00 to 8:20, employees whose names begin with "B" will go from 8:20 to 8:40, and so on. If you're unable to go at your allotted time, it will be necessary to wait until the next day when your turn comes again. In extreme emergencies, employees may swap their time with a co-worker. Both employees' supervisors must approve this exchange in writing. In addition, there is now a strict three-minute time limit in the stalls. At the end of three minutes, an alarm will sound, the toilet paper roll will retract, and the stall door will open.

LUNCH BREAK: Skinny people get an hour for lunch as they need to eat more so that they can look healthy; normal sized people get 30 minutes for lunch to get a balanced meal to maintain the average figure; fat people get five minutes for lunch because that's all the time needed to drink a Slim Fast and take a diet pill.

DRESS CODE: It is advised that you come to work dressed according to your salary. If we see you wearing $350 Prada sneakers and carrying a $600 Gucci bag, we assume you are doing well financially and therefore you do not need a raise.

Thank you for your loyalty to our company. We are here to provide a positive employment experience. Therefore, all questions, comments, concerns, complaints, frustrations, irritations, aggravations, insinuations, allegations, accusations, contemplations, consternations or input, should be directed elsewhere.

Have a nice week.

110   In North Carolina, a guy sees a sign in front of a house:

"Talking Dog for Sale."

He rings the bell and the owner tells him the dog is in the backyard.

The guy goes into the backyard and sees a black mutt just sitting there.

"You talk?" he asks.

"Yep," the mutt replies.

"So, what's your story?"

The mutt looks up and says, "Well, I discovered this gift pretty young and I wanted to help the government, so I told the CIA about my gift, and in no time they had me jetting from country to country, sitting in rooms with spies and world leaders, because no one figured a dog would be eavesdropping. I was one of their most valuable spies eight years running. The jetting around really tired me out, and I knew I wasn't getting any younger and I wanted to settle down. So I signed up for a job at the airport to do some undercover security work, mostly wandering near suspicious characters and listening in. I uncovered some incredible dealings there and was awarded a batch of medals. Had a wife, a mess of puppies, and now I'm just retired."

The guy is amazed. He goes back in and asks the owner what he wants for the dog.

The owner says, "Ten dollars." The guy says, "This dog is amazing. Why on earth are you selling him so cheap?"

The owner replies, "He's such a liar. He didn't do any of that stuff."

111   A fine looking lady walks into a Lexus dealership and browses around. Suddenly she spots the most perfect, beautiful car and walks over to inspect it.

As she bends forward to feel the fine leather upholstery, an unexpected little fart escapes her. Very embarrassed, she anxiously looks around to see if anyone has noticed and hopes a salesperson doesn't pop up right then.

As she turns back, there standing next to her is a salesman.

With a pleasant smile he greets her, "Good day, Madame. How may we help you today?"

Trying to maintain an air of sophistication and acting as though nothing had happened, she smiles back and asks, "Sir, what is the price of this lovely vehicle?"

Still smiling pleasantly, he replies, "Madame, I'm very sorry to say that if you farted just touching it, you are gonna shit yourself when you hear the price."

112   A young Aussie lad moved to London and went to Harrods looking for a job. The manager asked, "Do you have any sales experience?" The young man answered, "Yeah, I was a salesman back home." The manager liked the Aussie so he gave him the job. His first day on the job was challenging and busy, but he got through it. After the store was locked up, the manager came down and asked, "OK, so how many sales did you make today?" The Aussie said "One." The manager groaned and continued "Just one? Our sales people average 20 or 30 sales a day. How much was the sale for?" "£101,237.64." The manager choked and exclaimed, "£101,237.64? What the hell did you sell him?" "Well, first I sold him a small fish hook, then a medium fish hook, and then I sold him a new fishing rod. Then I asked him where he was going fishing and he said down at the coast, so I told him he would need a boat, so we went down to the boat department and I sold him that twin - engine Power Cat. Then he said he didn't think his Honda Civic would pull it, so I took him down to car sales and I sold him the 4 x 4 Suzuki". The manager, incredulous, said, "You mean to tell me...that a guy came in here to buy a fish hook and you sold him a boat and 4x4?"

No, no, no...he came in here to buy a box of tampons for his Misses and I said, "Well, since your weekend is screwed, you might as well go fishing."

113   A prostitute goes to a surgeon and tells him to create another hole. The doctor is curious, and before he starts, he asks, "Why?" The prostitute replies, "Business is going well and I want to create a new branch."

114   At one time in my life, I thought I had a handle on the meaning of the word "service." "It's the act of doing things for other people."

Then I heard these terms that reference the word.

SERVICE:

Internal Revenue Service

Postal Service

Telephone Service

Civil Service

City and County Public Service

Customer Service

Service Stations

Then I became confused about the word "service." This is not what I thought "service" meant. Then this morning, for no reason, I referred to my copy of the Farmer's Almanac and saw this tip to the farmers that suggested "renting" a bull to "service" their cows. BAM! It all came into perspective.

115   Subject Calls to Tech Support Helpdesk:

Helpdesk: What kind of computer do you have?

Customer: A white one...

Helpdesk: Click on the "My Computer" icon on the left of the screen.

Customer: Your left or my left?

Hi, good afternoon, this is Martha. I can't print.

Every time I try, it says '"Can't find printer." I've even lifted the printer and placed it in front of the monitor, but the computer still says he can't find it..."

Helpdesk: What's on your monitor now ma'am?

Customer: A teddy bear my boyfriend bought for me in the supermarket.

Helpdesk: Your password is the small letter 'a' as in apple, a capital letter 'V' as in Victor, and the number '7'.

Customer: Is that 7 in capital letters?

A customer couldn't get on the Internet.

Helpdesk: Are you sure you used the right password?

Customer: Yes, I'm sure. I saw my colleague do it.

Helpdesk: Can you tell me what the password was?

Customer: Yes, five stars.

Customer: I have a huge problem. A friend has placed a screensaver on my computer, but every time I move the mouse, it disappears!

Helpdesk: How may I help you?

Customer: I'm writing my first e-mail.

Helpdesk: OK, and what seems to be the problem?

Customer: Well, I have the letter 'a,' but how do I get the circle around it?

116   If you have any problems with the tax people, this may help.

At the end of the tax year, the IRS office sent an inspector to audit the books of a synagogue. While he was checking the books, he turned to the Rabbi and said, "I notice you buy a lot of candles. What do you do with the candle drippings?"

"Good question," noted the Rabbi. "We save them up and send them back to the candle makers, and every now and then they send us a free box of candles."

"Oh," replied the auditor, somewhat disappointed that his unusual question had a practical answer. But on he went, in his obnoxious way: "What about all these bread wafer purchases? What do you do with the crumbs?"

"Ah, yes," replied the Rabbi, realizing that the inspector was trying to trap him with an unanswerable question. "We collect them and send them back to the manufacturer, and every now and then they send us a free box of bread-wafers."

"I see," replied the auditor, thinking hard about how he could fluster the know-it-all Rabbi. "Well, Rabbi," he went on, "what do you do with all the leftover foreskins from the circumcisions you perform?"

"Here, too, we do not waste," answered the Rabbi. "What we do is save all the foreskins and send them to the tax office, and about once a year they send us a complete dick."

117   A Japanese company (Toyota) and an American auto company (General Motors) decided to have a canoe race on the Missouri River. Both teams practiced long and hard to reach their peak performance before the race. On the big day, the Japanese won by a mile. The Americans, very discouraged and depressed, decided to investigate the reason for the crushing defeat. A management team made up of senior management was formed to investigate and recommend the appropriate action. Their conclusion was the Japanese team had eight people steering and one person rowing. Feeling a deeper study was in order; American management hired a consulting company and paid them a large amount of money to get a second opinion. They advised, of course, that too many people were steering the boat, and not enough people were rowing. Not sure of how to utilize use that information, but wanting to prevent another loss to the Japanese, the rowing team's management structure was totally reorganized to four steering supervisors, three area steering superintendents and one assistant superintendent steering manager. They also implemented a new performance system that would give the one person rowing the boat greater incentive to work harder. It was called the "Rowing Team Quality First Program," with meetings, dinners and free pens for the rower. There was discussion of getting new paddles, canoes and other equipment, extra vacation days for practices and bonuses. The next year, Japanese won by two miles. Humiliated, the American management laid off the rower for poor performance, halted development of new canoes, sold the paddles, and canceled all capital investment for new equipment. The money saved was distributed to senior executives as bonuses and the next year's racing team was outsourced to India. Here is something to think about: Ford has spent many years moving some of its factories out of the U.S., claiming they can't make money paying American wages. Toyota has spent many years building many plants inside the U.S. Toyota makes money and Ford and GM lose money. We wonder why.

118   Smith started the day early having set his alarm clock (MADE IN JAPAN) for 6 a.m. While his coffeepot (MADE IN CHINA) was perking, he shaved with his electric razor! (MADE IN HONG KONG) He put on a dress shirt (MADE IN SRI LANKA), designer jeans (MADE IN SINGAPORE) and tennis shoes (MADE IN KOREA). After cooking his breakfast in his new electric skillet (MADE IN INDIA) he sat down with his calculator (MADE IN MEXICO) to see how much he could spend today. After setting his watch (MADE IN TAIWAN) to the radio (MADE IN INDIA) he got in his car (MADE IN GERMANY) and continued his search for a good paying AMERICAN JOB. At the end of yet another discouraging and fruitless day, Joe decided to relax for a while. He put on his sandals (MADE IN BRAZIL) poured himself a glass of wine (MADE IN FRANCE) and turned on his TV (MADE IN INDONESIA), and then wondered why he can't find a good paying job in - AMERICA...

119   Escort Screwed

A lawyer was visiting Bangkok. He went to the most exclusive escort agency and asked if he could take Sue-Lin to dinner. "Yes," said the Madam. "It will cost you $100 for Sue-Lin's company. No sex. And she must be back here at 12 a.m."

Sue-Lin was the most stunningly beautiful Eurasian creature the lawyer had ever seen. She was delicate, and statuesque with the perfect trim figure. He wined and dined her, and before returning her home, he gave her $1,000. "This is a gift", he said. Sue-Lin's eyes widened and she told him that he was a wonderful and generous man, and she slipped her hand inside his pants and gave him the best hand-job he had ever experienced.

Before she left him, he said, "Will you have dinner with me again tomorrow night?"

"Oh yes, most certainly," she replied." I will cancel all my previous engagements."

The next night, the lawyer wined and dined Sue-Lin again. He could not get over her beauty, and at the end of the evening, gave her another $1,000 and said, "Sue-Lin, this is a gift just for you."

Sue-Lin was overcome with gratitude and had a tear in her eye. "You are the most generous person I have ever met," she said and she lent over and gave him the most amazing blow-job he had ever experienced.

Before she left him he asked, "Sue-Lin, would you come to dinner with me again tomorrow night?"

"Of course I will!" said Sue-Lin. "I will do anything for such a kind, generous man."

So he wined and dined Sue-Lin again, and this time he invited her back to his apartment, where he gave her another $1,000. This truly overwhelmed Sue-Lin. She quickly undressed and fell into the lawyer's arms on the bed, where they made wild, passionate love until five in the morning in ways he did not know even existed. Then the lawyer told Sue-Lin that he had to leave as he was catching a plane for Sydney at seven o'clock that morning.

"Sydney!" said Sue-Lin. "You didn't tell me you came from Sydney! I have a sister who lives in Sydney!"

"Yes, I know", said the lawyer. "She is the one who sent you the $3,000."

120   The IRS decides to audit Ralph, and summons him to the IRS office.

The IRS auditor is not surprised when Ralph shows up with his attorney.

The auditor says, "Well, sir, you have an extravagant lifestyle and no full-time employment, which you explain by saying that you win money gambling. I'm not sure the IRS finds that believable."

"I'm a great gambler, and I can prove it," says Ralph. "How about a demonstration?"

The auditor thinks for a moment and says, "Okay. Go ahead."

Ralph says, "I'll bet you a thousand dollars that I can bite my own eye."

The auditor thinks a moment and says, "No way! It's a bet."

Ralph removes his glass eye and bites it.

The auditor's jaw drops. Ralph says, "Now, I'll bet you two thousand dollars that I can bite my other eye."

The auditor can tell Ralph isn't blind, so he takes the bet.

Ralph removes his dentures and bites his good eye.

The stunned auditor now realizes he has wagered and lost three grand, with Ralph's attorney as a witness.

He starts to get nervous. "Want to go double or nothing?" Ralph asks. "I'll bet you six thousand dollars that I can stand on one side of your desk, and pee into that wastebasket on the other side, and never get a drop anywhere in between."

The auditor, twice burned, is cautious now, but he looks carefully and decides there's no way this guy can manage that stunt, so he agrees again.

Ralph stands beside the desk and unzips his pants, but although he strains mightily, he can't make the stream reach the wastebasket on the other side, so he pretty much urinates all over the desk.

The auditor leaps with joy, realizing that he has just turned a major loss into a huge win. But Ralph's attorney moans and puts his head in his hands. "Are you okay?" the auditor asks. "Not really," says the attorney. "This morning, when Ralph told me he'd been summoned for an audit, he bet me twenty thousand dollars that he could come in here and piss all over an IRS official's desk and that you'd be happy about it."

121   On an application form for a job, what did Mr. Singh write for "sex"?

"Occasionally."

122   A gas station in Mississippi was trying to increase its sales, so the owner put up a sign that read, "FREE SEX with FILL-UP."

Soon a local redneck pulled in, filled his tank, and then asked for his free sex. The owner told him to pick a number from 1 to 10. If he guessed correctly, he would get his free sex. The redneck then guessed 8 and the proprietor said, "You were close. The number was 7. Sorry, no free sex this time."

A week later, the same redneck, along with a buddy, Bubba, pulled in for a fill-up. Again he asked for his free sex. The proprietor gave him the same story as last time, asking him to guess the correct number. This time the redneck guessed 2. And again the proprietor said, "Sorry, it was 3. You were close, but no free sex this time."

As they were driving away, the redneck said to his buddy, "I think that game is rigged and he doesn't really give away free sex."

Bubba replied, "No it ain't rigged, Billy Ray. My wife won twice last week!"

123   The boss wondered why one of his most valued employees was absent but had not phoned in sick. Needing to have an urgent problem with one of his main computers resolved, he dialed the employee's home phone number and was greeted with a child's whisper. "Hello?"

"Is your daddy home?" he asked.

"Yes," whispered the small voice.

"May I talk with him?"

The child whispered, "No."

Surprised and wanting to talk with an adult, the boss asked, "Is your Mommy there?" "Yes"

"May I talk with her?" Again the small voice whispered, "No."

Hoping there was somebody with whom he could leave a message, the boss asked, "Is anybody else there?"

"Yes," whispered the child, "a policeman."

Wondering what a cop would be doing at his employee's home, the boss asked, "May I speak with the policeman?"

"No, he's busy," whispered the child.

"Busy doing what?"

"Talking to daddy and mommy and the fireman and the priest," came the whispered answer.

Growing more worried as he heard a loud noise in the background, through the earpiece on the phone, the boss asked, "What is that noise?"

"A helicopter," answered the whispering voice.

"What is going on there?" demanded the boss, now truly apprehensive.

Again, whispering, the child answered.

"The search team just landed a helicopter."

Alarmed, concerned and a little frustrated, the boss asked, "Who are they searching for?"

Still whispering, the young voice replied with a muffled giggle…"Me!"

124   A man goes to a dance bar and meets a prostitute. He asks her what her profession is. She replies, I am a "Wholesaler" (hole seller).

125   A female customer had been trying the patience of the clerk, and he began to lose his temper. "Please get the manager," the woman ordered. "Perhaps he'll have a little more sense than you." "He does, madam. He left when you came in the door," says the clerk.

126   A Native American walked into a cafe with a shotgun in one hand and pulling a male buffalo with the other. He said to the waiter, "Want coffee." The waiter said, "Sure chief, coming right up." He got the Native American a tall mug of coffee. After drinking the coffee down in one gulp, the Native American turned and blasted the buffalo with the shotgun, and then walked out. The next morning the Native American returned. He has his shotgun in one hand, pulling another male buffalo with the other. He walked up to the counter and said to the waiter, "Want coffee." The waiter said, "Whoa, Tonto! We're still cleaning up your mess from yesterday. What the heck was all that about, anyway?" The Native American smiled and proudly said, "Training for upper management position. Come in, drink coffee, shoot the bull, leave a mess for others to clean up, and disappear for rest of day."

127   There were three parrots for sale at a pet shop. The first parrot was selling for 10,000 rupees because he could recite Geeta and Ramayan. The second parrot was selling for 20,000 rupees because he could not only recite Geeta and Ramayan, but also the Quaran and the Bible. The third parrot was selling for one lakh (one hundred thousand rupees). He couldn't recite anything, but that didn't matter since the other parrots called him boss.

128   A 16 year-old boy came home with a late-model Porsche. His parents began to yell and scream, "Where did you get that car?"
"I bought it just now," he said. "With what money?" his parents demanded. "We know what a Porsche costs!" "Well," said the boy, "this one cost me $15." The parents began to yell even louder, "Who would sell a car like that for $15?" "It was the lady up the street," said the boy. "I don't know her name...They just moved in. She saw me ride past on my bike and asked me if I wanted to buy a Porsche for $15." "Oh, good grief," moaned the mother, "she must be a child abuser. Who knows what she'll do next? John, you go right up there and see what's going on." So the boy's father walked up the street to the house where the woman lived and found her out in the yard, planting petunias. He introduced himself as the father of the boy to whom she had sold a Porsche for $15 and demanded to know why she did it. "Well," she said, "this morning I got a phone call from my husband. I thought he was on a business trip, but it seems he has run off to Hawaii with his secretary and doesn't intend to come back."
With the hint of a smile, she continued, "He asked me to sell his new Porsche and send him the money. So I did!"

Introduction

The author does not like blondes, he loves them. Truly speaking, blondes are beautiful creatures that God has created in the world, such as Marilyn Monroe. It is said that the late President John F. Kennedy was her admirer. Many people stereotype blondes as unintelligent but Mrs. Hillary Clinton, the U.S. Secretary of State, has proven that blondes are smart.

The jokes in this chapter are for fun and humor. We hope that no blondes will feel offended. The author asks for forgiveness if their feelings have been hurt.

129   A blonde is being bitten by mosquitoes all night due to a hole in the mosquito net. So the next night, she decides to sleep outside the net, thinking, "I'll sure fool those mosquitoes."

130   A brunette, a redhead and a blonde went on a camping trip. The brunette was the first one to go hunting for food. She came back with a pig. Her friends asked, "How did you find a pig?" "Easy. I followed the pig's foot tracks." The next day it was the redhead's turn. Sure enough, she was successful and came back with a deer. "Nice work," said her friends. "How did you find the deer?" "Easy. I followed the deer's foot tracks," she replied. The third day, the blonde went out for food. However, she came back all covered in blood, empty-handed. "What happened?" asked her friends. "Well, I followed some train tracks…"

131   A group of blondes were dancing for joy after learning that a fellow blonde had a brain tumor. "See?" one of them proclaimed. "It's proof we do have brains!"

132   A blonde girl asks her friend, "I wonder if I will be wealthy or pretty in my next life." Her friend replies, "Either way, it would be an improvement."

133   The blonde asked his servant to water the garden. The servant said that since it was raining, he wasn't going to water it. The blonde replied, "Just use an umbrella."

134   The blonde was color blind and mixed up socks of different colors. She suggested putting labels like B for blue, G for Green, etc., but still the problem continued because B is for blue, B is for black, B is for brown and B is for beige (not all problems have simple solutions).

135   How do you know if a blonde is a good housekeeper? If she gets to keep the house after the divorce.

136   The blonde called the fire department to report a fire. The dispatcher said, "Where is it?" "In my house," she replied. "What is the location?" "In my kitchen," she said. "How do we get there?" Confused, the blonde said, "Don't you have a fire truck?"

137   An interviewer asked the blonde to name the two days in a week that start with "T." After a long pause, she responded, "Today and tomorrow."

138   The blonde calls her friend and asks him to pick her up. "Where are you located?" "Near the traffic light." "What is the street name?" "Walk/Don't walk."

139   A lady asks God, "Can I be president of the USA?" Reply: "Not in your life." "Can a blonde become President of the USA?" Reply: "Not in my life."

140   Inspired by the feat of putting a man on the moon, a blonde petitioned NASA to send someone to the sun. NASA replied, "No can do that. It's too hot." Not to be discouraged, the blonde said, "We can go at night."

141   The blonde goes to a pet shop and buys 60 cockroaches. The clerk asks him, "Why do you need so many cockroaches?" "Well," he replies, "It says in my lease I have to leave the apartment in the same condition as when I moved in."

142   A teacher asked her blonde student to spell Mississippi. "Which one? The river or the State?"

143   A blonde is filling out a job application. Sex: 2 times a week. Male or Female: Both. Either one is OK.

144   A blonde traveling coach class to Hawaii insisted that she be allowed to travel in first class because she is beautiful, smart and works for the government. The flight attendant tried to convince her to stay in coach, but to no avail. The pilot got involved and whispered something in the blonde's ear that settled the issue. Curious, the flight attendant asked the pilot what he said. "I just told her the front portion of the plane goes to Jamaica, and the rear portion goes to Hawaii."

145   The blonde bought a thermos which keeps hot things hot and cold things cold. She put ice cream and hot coffee in it.

146   The blonde's pants fell down in the well. The good news is - she was not inside the pants.

147   Twin blonde sisters were given a pair of identical horses for their 21st birthday. At first they were puzzled as to how they would be able to tell them apart. Then Tammy got the idea of cutting the mane off her horse; but in time it grew back again. Then Pammy trimmed the tail off her horse but it also grew back.

Finally Tammy said, "This is silly. Why don't we measure them? Maybe one horse is taller than the other." The measurement was taken and to the delight of both sisters, the problem was solved. The black horse was 3 inches taller than the white one.

148   A blonde called up a long distance operator and asked, "Could you please tell me the time difference between India and Dubai?" The operator replied, "Yes. Just a minute." The blonde replied, "That's great! Thank you!" and hung up the phone.

149   A young blonde woman in Indiana was so depressed that she decided to end her life by throwing herself into the Ohio River. She went down to the docks and was about to leap into the frigid water when a handsome young sailor saw her tottering on the edge of the dock, crying. He took pity on her and said, "Look, you have so much to live for. I'm off to Europe in the morning, and if you like, I can stow you away on my ship. I'll take good care of you and bring you food every day." Moving closer, he slipped his arm around her shoulders and added, "I'll keep you happy, and you'll keep me happy."

The girl nodded yes. After all, what did she have to lose? Perhaps a fresh start in Europe would give her life new meaning.

That night, the sailor brought her aboard and hid her in a lifeboat. From then on, every night he brought her three sandwiches and a piece of fruit,

and they made passionate love until dawn.

Three weeks later during a routine inspection, the captain discovered her. "What are you doing here?" the captain asked.

"I have an arrangement with one of the sailors," she explained. "I get food and a trip to Europe, and he's screwing me."

"He certainly is," the captain said. "This is the Argosy Casino, and we never leave the Ohio River."

150   At a bar in New York, a man to a blonde's left tells the bartender, "Johnny Walker, single." The man's companion says, "Jack Daniels, single. The bartender approaches the blonde and asks, "And you, ma'am?" The blonde replies, "Susie Sproket, married."

151   After working on a jigsaw puzzle for quite some time, a blonde proudly shows off the finished puzzle to a friend. "It took me only five months to do it,"

"Five months? That's too long," the friend exclaims. "You are a fool," the blonde replies. "It says on the box 'Four to seven years.'"

152   A doctor told a blonde that if he ran eight miles a day for 300 days, he would lose 34 pounds. At the end of 300 days, the blonde called his doctor to report he had lost the weight but he had a problem. "What is the problem?" asked the doctor. The blonde replied, "I am 2,400 miles away from home."

153   A blonde was playing Trivial Pursuit one night. It was her turn. She rolled the dice and she landed on Science and Nature. Her question was, "If you are in a vacuum and someone calls your name, can you hear it?"   She thought for a moment and then asked, "Is it on or off?"

154   A girl was visiting her blonde friend, who had acquired two new dogs, and asked her what their names were. The blonde responded by saying that one was named Rolex and the other was named Timex. Her friend said, "Whoever heard of someone naming dogs like that?"   "Hellllooooo!" answered the blond. "They're watch dogs."

155   A police officer stops a blonde for speeding and asks her very nicely if he can see her license. She replies in a huff, "I wish you guys would get your act together. Just yesterday you took away my license and then today you expect me to show it to you?"

156   A blonde is walking down the street with her blouse open and her right breast hanging out. A policeman approaches her and says, "Ma'am, are you aware that I could cite you for indecent exposure?"   She says, "Why officer?"
"Because your breast is hanging out," he says. She looks down and says, "OH MY GOD, I left the baby on the bus again!"

157   There's this blonde out for a walk. She comes to a river and sees another blonde on the opposite bank. "Yoo-hoo!" she shouts, "How can I get to the other side?"   The second blonde looks up and down the river and shouts back, "You ARE on the other side."

158   A highway patrolman pulled alongside a speeding car on the freeway. Glancing at the car, he was astounded to see a blonde behind the wheel knitting! Realizing that she was oblivious to his flashing lights and siren, the trooper cranked down his window, turned on his bullhorn and yelled, "PULL OVER!" "NO!" the blonde yelled back, "IT'S A SCARF!"

159   A blonde went to a shoe store to buy a pair of shoes made of crocodile skin. She was shocked when she looked at the price: $2,000. So, she went to a nearby zoo and shot a crocodile. After looking at it more closely, she got upset and huffed, "This crocodile isn't wearing any shoes!"

160 A blonde was carrying three sets of eye glasses: one for reading, one for driving and one for figuring out which one is for reading and which one is for driving.

161 On a romantic day, a boy asks his blonde girlfriend, "If we got engaged, would you give me a ring?" "Of course," she replies. "On your landline or cell?"

162 The sign in the parking lot read, "Parking for Two-Wheelers Only." "Oh great. This is going to make me late," the blonde said as she started to remove her two front tires.

163 A friend asked a blonde, "What kind of car do you have?" "I'm not sure," she said. "But it starts with a "T." At this point another blonde chimed in, "Mine starts with gasoline."

164 A blonde was trying to put a bomb in a car. His friend asked, "What would you do if the bomb exploded while you are installing it?" "No problem," he replied. "I have an extra one in my briefcase."

165 A blonde kept getting bitten by mosquitoes while she was sleeping. Frustrated, she decided to drink some poison so that they would die when they sucked her blood.

166 A blonde in a museum accidentally broke a statue. The museum administrator exclaimed, "You just broke a 500-year-old statue." "Wheww!" the blonde replied. "I would have felt horrible if it were new."

167 How do you sink a submarine full of blondes?
Knock on the door.

168 Why do blondes smile when there is lightening?
Because they think someone is taking their picture.

169 Two blondes go camping and pack a cooler with sandwiches and beer. After three days of walking, they arrive at a great spot but realize they've forgotten the bottle opener. The first blonde turns to the second and says, "You've gotta go back and get the opener." "No way," says the second. "By the time I get back, you will have eaten all the food." "I promise I won't," says the first. "Just hurry!" Nine full days pass and there's still no sign of the second blonde. Exasperated and starving, the first blonde digs into the sandwiches. Suddenly, the second blonde pops out from behind a rock and yells, "That's it! I knew it. Now I'm not going!"

170   Two women were filling up at a gas station and the first woman says to her blonde friend, "I bet these awful gas prices are going to go even higher."
The blonde woman replies, "Won't affect me. I always put in just $20 worth."

171   A blind man enters a bar, finds his way to a bar stool and orders a beer. After sitting there for a while, he yells to the bartender, "Hey, you wanna hear a blonde joke?" The bar immediately falls absolutely quiet. In a very deep, husky voice, the woman next to him says, "Before you tell that joke, sir, I think it's fair, given that you are blind, that you know five things:
#1 - The bartender is a blonde girl.
#2 - The bouncer is a blonde girl.
#3 - I'm a 6 feet tall, 220 lb. blonde woman with a black belt in karate.
#4 - The woman sitting next to me is blonde and is a professional weight lifter.
#5 - The lady to your right is a blonde and is a professional wrestler.
Now think about it seriously, mister. Do you still wanna tell that joke? The blind man thinks for a second, shakes his head, and says, "Nah. Not if I'm gonna have to explain it five times."

172   Sam urgently needed to take a few days off work, but knew the boss wouldn't let him. Sam thought that maybe if he acted "crazy" then he would tell him to take a few days off. So, Sam hung upside down on the ceiling and made funny noises. Sam's blonde co-worker asked what he was doing. Sam told her that he was pretending to be a light bulb so that the boss would think he was crazy and give him a few days off. A few minutes later the boss came into the office and asked, "What are you doing?" Sam replied, "I'm a light bulb!" The boss said, "You are clearly stressed out.
Go home and recuperate for a couple of days." Sam jumped down and walked out of the office. Sam's co-worker followed Sam out the door, prompting the boss to ask her, "And where do you think you're going?"
She said, "I'm going home, too. I can't work in the dark."

173   One day a housework-challenged blonde husband decided to wash his sweatshirt. Seconds after he stepped into the laundry room, he shouted to his wife, "What setting do I use on the washing machine?" It depends," she replied. "What does it say on your shirt?" He yelled back, "University of North Carolina."

174   Why does a blonde keep empty beer bottles in her fridge? They're there for those who don't drink.

175   A little boy asked his dad, "Why do you spank me? Did my grandfather also spank you? Did my great-grandfather spank my grandfather?" His dad replied, "Yes." The little boy exclaimed, "For how long and for how many generations will this violent behavior continue?"

176   Newly born boy and girl are sleeping in a crib. Girl asks the boy, "prove you are a boy." Boy pulls up his gown and shows his blue booties (socks).

177   A child is born without ears. The neighbor's son came over and didn't want to say anything about the baby's ears but asked his dad, "When he grows up, if his eyesight is less than 20/20, how would he wear glasses?"

178   A set of twins had been learning about the environment in school. They asked their dad, who was an accountant, "What does carbon do?" "It makes copies," he replied. "Is that how we were born?" they asked.

179   A man comes home with a toy and tells his five kids that the one who is obedient and never talks back will be rewarded with the toy. One kid says, "Dad you should get the toy."

180   Three boys were bragging about their father. The first one says, "My father shot an arrow and ran to the deer before the arrow got there." The second boy says, "My father shot a tiger and he reached it before the tiger fell to the ground." The third boy says, "That's nothing. My father works till 5 PM and reaches home at 4:30 PM."

181   What do train sets and breasts have in common? They are both meant for kids, but the dad's end up playing with them.

182   A boy asks his friend, "How old is this river?" His friend replies - 3 million and 20 years old. The boy says, "Wow, that's really exact. How do you know that?" The friend replies, "Because my dad told me 20 years back that it was 3 million years old."

183   A kid asks why do bride's dress up in white. Reply: It is sign of purity, happiness and peace. Then why do grooms wear black? Reply: Because they are not sure if the marriage will be happy with the bride.

184   What's the difference between radio and television? When parents fight and argue inside the house and the neighbors can hear, that's radio. When parents fight on the front lawn, that's television.

185   Why doesn't Mr. Singh like to play hide and seek? Because he's afraid no one will try to find him.

186   Knowing her husband's habit of sampling everything she bakes, a woman left a note on a dozen tarts reading: "Hands off. One dozen." When she returned, she noticed that two of the tarts had disappeared and the note now read: "Think metric."

187   Mother was setting the table for breakfast when three-year-old Jacquie asked, "Is my supper ready, mom?"
"You don't mean supper," said mother. "What meal do we have in the morning?"
"Oatmeal."

188   A group of kindergarten children visited the local police station and saw pictures of the 10 most wanted men.
One child pointed to a picture and asked if it really was the photograph of the wanted person.
"Yes," answered the policeman guide.
"Well, why didn't you keep him when you took his picture?"

189   A 10-year-old boy wanders into an office building and enters an old-fashioned manned elevator. "What floor please?" asks the attendant.
"Eight," says the boy.
When the elevator reaches the eighth floor, the attendant opens the door and says, "Floor eight, son."
The boy snaps, "Don't call me son. You are not my father!"
The attendant paused for a moment and then answered, "Well, I brought you up, didn't I?"

190 Two new chemical elements have recently been discovered. Here for the first time is a description of their properties:

Element Name: WOMAN

Symbol: WO

Atomic weight: (Don't even go there!)

Physical properties: Generally round in form. Boils at nothing and may freeze any time. Melts whenever treated properly. Very bitter if not used well.

Chemical properties: Very active. Highly unstable. Possesses strong affinity to gold, silver, platinum and precious stones. Violent when left alone. Able to absorb great amounts of exotic food. Turns slightly green when placed next to a better specimen.

Usage: Highly ornamental. An extremely good catalyst for dispersion of wealth. Probably the most powerful income reducing agent known.

Caution: Highly explosive in inexperienced hands.

Element Name: MAN

Symbol: XY

Atomic weight: (180 +/-50)

Physical properties: Solid at room temperature but gets bent out of shape easily. Fairly dense but sometimes flaky. Difficult to find a pure sample. Due to rust, aging samples are unable to conduct electricity as easily as young samples.

Chemical properties: Attempts to bond with WO any chance it can get. Also tends to form strong bonds with itself. Becomes explosive when mixed with KD (Element: Child) for prolonged period of time. Neutralize by saturating with alcohol.

Usage: None known. Possibly good methane source. Good samples are able to produce large quantities on command.

Caution: In the absence of WO, this element rapidly decomposes and begins to smell.

191 A young couple was discussing the imminent arrival of their second child and mentioned that they would have to move to a bigger house. Their first born listened gravely, then shook his head "That would not work," he said. "He'd follow us."

192 One day, a little girl was sitting and watching her mother do the dishes at the kitchen sink. She suddenly noticed that her mother had several strands of white hair sticking out in contrast to her brunette hair.

She looked at her mother and inquisitively asked, "Why is some of your hair white, mom?" Her mother replied, "Well, every time that you do something wrong and make me unhappy, one of my hair turns white."

The little girl thought about this revelation for a while and then asked, "Mom, how come all of grandma's hair is white?"

193   Sue arrives in London on a rainy day. She wakes up the next day and it's raining. It also rains the day after that, and the day after that.

Going out to lunch, she sees a young child and out of despair asks, "Hey kid! Does it ever stop raining around here?" The child replies, "How should I know? I'm only 8."

194   Mr. Singh is filling out his fourth child's birth certificate.

Mother: Sikh. Father: Sikh. Kid: Chinese.

The clerk asks, "How come you wrote Chinese when you and your wife are Sikh?

"Aah," said Mr. Singh, "I read in a newspaper that every fourth person born on the Earth now is Chinese."

195   The mother of two teenagers said to her friend, "I am worried about my kids' failing eyesight."

"Oh, why is that?" asked the friend.

"My daughters can't find anything to wear in a closet full of clothes and my son can't find anything to eat in a refrigerator full of food."

196   A woman received a letter from her sister in which she announced that she had married an Australian. She shared the letter with her young children. "Aunt Christina has married a native of Australia."

Some days later, the family went to visit the local zoo. "And this here," explained a guide pointing to a kangaroo, "is a native of Australia."

Shocked, the youngest child exclaimed, "And to think, Aunt Christina married one of them."

197   A six-year-old boy asked his grandpa, "Why don't dogs like to sit outside in the sun?" "Well," the grandpa says, "They don't want to become hot dogs."

198   Mr. Singh goes to a dinner to honor his friend's late father. He asks, "How did your father die?" His friend replies, "A snake bit him near his left eye." Mr. Singh says, "Lucky that it did not bite him in the eye, otherwise he would have gone blind, too."

199   One day Mr. Singh's wife asked him, "Do you prefer to be buried or cremated after your death?" He replied, "Surprise me."

200   A man goes to a cemetery to visit a recently departed friend. The tombstone reads, "Here lies Joe, a great lawyer and an honest man." The man is very upset and asks the caretaker, "How can you bury two people on one site?"

201   A man ran into a friend of his. His friend noticed that he looked a little down. The man said, "Yes. Money is a little tight right now. Last month I got $5,000 when my dad died. Two months ago I got $10,000 when my grandfather died. Unfortunately, this month no one has died."

202   One day a friend asked Mr. Singh, "Do you want to go to heaven or hell?" Mr. Singh thought for a moment and said, "Hmmm. I'm pretty sure my wife will make it to heaven, so put me down for hell."

203   Once a kid heard some people talking about how dead people go to hell. Confused, she asked her mother, "What is hell?" The mom didn't quite know how to reply, so she said, "Hell is a place where there is no food, water or television." The kid replied, "So dead people come to our house?"

204   Three people died and went to heaven. God asked, "What would you like your friends to say at your viewing?" The first said, "I want to hear that I was a great professor." The second said, "I want to hear that I was a great friend."   The third said, "I want to hear, 'Look! His finger is moving!'"

205   Condolence visit – the younger son did not know what to say so he told his relative, "It is good that your daughter died so now you can save money from her dowry." The relative was upset so the father sent his older son to console and rectify the situation. The older son said, "I am sorry that my brother offended you. But next time, when your son dies, I will come for the condolence visit."

206   A son-in-law on vacation received a telegram saying that his mother-in-law died. The telegram also said, "Advice needed: should we bury or cremate her?" The son-in-law replied, "Use both methods. I don't want to take any chances."

207 The neighbor's second wife died and the husband refused to visit for condolences because he never came to console me.

208 A lady decided to have her portrait made wearing a lot of jewelry that she did not own. When her friend asked her why, she replied, "Well, if my husband remarries, I know she's going to ask, "Hey? Where's all that jewelry?"

209 An American, a Russian and an Indian were fed up with eating the same thing for lunch every day, so instead of enduring the same thing each day, they decided to commit suicide. The American always ate hotdogs. The Russian always ate potatoes. All the wives felt guilty about this, except for the Indian lady. When asked why she didn't feel remorse, she responded, "He packed his own lunch every day."

210 "Young man," asked the supervisor, "Do you believe in life after death?"
"Yes sir," answered the sales clerk.
"Good. Now everything makes sense," said the boss. "Remember yesterday when you left work to attend your grandfather's funeral? Well, about 30 minutes later he dropped in to say hello."

211 At a Rotary dinner, Mr. Singh was honored by the district governor for his nearly 60 years of membership. After the dinner, a newcomer to the community asked Mr. Singh, "Have you spent all of your life in Madison County?"
"Not yet," he replied, "not yet."

212 At their last home game of the season, the coach of a very popular football team noticed an empty seat in the front row behind the coaches' bench. The stadium had been sold out for many years, so he was quite surprised.
It bothered him so much that at halftime he decided to speak to the woman sitting next to the empty seat to see if she knew anything about it. "Pardon me, ma'am but do you know who is supposed to be sitting here?"
"Oh, yes," she said. "It was my husband's seat but he died."
"Well, you certainly have my sympathy," replied the coach. "But don't you have a relative or friend you could offer the seat to?"
"Sure, but not now," the woman responded. "They are all at the funeral."

213 A rich family commissioned a well-known author to write their history, but pointed out that he should soft pedal the fact that one of the uncle's life of crime had ended with a death sentence in the electric chair. "Don't say it straight out," they told the writer. "Skirt around a bit."

The author wrote: "Uncle William occupied a chair of applied electronics in one of the leading government institutions. He was held to the post by the closest of ties, and his death came as a real shock."

214 Mr. Singh died and went to heaven. When he got to the pearly gates St. Peter told him that new rules were in effect due to the advance in education on Earth.

"In order to gain admittance, a prospective heavenly soul must answer two questions.

First, name two days of the week that begin with T.

Second, how many seconds are in a year?"

Mr. Singh thought for a minute and answered.

"First question. The two days of the week with letter T are today and tomorrow.

Second question. There are 12 seconds in a year."

St. Peter said, "Ok, I will buy today and tomorrow even though that wasn't quite what I was looking for. But how did you get 12 seconds in a year?"

Mr. Singh replied, "Well, January 2nd, February 2nd, March 2nd..."

215 George went on a vacation to the Middle East with most of his family, including his mother-in-law. During their vacation, and while they were visiting Jerusalem, George's mother-in-law died.

With the death certificate in hand, George went to the Australian Consulate Office to make arrangements to send the body back to Australia for a proper burial.

The Consul, after hearing of the death of the mother-in-law, told George that the sending of a body back to Australia for burial is very, very expensive. It could cost as much as $5,000. The Consul continued, in most cases the person responsible for the remains normally decides to bury the body here. This only costs $150.

George thinks for a moment and answers, "I don't care how much it will cost to send the body back; that's what I want to do."

The Consul, after hearing this says, "You must have loved your mother-in-law very much considering the difference in price."

"No, it's not that," says George. "You see, I know of a case many years ago of a person who was buried here in Jerusalem. On the third day, he arose from the dead. I just can't take that chance."

216   Due to inherit a fortune when his sickly, widower father died, Charles decided he needed a woman to enjoy it with. Going to a singles bar, he spotted a woman whose beauty took his breath away.

"I'm just an ordinary man," he said, walking up to her, "but in just a week or two, my father will die and I'll inherit $20 million."

The woman went home with Charles, and in four days she became his stepmother.

217   Karen lost her husband almost four years ago and still hasn't gotten out of her mourning stage. Her daughter is constantly calling her and urging her to get back into the world. Finally, Karen says she'll go out, but that she doesn't know anyone. Her daughter immediately replies, "Mom! I have someone for you to meet."

Well, it was an immediate hit. They took to one another and after dating for six weeks, he asks her to join him for a weekend in the Catskills.

Their first night there, she undresses as he does. There she stands nude except for a pair of black lacy panties and he is in his birthday suit. Looking at her he asks: "Why the black panties?" She replies, "My breasts you can fondle, my body is yours to explore, but down there I am still in mourning." He knows he's not getting lucky that night. The following night, the same scenario. She's standing there with the black panties on, and he is in his birthday suit — except that he is wearing a black condom. She looks at him and asks, "What's with the black condom?" He replies, "I want to offer my deepest condolences."

218 A rich person wants to get an honorary PhD. He goes to the University president who says that if you pay $1 million, we will give you an honorary PhD by organizing a special commencement ceremony. The person asks the University president if he would be kind enough to also give a degree to his father, who has been very supportive of his education. The president asks for another $1 million. Then the person asks for a degree for his pet horse. The president replies, I'm sorry, but we only give honorary degrees to donkeys, not horses."

219 A teacher wants all female students to be in the back on the upper level of the classroom. Male students are to be in the front on the lower level. So he says that he wants "all frocks up and pants down."

220 One day Mr. Singh asks his wife, "Please don't talk loudly. It echoes in my head." "Sure dear," she replies. "I'm not sure that's going to help. It's a principle of physics that sound echoes in hollow places."

221 A man's son got some girls pregnant at school. The father had to pay hush money to the girls to protect his son's reputation. Later that year, the daughter of the man got pregnant. He was filled with joy. His daughter was confused that he wasn't upset. "It's my turn to collect money now!"

222 A lazy teacher asked his students, "Do you know what I am going to teach today?" The students replied, "No." The teacher then said, "Since you don't know what I am going to teach today, I'm going home." The second day the teacher asked the same question, "Do you know what I am going to teach today?" And the students replied, "Yes." The teacher said, "If you know what I am going to teach then I'm going home." The third day the teacher asked the same question. Fifty percent of the students said yes. The remaining fifty percent said no. The teacher then said, "Those students who know what I am going to teach will teach the other students who don't know, and I am going home."

223 An English professor asks all students to punctuate the following sentence: Woman without her man is nothing. The boys write, "Woman, without her man, is nothing." The girls wrote, "Woman! Without her, man is nothing."

224 Blackout in girl's dormitory. Girls request boys to come out and help. Reply: Boys are not available, use candles.

225 Four students skipped school and told the teacher that they had a flat tire. The teacher agreed to let them take a make-up test. When they arrived, he asked each one to go in a different room. The test had one question: Which tire?

226   A student did not do his homework and was trying to think of a way to get out of it. "Teacher," the boy said, "I saw your father in a dream and he told me not to do homework and that you won't punish me." This excuse continued for many days. One day the teacher said he also had a dream and his father told him to punish him if he did not do his homework. The student got furious and said, "Your father is a hypocrite."

227   What is the difference between a Ph.D. and an M.D.? The Ph.D. is a Poor Hungry Doctor and the M.D. is a Money Doctor.

228   A teacher asks his class, "What is red and juicy?" Tommy says, "Apple!" The teacher says, "It's a tomato, but I'm glad you were thinking." Then Tommy asks the teacher while putting his hand in his pocket, "What is in my hand? It's long, hard and has a pink tip?" The teacher says, "You have a dirty mind." Tommy says, "It's my pencil but I'm glad you are thinking."

229   A teacher asks his students, "If I lay 5 eggs every day how many eggs would I lay in 7 days?" A student says, "You can't lay eggs. You're not a chicken!"

230   A father, upon seeing his kid's test results, asks, "Why did you fail this test?" His son replies, "It's not my fault. The kid sitting next to me didn't study."

231   A friend in London was explaining the concept of logic to Mr. Singh. "If you feed the fish, it means you love fish. If you are married, it means you are not gay." "I see," said Mr. Singh, and so then he tried to explain the concept of logic to his friend in India. "Are you married?" he asked a friend. "No" "Then you're gay."

232   A teacher tells her class on Thursday, "If you answer a question correctly, then you can have Friday off." She asks the question: "How many stars are in the sky?" No one answers so she says, "See you tomorrow." The next week, she asks, "How many gallons of water are in all the oceans?" Again, there is no answer so she says, "See you tomorrow." One of the students, Ernie, is getting angry because the questions are too tough. So, one night when he's at home he takes two marbles and paints them black. The next day at school when the teacher is getting ready to ask the weekly question, Ernie rolls the two marbles slowly toward her. She asks, "Okay, who's the comedian with the two black balls?" Ernie says, "Bill Cosby. See you on Monday."

233   An email is like a fart. Once it's gone, you can't get it back.

234   One day a dad was talking to his son about discovery and invention. "When I discovered your mother, you were invented."

235   A teacher was explaining to his students, "In our time, our education level was very high." "I assume in your time teachers were very good too," replied one of the students.

236   A teacher was explaining how heat makes things expand and cold makes them contract. "Give me an example, Nancy," he said. "Well, in the summer the days are long and in the winter they are short."

237   Dolly came home from her first day at school.
"Well, darling," asked her mother, "what did they teach you?"
"Not much," Dolly said. "I have to go again tomorrow."

238   What's the plural of baby? Twins…

239   A government speaker addressed the grade school about the danger of rats. One boy was so impressed that he wrote to the speaker, "We didn't know what a rat was like till you came here."

240   The definition of kiss, according to different professors:
Professor of algebra: Kiss is infinity because two can be divided by nothing.
Professor of geometry: Kiss is shortest distance between two lips.
Professor of physics: Kiss is the contraction of the mouth due to expansion of the heat.
Professor of chemistry: Kiss is the reaction of the interaction between two hearts.
Professor of zoology: Kiss is the interchange of salivary bacteria.
Professor of Physiology: Kiss is the just a position of two orbicular muscles in the state of contraction.
Professor of dentistry: Kiss is infectious and antiseptic.
Professor of accountancy: Kiss is a credit because it is profitable when returned.
Professor of economics: Kiss is that thing for which the demand is always higher than the supply.
Professor of statistics: Kiss is an event whose probability depends on the vital statistics of 36-24-36.
Professor of philosophy: Kiss is the persecution for the child, ecstasy for the youth and homage for the old.
Professor of English: Kiss is a noun that is used as a conjunction; it is more common than proper.
Professor of comparative sciences: Kiss is an undefined variable.
Professor of architecture: Kiss is a process that builds a solid bond between two dynamic objects.

241 A high school teacher was telling her students, "Remember, you can't all be first. Even great men have to be second sometimes."

"What about George Washington?" challenged a student. "He was the first U.S. president, first in war, first in peace and first in the hearts of our countrymen!"

"True," replied the quick-thinking teacher. "But don't forget, he married a widow."

242 Sociology: The study of people who do not need to be studied by people who do.

Optimist: A husband who goes to the registry office each year to see if his marriage license has expired.

243 A teacher asked her Sunday school class to tell the story of Creation. A little girl raised her hand and said, "First God created Adam. Then He looked at him and said, 'I think I could do better if I tried it again.'

So he created Eve."

244 A university alumnus sees a list of examination questions by his old economics professor, and exclaims, "Why, those are the same questions you asked when I was in school 20 years ago!"

"Yes," said the professor. "We ask the same questions every year."

"But surely you know that students pass along the questions from one year to the next."

"Of course," said the professor. "But in economics, we change the answers."

245 A teacher was working with a group of children trying to broaden their horizons through sensory exploration. With their eyes closed, they would feel objects from pumice stones to pine cones and smell aromatic herbs and exotic fruits. Then one day, the teacher brought in a great variety of Lifesavers Candy, more flavors than you could ever imagine.

"Children, I'd like you to close your eyes and taste these," announced the teacher. Without difficulty, they managed to identify the taste of cherries, lemons and mint, but when the teacher had them try a honey-flavored one, all of the children were stumped.

"I'll give you a hint," said the teacher. "It's something your daddy and mommy probably call each other all the time."

Instantly, one of the children spat the Lifesaver out of his mouth and shouted, "Spit 'em out, you guys. They're assholes!"

246 Marriage advice from the 1950s:

Have dinner ready: Plan ahead, even the night before, to have a delicious meal – on time. This is a way of letting him know that you have been thinking about him and are concerned about his needs. Most men are hungry when they come home and the prospects of a good meal are part of the warm welcome needed.

Prepare yourself: Take 15 minutes to rest so you will be refreshed when he arrives. Touch up your makeup, put a ribbon in your hair and be fresh looking. He has just been with a lot of work-weary people. Be a little happy and a little more attractive. His boring day may need a lift.

Clear away clutter: Make one last trip through the main part of the house just before your husband arrives, gathering up school books, toys, paper, etc. Then run a dust cloth over the tables. Your husband will feel he has reached a haven of rest and order, and it will give you a lift, too.

Prepare the children: Take a few minutes to wash the children's hands and faces if they are small, comb their hair, and if necessary, change their clothes. They are little treasures and he would like to see them playing the part.

Minimize the noise: At the time of his arrival, eliminate all noise coming from the washer, dryer and vacuum. Try to encourage the children to be quiet. Greet him with a warm smile and be glad to see him.

Some don'ts: Don't greet him with problems or complaints. Don't complain if he's late for dinner. Count this as minor compared with what he might have gone through that day.

Make him comfortable. Have him lean back in a comfortable chair or suggest he lay down in the bedroom. Have a cool or warm drink ready for him. Arrange his pillow and offer to take off his shoes. Speak in a low, soft, soothing and pleasant voice. Allow him to relax and unwind.

Listen to him: You may have dozens of things to tell him, but the moment of his arrival is not the time. Let him talk first.

Make the evening his: Never complain if he does not take you out to dinner or to other places of entertainment. Instead try to understand his world of strain and pressure and his need to be home and relax.

The goal: try to make your home a place of peace and order so your husband can relax.

Here is the reality check for 21st century:

Have dinner ready: Make reservations ahead of time. If your day becomes too hectic just leave him a voicemail message regarding where you would like to eat and at what time. This lets him know that your day has been crappy and gives him an opportunity to change your mood.

Prepare yourself: A quick stop at the Clinique counter on your way home will do wonders for your outlook and will keep you from becoming irritated every time he opens his mouth.

Clear away the clutter: Call the housekeeper and tell her that any miscellaneous items left on the floor by the children can be placed in the Goodwill box in the garage.

Prepare the children: Send the children to their rooms to watch television or play Nintendo.

Minimize the noise: If you happen to be home when he arrives, be in the bathroom with the door locked.

Some don'ts: Don't agree with problems and complaints. Let him speak first, and then your complaints will get more attention and remain fresh in his mind throughout dinner. Don't complain if he's late for dinner, simply remind him the leftovers are in the fridge and you left dishes for him to do.

Make him comfortable: Tell him where he can find a blanket if he's cold. This will really show you care.

Listen to him: But don't ever let him get the last word.

Make the evening his: Never complain if he does not take you out to dinner or other places of entertainment; go with a friend or go shopping. (You can use his credit card!) Familiarize him with the phrase "Girl's Night Out!"

The Goal: Try to keep things amicable without reminding him that he only thinks the world revolves around him. Obviously he's wrong, it revolves around you.

247   One day, a 6-year-old girl was sitting in a classroom. The teacher asked one of the other students, "Tommy, do you see the grass outside?" "Yes," he said. Then the teacher asked, "Do you see a tree outside?" "Yes," he replied. Again the teacher asked, "Do you see grass outside?" "Yes," Tommy said. "Did you see God outside?" Tommy replied, "No."

The teacher said, "That is my point, we cannot see God because he is not there. He does not exist."

Then the girl asked Tommy the same questions about the grass, the tree and the sky. She then added, "Do you see the teacher?" "Yes," "Do you see her brain?" she asked. He said, "No." The little girl said, "Then according to what we were taught today in school, the teacher must not have a brain."

248   A scientist was studying the behavior of frogs. He instructed the frog to jump, and the frog jumped four feet. So he wrote in his notebook: A frog with all four feet jumps four feet.

The scientist then cut off one leg. He instructed the frog to jump, and the frog jumped three feet. The scientist wrote in his notebook: A frog with three feet jumps three feet.

The scientist then cut off one more leg. He instructed the frog to jump, and the frog jumped two feet. The scientist wrote in his notebook: A frog with two feet jumps two feet.

The scientist cut off one more leg. He instructed the frog to jump, and the frog jumped one foot. The scientist wrote in his notebook: A frog with one foot jumps one foot.

The scientist then cut off the last leg. He told the frog to jump, jump, JUMP!

But the frog did not jump. The scientist wrote in his notebook: A frog with no legs becomes deaf.

249 Here is a barnyard course in economics based on definitions of major social orders:

a. Socialism: You have two cows; you give one to your neighbor.

b. Communism: You have two cows; the government takes both of them and gives you the milk.

c. Fascism: You have two cows; the government takes both of them and sells you the milk.

d. Bureaucracy: You have two cows; the government takes both of them, shoots one, milks the other and pours the milk down the drain.

e. Capitalism: You have two cows; you sell one and buy a bull!

250 A first grade teacher, Ms. Brooks, was having trouble with one of her students. The teacher asked, "What is your problem?" Tommy answered, "I'm too smart for the first grade. I want to be in the third grade. My sister is in the third grade too." Ms. Brooks had had enough. She took Tommy to the principal's office. While Tommy waited in the outer office, the teacher explained the situation to the principal. The principal told Ms. Brooks he would give the boy a test and if he failed to answer any of the questions, he would remain in the first grade and have to behave. She agreed. Tommy was brought in and the conditions were explained to him and he agreed to take the test. Principal: "What is 3x3?" Tommy: "9." Principal: "What is 6x6?" Tommy: "36." And so it went with every question the principal thought a third grader should know. The principal looked at Ms. Brooks and told her, "I think Tommy can go to third grade." Ms. Brooks says to the principal, "Let me ask him some questions." The principal and Tommy both agreed. Ms. Brooks asked, "What does a cow have four of that I have only two of?" Tommy, after a moment, replied, "Legs." Ms. Brooks: "What do you have in your pants that I do not have in mine?" The principal wondered, why does she ask such a question? Tommy replied: "Pockets." Ms. Brooks: "What starts with a C and ends with a T, is hairy, oval, delicious, and contains thin whitish liquid?" Tommy: "Coconut." Ms. Brooks: "What goes in hard and pink then comes out soft and sticky?" The principal's eyes open wide and before he could stop the answer, Tommy: "Bubble gum." Ms. Brooks: "What does a man do standing up, a woman does sitting down and a dog does on three legs?" Tommy: "Shake hands." Ms. Brooks: "What word starts with an F and ends in K that means a lot of heat and excitement?" Tommy: "Fire truck". The principal breathed a sigh of relief and told the teacher, "Put Tommy in the fifth grade; I got the last six questions wrong."

251 A fourth grade teacher was giving her pupils a lesson in logic. "Here is the situation," she said. "A man is standing up in a boat in the middle of the river, fishing. He loses his balance, falls in, and begins splashing and yelling for help. His wife hears the commotion, knows he cannot swim and runs down to the bank. Why do you think she ran to the bank?"
A girl raised her hand and asked, "To draw out all his savings?"

252   One day in Contract Law class, the professor asked one of his better students, "Now if you were to give someone an orange, how would you go about it?

The student replied, "Here is an orange."

"No, no, think like a lawyer!" the professor instructed.

The student then recited, "OK, I'd tell him, 'I hereby give and convey to you all and singular, my estate and interests, rights, claim, title, claim advantages of and in, said orange together with its rind, juice, pulp, and seeds, and all rights and advantages with full power to bite, cut, freeze and otherwise eat, the same, or give the same away with and without pulp, juice, rind and seeds, anything herein before or herein after or in any deed, or deeds, instruments of whatever nature or kind whatsoever to the contrary in anywise notwithstanding.'"

253   A language instructor was explaining to her class that French nouns, unlike their English counterparts, are grammatically designated as masculine or feminine. Things like "chalk" or "pencil," she described, have a gender association, although in English these words were neutral.

Puzzled, one student raised his hand and asked, "What gender is computer?"

The teacher was not certain, so she divided the class into two groups and asked them to decide if computer should be masculine or feminine. One group was composed of women and the other group was of men. Both groups were asked to give four reasons for their recommendation.

The group of women concluded that computers should be referred to as masculine gender because:

In order to get their attention, you have to turn them on.

They have a lot of data, but are clueless.

They are supposed to help you solve problems, but half the time they are the problem.

As soon as you commit to one, you realize that, if you had waited a little longer, you could have a better model.

The men, on the other hand, decided that computers should definitely be referred to as feminine gender because:

No one but their creator understands the internal logic.

The native language they use to communicate with other computers is incomprehensible to everyone else.

Even your smallest mistakes are stored in long-term memory for later retrieval.

254   How computers have changed our perspective? Remember when:

An application was for employment. A program was a television show. A cursor was profanity. A keyboard was a piano!

Memory was something you lost with age; a CD was a bank account.

And if you had a 3½ inch floppy, you hoped nobody ever found out.

Compress was something you did to garbage, not something you did to a file;

and if you unzipped anything in public, you would be in jail for a while.

Log on was adding wood to fire; a hard drive was a long trip on the road;

a mouse pad was where a mouse lived; and a backup happened to your commode.

Cut you did with a pocket knife; paste you did with glue;

a web was a spider's home; and a virus was the flu.

I guess I will stick to my pad and paper, and the memory in my head;

nobody's been killed in a computer crash, but when it happens they wish they were dead.

255   A frustrated professor asked his class, "If there are any dumbbells in the room, please stand up."

After a long pause, a lone freshman stood up.

The professor asked, "Do you consider yourself a dumbbell?

The freshman replied, "Well, not exactly that, sir, but I hate to see you standing all alone."

256   "Can anyone tell me how fast light travels?" asked the third grade teacher.

"I don't know how fast it travels," answered Tommy, "but I know it comes too early in the morning for me."

257   A teacher was trying to motivate an underperforming pupil. "When George Washington was your age," she said, "he was head of the class."

"Yes, I know," answered the student. "And when he was of your age, he was the president of the United States."

258   A university lecturer asked her students to describe in a page or less the difference between ignorance and apathy. The top mark went to a student who wrote, "I don't know and I don't care."

259   A teacher gave his kindergarten class a homework assignment asking them to find out about something exciting and relate it to the class next day.

When the time came for the little kids to give their reports, the teacher called on them one at a time.

He was reluctant to call upon Johnny, knowing that sometimes he could be a bit crude. But eventually his turn came.

Johnny walked up to the front of the class and made a small dot on the chalkboard and sat back down.

The teacher could not figure out where Johnny was going with this, so he asked him what it was.

"It is a period," reported Johnny. "Well I can see that but what is so exciting about a period?" the teacher asked.

"Damned if I know," said Johnny. "But this morning my sister said she missed one. Then daddy had a heart attack, Mommy fainted and the man next door shot himself."

260   The first-grade teacher was starting a new lesson on multi-syllable words and asked a few of the children for examples of words with more than one syllable.

Johnny raises his hand and says, "I know, I do I do!"

Knowing Johnny's more mature sense of humor she calls on Mike instead.

Mike says, "Saturday." The teacher says, "Great! That has three syllables."

Johnny says, "I know a four syllable word."

Teacher reluctantly asked him to say the word. Johnny proudly says, "Mas…tur…ba…tion."

The shocked teacher says, "Wow, Johnny. A four syllable word is certainly a mouthful."

Johnny, "No ma'am, you are thinking of 'blowjob' and that is only two syllables."

261   Mr. Singh came to Miami University to study and the foreign student advisor introduced him to a host family so that he could learn American customs. The host explained to Mr. Singh that if there is an emergency, such as a fire, you should dial 911 for help. When Mr. Singh moved to his apartment, he started a fire while cooking. The next day he talked to his host and told him about the fire. The host asked, "Why didn't you call 911?" "I tried," Mr. Singh said. "But I could not find the number "11" on my phone.

262   One Friday afternoon a teacher announced, "Whoever answers these questions first gets to go home early."

The teacher asked, "Which president said 'the buck stops here?'" Susie shouted out, "Nixon!"

Next the teacher asked, "Who said 'read my lips?'" Little Annie shouted out, "George Bush!"

The teacher said, "Very good, see you Monday."

Little Johnny was pissed off and muttered, "I wish those girls would keep their f…..
mouths shut."

The teacher very angrily said, "Who said that?"

Little Johnny shouted, "Bill Clinton, see you Monday."

263   A Sunday school teacher of preschoolers was concerned that her students might be a little confused about Jesus Christ because of the Christmas season's emphasis on his birth. She wanted to make sure they understood that the birth of Jesus occurred a long time ago, that he grew up, etc. So she asked the class, "Where is Jesus today?" Steven raised his hand and said, "He is in heaven."

Mary was called on and answered, "He's in my heart."

Little Johnny, waving his hand furiously, blurted out, "I know, I know! He is in our bathroom!"

The teacher was completely at a loss. Finally she gathered her courage and asked Little Johnny how he knew this.

Little Johnny said, "Well, every morning my father gets up, bangs on the bathroom door and yells, 'Jesus Christ, are you still in there?'"

264 It was the first day of school and a new student named Krishna entered the fourth grade.

The teacher said, "Let's begin by reviewing some American history. Who said, "Give me liberty or give me death"?

She saw a sea of blank faces, except for Krishna, who had his hand up. "Patrick Henry, 1775" he said. "Very good! Who said, "Government of the people, by the people, for the people, shall not perish from the Earth?" Again, no response except from Krishna. "Abraham Lincoln, 1863." The teacher snapped at the class, "Class, you should be ashamed. Krishna, who is new to our country, knows more about its history than you do." She heard a loud whisper: "F**k the Indians." "Who said that?" she demanded.

Krishna put his hand up. "General Custer, 1862." At that point, a student in the back said, "I'm gonna puke."   The teacher glared around and asked, "All right! Now, who said that?" Again, Krishna said, "George Bush to the Japanese prime minister, 1991."

Now furious, another student yelled, "Oh yeah? S*ck this!"

Krishna jumped out of his chair waving his hand and shouts to the teacher, "Bill Clinton, to Monica Lewinsky, 1997!" Now with almost mob hysteria someone shouted, "You little shit. If you say anything else, I'll kill you."

Krishna frantically yelled at the top of his voice, "Gary Condit to Chandra Levy, 2001."

The teacher fainted. And as the class gathered around her on the floor, someone said, "Oh shit, we're f**ked!" and Krishna said quietly, "George Bush, Iraq, 2005."

265   A not necessarily well-prepared student sat in his life science classroom, staring at a question on the final exam paper. The question directed said, "Give four advantages of breast milk."

What to write? He sighed and began to scribble whatever came into his head, hoping for the best:

1. No need to boil.

2. Never goes sour.

3. Available whenever necessary.

"So far so good," he thought. "But I still need one more answer."

He sighed. He frowned. He scowled, and then sighed again. Suddenly, he brightened. He grabbed his pen and triumphantly scribbled his definitive answer:

4. Available in attractive containers of varying sizes.

266   Mr. Singh is very disappointed in the singer he hired for a function and charges the stage with a baseball bat. The singer starts to get scared and run away. Mr. Singh says, "You are our guest. Please continue to sing. I'm looking for the organizer who invited you to perform here."

267   The host of the party asked Mr. Singh not to wear smelly socks at his next party since they smell like a dead mouse. A few weeks later, Mr. Singh went to another party hosted by the same person. The host, very angry, approached Mr. Singh and said, "I thought I told you not to wear those dirty socks at my party." Mr. Singh replied, "I'm not wearing those dirty socks. I brought them here in my pocket to prove that I'm not wearing them."

268   A perfect couple bought a perfect car and went for a ride and met Santa Claus, who was in desperate need of a ride. They had an accident and two of the three died. Who survived? The wife. After all, there is no such thing as a perfect husband, and there is no Santa Claus.

269   Mr. Singh complained that all other government officials have a refrigerator except him. They went to inspect and found that he has a refrigerator. They opened the door and found that all of his shoes are in the refrigerator because Mr. Singh thought it was a shoe closet.

270   Mr. Singh took a group photograph of 50 people. He insisted that the whole group move back three feet in order to frame the picture properly rather than moving back three feet himself.

271   Mr. Singh is tired and goes to take a nap. He heads to his room and starts to put on brand new underwear, a shirt, a tie, and a turban. "What on Earth are you doing? Aren't you going to bed?" his wife asks. "Yes, but I want to be ready in case company comes."

272   Mr. Singh receives a telegram from his wife. He tells the delivery person, "I will not acknowledge this telegram. That's not my wife's handwriting."

273   An Egyptian was bragging that they discovered copper wire in ancient ruins. Mr. Singh said that in India, they were digging in North India and didn't find any wire — proof that they were so advanced that they had a wireless system.

274   A teenage girl was about to leave the house wearing very tight clothes. Her dad said, "Those clothes will stop your blood circulation." "Yes, dad. But they will increase my social circulation."

275   A man asked the head of the village if he could borrow his horse for one day. The owner didn't want to lend him the horse so he lied and said that the horse had gone somewhere. The man heard the horse's as he was walking out the gate. He immediately turned around and told the owner that he just heard the horse's voice through the barn. The owner got very upset and replied, "Mister you understand the language of the animal but not the language of human beings."

276   What's a benefit to dating a homeless girl? You can drop her off anywhere you like.

277   A New Yorker passing through Kentucky went to a restroom. While in the restroom a quarter fell from his pocket into the toilet. The New Yorker did not want to put his hand in the dirty toilet water to get the quarter out so he put a twenty dollar bill in the toilet. He then put his hand in the toilet bowl and pulled out both the twenty dollar bill and the quarter.

278   A survey was done on all bald men. Turns out, men who are bald in the back of their head are thinkers. Men who are bald in the front of their heads are lovers. Those who are completely bald think that they are lovers.

279   Mr. Singh is very happy because his brother is expecting a child. His friends ask him, "Are you going to be an uncle or an aunt?" Mr. Singh replies, "I don't know if the child is a boy or a girl."

280   Two servants were talking about their masters' stupidity. The first servant said, "My master asked me to buy a BMW for fifty dollars, how stupid is that request?" The second servant said, "My master asked me to call him at his home to find out if he is at home."

281   Three people exaggerating about their countries' achievements: an American says, "We have airplanes that can almost touch the sky, only two centimeters below the sky." A Russian man says, "We have submarines that can go two centimeters above the bottom of the ocean and almost touch it." Mr. Singh says, "In India we can eat from just two centimeters below the nose."

282   Mr. Singh always scolds the children in his neighborhood for not being knowledgeable. He asked them, "Do you know where the Taj Mahal is, do you know where the White House is, do you know where London Bridge is?" The children did not know. Well, one day the children asked Mr. Singh if he knew who Tom Cruise was. Mr. Singh did not know. The children said, "Mr. Singh, sometimes you should see who comes into your house when you go out. You know the whole world but you do not know what happens in your house."

283   An Indian man who had been living in America returned home to India. Every day, he kept saying how great America was because there weren't electricity or water shortages, etc. His relatives were getting pretty tired of his uncle's statements implying that India wasn't that good. "When you were happy in America," he said, "we were very happy in India."

284   A man asked his friend in a theater, "Where should I spit out my chewing tobacco?" "Spit in your neighbor's coat pocket?" Then the man said, "He might get upset and beat me up." The friend said, "Did you notice it when I spit in your pocket?"

285   Mr. Singh told his wife that he would like to be on the bottom while making love. The next day he arrived home to find bunk beds in their bedroom.

286   A man wears a hat before opening the door to avoid unwanted guests. If someone comes who he doesn't want to see, he says that he is about to leave.

287   Why did Mr. Singh climb the glass wall? He wanted to see the other side.

288   How do you keep Mr. Singh busy? Give him a bag full of M&Ms and ask him to put them in alphabetical order.

289   A man accidentally killed a farmer's pig. "Don't worry," the man said. "I will replace your pig." The farmer says, "That's awful nice of you, but you are not nearly as fat as my pig."

290   A young lady realizes that she does not have money to pay the taxi fare. The driver says, "No problem, lady. Just give me your panties." The lady says, "But they are only worth $2 while the fare is $20."

291   A man who stutters was trying to convince people that everyone has some sort of peculiarity. He points to his friend and asks, "Take you, for example. Do you stir your tea with your right hand?" "Yes," his friend replied. "That's funny," said the man. Everyone else uses a spoon."

292   Mr. Singh, calling his friend from the top of the Empire State building, uses binoculars and talks very slowly because he thinks people are very close.

293   A burglar broke into a house looking for money. The poor house owner wakes up and says, "Hey. Let me know if you find any."

294 An ape died in a zoo and the zoo decided to replace it with a man dressed up like an ape. He mistakenly jumped into the lion's den and started screaming. The lion came close and said, "Shut up! I am also a man dressed up as a lion and if you keep screaming, we'll both loose our jobs."

295 A friend said to his classmate, "You are very fat." The man replies, "I'm not fat, I'm just short for my weight."

296 A son tells his brother, "Keep digging in the lawn because Dad put a lot of money in it."

297 Mr. Singh was robbed and lost two dollars. The judge asked him, "Why are you suing him for just two dollars?" Reply: "I do not want to expose my poor financials to a stranger."

298 A barber decided to give back to his community so he decided to give free haircuts. Some local struggling students were very appreciative so they sent 12 roses as a token of gratitude. A few local businesses sent the barber 12 donuts and a thank-you. Indians sent 12 fellow Indians for a free haircut.

299 The wait staff at a local restaurant was told by management not to announce to patrons when they ran out of something, but to instead offer a substitute. When they ran out of milk, one inventive waiter tried to trick the customers and used facial powder for the coffee, hoping no one would notice.

300 A man was looking for shelter. He knocked on doors in a neighborhood and asked the owner of a house "Do you have any rooms available?" The owner said, "Sorry, but no. I have young girls in the house." So the man went to the next house and asked, "Do you have a room for the night and do you have young girls in the house?"

301 What does a dog do on three legs, a man does standing up, and a woman does sitting down? Shake hands.

302 Mr. Singh comes to the U.S. and sees a sign that says "Deer Crossing." He thinks, "Wow. The U.S. road system is so organized that even the deer are trained."

303 Mr. Singh couldn't eat any more because he was full but he couldn't resist his favorite dessert and had three servings. "Wow," The waiter said. "I thought you were full. How did you have room for all that dessert?" Mr. Singh replied, "Well, it's like when the president decides to come to a sold-out show. People create room."

304   A lady took her car in for a repair estimate and got into an argument with the mechanic and said, "I would like to get a second opinion." He said, "I think you're ugly, too."

305   Mr. Singh couldn't tell if brown stuff in front of his house was cow shit or chocolate. After tasting it he said, "I am soooo glad I didn't put my foot in it."

306   Two friends saw a tiger running in the forest. One friend started running very fast. His friend said, "You can never beat a tiger." He replied, "I am trying to beat you, not the tiger."

307   A beggar asked a gentleman to give him money, food or clothes. The man replied, "I don't have anything." The beggar said, "Well then, why don't you join me? We can start our own business."

308   A lady just came out of the shower when the doorbell rings. She sees out of the window that it is her blind friend. She doesn't bother putting on any clothes and opens the door. He is standing there with a box of chocolates to celebrate his successful eye operation.

309   Mr. Singh opened a bottle and asked the genie for three wishes. "I would like a liquor bottle that never empties." Then he asked for two more bottles.

310   Mr. Singh was having a headache and a friend told him to put his head in his wife's bosom. "That's crazy!" he said. His friend replied, "It worked for me."

311   A very shy young man and a young girl had to share a bed separated by a pillow. The next morning the girl asks, "What are you doing in Calcutta?" The man replies, "I came to cross the Bay of Bengal." The girl laughs and says, "If you cannot cross this pillow, how could you cross the Bay of Bengal?"

312   A friend asks Mr. Singh, "What is your address?" Reply: "Which one: Indian, American or Mexican?" "Your car plate #?" Reply: "Which car, Mercedes, Chevrolet or BMW?" "What is your Father's name?" Reply: "Which father?"

313   A host asks his guest if he would like to have some tea. Reply: "Yes." Q1: "Tea in a kettle or pot?" Q2: "With milk or without milk?" Q3: "With or without sugar?" Q4: "With spices or no spices?" Q5: "Teabag or loose tea?" Q6: "Now or later?" The guest got so annoyed that he said, "Don't ask me if I want to have tea here or at home."

314   Too many family relatives – should I make a family tree or forest?

315 Mr. Singh bought a new house and a new car.
Thinking he was in a spending mood, his wife asked for a vacation. "I have the perfect idea! He said, "We will sit in our house and watch our car and when we get tired of that we will sit in our car and watch our house."

316 There was this international milking competition. The Russian team milked 200 liters. The American team milked 100 liters and an Indian milked 40 liters because he tried to milk a bull.

317 Being pissed off is better than being pissed on.

318 A servant went to buy three chocolates for his master and ate one on his way home. When he got home his master asked, "How did one of the chocolates disappear?" "Easy," the servant replied as he popped another one in his mouth.

319 A beggar asks for 10 cents and the donor says, "Why are you asking for so little?" The beggar replied, "I operate on a sliding scale."

320 Mr. Singh asked the joke teller to wait while he called his four sons. The joke teller refused, saying "I'm not going to tell the same joke five times."

321 A lady asked a genie, "Make me two times wiser than my friends." The genie granted her the wish. Then she said, "Make me 10 times wiser." Again, the genie complied. For her third wish, she said, "Make me 1,000 times wiser." Then, poof! The genie turned her into a man.

322 A lady on a bus, wearing a very tight skirt, tried twice to unzip it. A man standing behind her reached over and unzipped her skirt a little bit. The lady got mad. The man replied, "You tried to zip my pants twice and I didn't get mad."

323 A blind man's dog was misbehaving so he asked a policeman to show him where the dog's mouth was. "Why do you want to know that?" the policeman asked. "So I can kick his ass."

324 Mr. Singh decided to paint his house and put on two jackets. His wife asked, "Why are you wearing two jackets?" "Well," he replied, "It says on the can, 'Put on two coats for long-lasting results.'"

325 An artist was tired of giving autographs so he decided to draw a monkey instead. Upon seeing it, one fan said, "I asked for an autograph, not a photograph."

326   Mr. Singh was asked to buy a cat and he bought cat food; he was asked to buy a dog and he bought dog food; he was asked to buy toilet tissue paper but bought a plastic bag full of shit.

327   One day there was a major snow storm on a farm. The Indian farmer said, "We got so much cold weather that while milking a cow, the milk turned into ice cream."

328   Two friends were walking and a bird shits on Singh's shirt. His friend brings toilet paper to clean his friend's shirt. Mr. Singh says, "The bird is gone so we don't need toilet paper."

329   What is your opinion about eating meat? An Indian says, "What is meat?" An Ethiopian says, "What is eating?" And an Iranian says, "What is meant by opinion?"

330   A farmer has stopped giving water to his cow. Confused, his wife asks, "Why aren't you giving the cow water anymore?" He replies, "I want her to produce powdered milk."

331   A lady says to her neighbor, "The social atmosphere is not very good here so we are moving." The neighbor replies, "Once you move out, the atmosphere will improve."

332   A lady gives blessings to a man. Her husband asks, "Why did you do that?" She replies, "He touched my feet." Husband: "The man was simply measuring your shoe size."

333   Bernard Shaw, while walking, faced the king who said, "I don't yield the way to people." Shaw said, "But I do yield to fools."

334   What are a woman's four best animal friends? A mink on the back, a Jaguar in the garage, a Tiger in bed, and a Jackass to pay the bills.

335   Mr. Singh was laughing while being beaten up by the police because he was the wrong guy.

336   Mr. Singh was having trouble measuring the height of a flagpole. He tried and tried, and even asked his relatives to stand on top of each other to reach the top. Then a friend passed by and suggested, "Why don't you pull the flagpole out, lay it on the ground and measure it that way?" Mr. Singh said in an angry voice, "I'm supposed to measure the height of the pole, not the length."

337   A buffalo was trying to pass through a door but its horns and legs were too big for him to get through. Mr. Singh thought, "I know! Let's dig a hole in the floor so that it can fit through!"

338   A lady with only three hairs goes to a beauty salon and asks to have it braided. While braiding it one hair falls out. Without feeling bad, she asks the barber to make a bun with the remaining two hairs. Then a second hair falls out. She tells the barber, "Just keep it untied. I like that way too."

339   A man was hopping around and friend asked if he lost a shoe. Reply: "No, I found a shoe."

340   A man bought a watch dog who watched a thief steal but did not bark. When the man complained to the seller, he replied, "He's a watch dog, not a bark dog."

341   A modern artist painted a painting titled, 'A Cow Grazing'. Mr. Singh asked, "Where is the grass?" The artist replied, "The cow ate the grass." Mr. Singh asked, "Where is the cow?" The artist replied, "After eating the grass, she went to a different pasture."

342   Mr. Singh told all of his employees to shred all documents. Worried about losing important records he asked, "But be sure to make copies first."

343   The Benefits of Smoking: You never get old because you die young and you will never have any theft because you cough all night.

344   A woman desires two men in her life – one to cook and the second to do the dishes.

345   Mr. Singh pulled out six firefighters from a burning building filled with people. After his heroic feat he was arrested. "But officer," he asked, "What's the charge?" "Interfering with a rescue operation."

346   A wife told her husband she thought there was a thief in the house. Her husband ran to the kitchen and found a thief stealing things. He knocked the thief down, sat on him and asked his son to run to the police station. After 10 minutes his son was still in the house. The father asked his son, "Why haven't you gone to police station?" "I cannot find my shoes," he replied. The thief told the boy, "You can use my shoes but go fast because I cannot bear the heavy weight of your father."

347   Mr. Singh was looking for his wife, who was shopping in the mall, and ran into his friend who was also looking for his wife at the mall. Mr. Singh described his wife as beautiful, with blue-eyes, a fair complexion and with looks like an actress. His friend said, "Let's find your wife first."

348   What a benefit to smoking? You never get old because you die young.

349 Mr. Singh ran into a friend who asked him, "Is that beautiful car yours?"

"It is and it isn't," replied Mr. Singh.

"What do you mean?"

"When it is necessary to go shopping, it belongs to my wife. When there is a party, it's my daughter's. When the guys are getting together, it belongs to my son. And when it needs an oil change or repairs, it is mine."

350 The tenant complained to his landlord, "The couple in the upstairs apartment annoyed me again last night with their stomping and banging on the floor until well after midnight."

"Did they awaken you?" inquired the landlord.

"Well, no," answered the tenant. "As it happened, I was still up practicing my tuba."

351 A man met another man in a big city. He asked him, "What happened to you, Anderson? You used to be a tall man, now you are a small man. You used to have a black beard, now you have a red beard. What has this city done to you?"

The second man replies, "My name is not Anderson."

"So, you changed your name, too?"

352 The suburban housewife had been reading about Cleopatra and the milk baths she took to enhance and preserve her legendary beauty. The housewife confronted her milkman at the door and asked, "How much milk would it take to fill a bathtub?"

"Pasteurized?" asked the milkman.

"No," said the lady, "I think up to the shoulders would do."

353 A young boy leading a donkey passed by an army camp. A couple of soldiers wanted to have some fun by teasing the boy.

"Why are you holding your brother so tight, lad?" one of the men asked.

"So he won't join the army," the kid replied.

354 Two counterfeiters with a talented but not-so-smart engraver found themselves with a large quantity of almost perfect bills in their hands. The trouble was they were all $18 bills. The crooks decided to go far into the hill country to dispose of the bills, because, as one explained to the other, "Nobody up there sees much money."

Deep in the mountains, they entered a tiny out-of-the-way store and talked the storekeeper into changing the bill.

"How do you want it?" the storekeeper asked. "Would two sevens and a four be all right?"

355 An actor in Hollywood was complaining about the inefficient postal system in Los Angeles. "I'm not saying the mail in Hollywood is slow, but I just got my invitation to Elizabeth Taylor's first wedding."

356 A beggar walked up to a well-dressed woman shopping on Rodeo Drive and said, "I haven't eaten anything in four days." She looked at him and said, "God, I wish I had your willpower."

357 Things to think about:
To steal ideas from one person is plagiarism, to steal from many is research.
Why is abbreviation such a long word?
Many people quit looking for work as soon as they find a job.
If you think nobody cares about you, try missing a couple of payments.
What happens if you get scared half to death twice?

358 Sherlock Holmes and Dr. Watson went on a camping trip. After a good meal and a bottle of wine they lay down for the night and went to sleep. Some hours later, Holmes awoke and nudged his faithful friend. "Watson, look up at the sky and tell me what you see." Watson replied, "I see millions and millions of stars."
"What does that tell you?" inquired Holmes. Watson pondered for a minute and said, "Astronomically, it tells me that there are millions of galaxies and potentially billions of planets. Astrologically, I observe that Saturn is in Leo. Horologically, I deduce that the time is approximately a quarter past three. Theologically, I can see that God is all-powerful and that we are small and insignificant. Meteorologically, I suspect that we will have a beautiful day tomorrow. What does it tell you?"
Holmes was silent for a minute, and then spoke.
"It tells me some bastard has stolen our tent."

359 Americans are getting stronger. Fifty years ago, you needed a station wagon to hold $10 worth of groceries; Twenty years ago, it took two people to carry $10 worth of groceries. Now a five year old can handle it.

360 My face in the mirror isn't wrinkled or drawn.
My house is not dirty. My cobwebs are gone.
My garden looks lovely and so does my lawn.
I think I might never put my glasses back on.

361   My neighbor was bitten by a stray, rabid dog. I went to see how he was, and found him writing frantically. I told him rabies can be cured and that he didn't have to worry about a will. He said, "Will? What will? I am making a list of the people I want to bite!"

362   A bus stopped and two Italian men got on. They sat down and engaged in animated conversation. The lady sitting behind them ignored their conversation at first, but her attention was galvanized when she heard one of the men say the following:
"Emma come first, Denna I come. Two asses, they come together. I come again. Two asses, they come together again. I come again and pee twice. Then I come once more."
"You foul mouthed swine," said the lady. "In this country we don't talk about our sex lives in public!" "Hey, cool down lady," said the man. "Imma just telling my friend howa to spella MISSISSIPPI."

363   How many times has someone said to you, "You don't know Jack Schitt"?
This phrase is usually used in a heated argument to basically tell the other person they are stupid. Now you will learn the entire story.
Jack Schitt is the only son of O. Schitt and Awe Schitt. O. Schitt, the fertilizer magnate, married Awe Schitt, who later ran the Kneedeep Inn – Schitt. Jack Schitt eventually married Noe Schitt, and together they produced six children. Holy Schitt, their first child passed away shortly after birth. Next came twin sons, Deep Schitt and Dip Schitt and then two daughters, Fulla Schitt and Giva Schitt. Their final child, another son, named Bull Schitt. In the meantime, Deep Schitt married Dumb Schitt, a high school dropout. Dip Schitt married Lotta Schitt and they have a son Chicken Schitt. Full Schitt and Giva Schitt married the Happens Brothers. The Schitt –Happens children are Dawg Schitt, Bird Schitt and Horse Schitt. Bull Schitt just married a spicy number, Pisa Schitt and they are expecting the arrival of Baby Schitt.

364   One day the different parts of the body were having an argument to see which one should be in charge.

The brain said, "I do all the thinking so I'm the most important and I should be in charge."

The eyes said, "I see everything and let the rest of you know where we are, so I'm the most important and I should be in charge."

The hand said, "Without me we would not be able to pick anything up or move anything. So I'm the most important and I should be in charge."

The stomach said, "I turn the food we eat into energy for the rest of you. Without me, we'd starve. So I am the most important and I should be in charge."

The legs said, "Without me we would not be able to move anywhere. So I am important and I should be in charge."

Then the rectum said, "I think I should be in charge." All the rest of the parts said "YOU? You don't do anything. You are not important so you should not be in charge."

So the rectum closed up.

After a few days, the legs were all wobbly, the stomach was queasy, the hands were all shaky, the eyes were watery, and the brain was cloudy. They all agreed that they could not take any more of this and agreed to put the rectum in charge.

The moral of the story?

You don't have to be the most important to be in charge, you just have to be an asshole.

365   Life is full of contradictions:

Why is it called rush hour when your car barely moves?

If Superman is so clever, why did he wear his underwear on the outside?

If a 7-11 is open 24 hours a day, 365 days a year, why are there locks on the doors?

If it is a circular drive, how do you get out?

Why does sour cream have an expiration date?

Why is it that when you deliver by car, it's called a shipment and when you deliver by boat, it is called cargo?

How do "Don't walk on the Grass" signs get there?

Why are cigarettes sold at gas stations when smoking is prohibited there?

If olive oil comes from olives, where does baby oil come from?

Why do they call it a garage sale, when the garage is not for sale?

If a word in the dictionary were misspelled, how would we know?

366   Only in America do drugstores make the sick walk all the way to the back of the store to get their prescriptions while healthy people can buy cigarettes at the front.

Only in America do people order double cheeseburgers, large fries, and a diet coke.

Only in America do banks leave both doors open and then chain the pens   to the counters.

Only in America do we leave cars worth thousands of dollars in the driveway and put our useless junk in the garage.

Only in America do we buy hot dogs in packages of ten and buns in packages of eight.

Only in America do we use the word "politics" to describe the process so well: "Poli" in Latin meaning "many" and "tics" meaning "bloodsucking creatures."

Only in America do they have drive-through ATMs with Braille lettering.

Ever wonder why the sun lightens our hair, but darkens our skin?

Why can't women put on mascara with their mouth closed?

Why don't you ever see the headline "Psychic Wins Lottery?"

Why is "abbreviated" such a long word?

Why is it that doctors call what they do "practice?"

Why is lemon juice made with artificial flavor and dishwashing liquid made with real lemons?

Why is the man who invests all your money is called a broker?

Why isn't there mouse-flavored cat food?

Why didn't Noah swat those two mosquitoes?

Why do they sterilize the needle for lethal injections?

You know that indestructible black box that is used on airplanes? Why don't they make the whole plane out of that stuff?

Why don't sheep shrink when it rains?

Why are they called apartments when they are all stuck together?

If con is the opposite of pro, is Congress the opposite of progress?

If flying is so safe, why do they call the airport the terminal?

367   The editor of a town's newspaper was known for being stubborn and hardheaded. "You always think you're right," a reader told him. "Can't you admit there are times when you may be wrong?"

"Yes," said the editor. "I remember one time when I was wrong."

"Aha! And when was that?'

"It happened once," the editor said, "When I thought I was wrong but I wasn't."

368   A teacher asked his students, What's the difference between a hill and a pill?" One student replied, "The first one is difficult to get up and the second one is difficult to get down."

369   A doctor asked Mr. Singh how his father died.   He answered, "My father had a habit of forgetting things, and one day he forgot to breathe."

370   A dad asked his son, "How many candies can you eat on an empty stomach?" His son said, "A whole bag full!" The dad said, "No. You can only eat one candy, because after you eat one, your stomach is no longer empty."

371   A criminal was asked before being hung, if he had a last wish. "Yes," he replied. "Would you take my place?"

372   Two middle-aged longtime friends were chatting. "Have you ever realized any of your childhood hopes?" asked one friend to another.
"Yes, unfortunately," said Pete.
"Oh?"
"When my mother used to comb my hair, I often wished I didn't have any."

373   A man convinced his frugal friend to buy two tickets for the big sweepstakes. The friend won the drawing, but did not seem too happy. "What is wrong with you?" the man asked. "You just became a millionaire!"
"I know," his friend groaned, "But I'm wondering why I bought the second ticket!"

374   A girl visiting a museum of prehistoric animals was admiring a dinosaur on display. She asked the attendant, "How old is this dinosaur?"
He replied, "Three million years and seven months."
"That's amazing!" said the girl. "How can they calculate the age so accurately?"
"Well," explained the attendant, "When I came to work here it was three million years old, and I have been here for seven months."

375   The cop got out of his car and the kid who was stopped for speeding rolled down the window.

"I have been waiting for you all day long," the cop said.

The kid replied, "Yeah, well I got here as fast as I could."

376   What equals 100%? What does it mean to give more than 100%? Ever wonder about those people who say they are giving more than 100%?

We have all been to those meetings where someone wants you to give over 100%. How about achieving 103%? What equals 100% in life?

Here's a little mathematical formula that might help you answer these questions:

If: A B C D E F G H I J K L M N O P Q R S T U V W X Y Z is represented as:

1 2 3 4 5 6 7 8 9 10 11 12 13 14 15 16 17 18 19 20 21 22 23 24 25 26.

H-A-R-D-W-O-R-K = 8+1+18+4+23+15+18+11

= 98%

K-N-O-W-L-E-D-G-E = 11+14+15+23+12+5+4+7+5

= 96%

But, A-T-T-I-T-U-D-E = 1+20+20+9+20+21+4+5

=100%

And,

B-U-L-L-S-H-I-T = 2+21+12+12+19+8+9+20 =103%

AND, look how far ass-kissing will take you.

A-S-S-K-I-S-S-I-N-G

1+19+19+11+9+19+19+9+14+7 = 118%

Therefore, one can conclude with mathematical certainty that: While hard work and knowledge will get you close, and attitude will get you there, it's the bullshit and ass-kissing that will put you over the top!!!

377   The difference between 1974 and 2004:

1974: Long hair

2004: Longing for hair

1974: KEG

2004: EKG

1974: Acid rock

2004: Acid reflux

1974: Moving to California because it's cool

2004: Moving to California because it's warm

1974: Trying to look like Marlon Brando or Liz Taylor

2004: Trying NOT to look like Marlon Brando or Liz Taylor

1974: Seeds and stems

2004: Roughage

1974: Hoping for a BMW

2004: Hoping for a BM

1974: Going to a new, hip joint

2004: Receiving a new hip joint

1974: Rolling Stones

2004: Kidney Stones

1974: Being called into the principal's office

2004: Calling the principal's office

1974: Screw the system

2004: Upgrade the system

1974: Disco

2004: Costco

1974: Parents begging you to get your haircut

2004: Children begging you to get their heads shaved

1974: Passing the driving test

2004: Passing the vision test

1974: Whatever

2004: Depends

378 I want to live my next life backwards.

You start out dead and get that out of the way right off the bat.

Then you wake up in a nursing home feeling better every day and then get kicked out for being too healthy.

You spend several years enjoying your retirement and collecting Social Security checks.

Then when you start work, you get a gold watch on your first day.

You work 40 years or so, getting younger every day until pretty soon you're too young to work.

Then you go to high school: play sports, date, drink, and party.

As you get even younger, you become a kid again. You go to elementary school, you play, and have no responsibilities.

In a few years you become a baby and everyone runs themselves ragged keeping you happy.

You spend your last 9 months floating peacefully in luxury, spa-like conditions: central heating, room service on tap.

Until finally, you finish off as an orgasm.

379 There was a man who lost one of his arms in an accident. He became very depressed because he loved to play the guitar. One day he had enough and decided to commit suicide. He got on an elevator and went to the top of a building to jump off. He was standing on the ledge looking down and saw this man skipping along, whistling and kicking up his heels. He looked closer and saw this man didn't have any arms at all. He started thinking, what am I doing up here feeling sorry for myself, I still have one good arm to do things with? There goes a man with no arms skipping down the sidewalk happy and going on with his life. He hurried down and caught the man with no arms. He told him how glad he was to see him because he had lost one of his arms and felt ugly and useless and was going to kill himself. He thanked him again for saving his life and he knew he could make it with one arm if that guy could go on with no arms. The man with no arms began dancing and whistling and kicking up his heels again.

He asked, "Why are you so happy anyway?"

He said, "I'm not happy — my back itches."

380   An old man lived alone in Idaho. He wanted to spade his potato garden, but it was very hard work. His only son, Bubba, who used to help him, was in prison. The old man wrote a letter to his son and described his predicament.

Dear Bubba,
I am feeling pretty bad because it looks like I won't be able to plant my potato garden this year. I'm just getting too old to be digging up a garden plot. If you were here, all my troubles would be over. I know you would dig the plot for me.
Love,
Dad

A few days later he received a letter from his son.

Dear Dad,
For heaven's sake, Dad, don't dig up that garden, that's where I buried the bodies.
Love,
Bubba

At 4 a.m. the next morning, F.B.I. agents and local police showed up and dug up the entire area without finding any bodies. They apologized to the old man and left. That same day the old man received another letter from his son.

Dear Dad,
Go ahead and plant the potatoes now. It's the best I could do under the circumstances.
Love,
Bubba

381   Meet the 12 members of the Tate Family.
You may have heard about the Tate family. They're in every organization.
There is Dic-Tate, who wants to run everything. Ro-Tate is always trying to change things. Agi-Tate stirs up trouble wherever possible, with the help of Irri-Tate.Every time new ideas are suggested, Hesi-Tate and Vege-Tate are there who say the ideas won't work. Imi-Tate wants to copy other organizations and not do anything new. Devas-Tate loves to be disruptive; Poten-Tate wants to be the big shot. But it's Facili-Tate, Cogi-Tate and Medi-Tate who always save the day and get everyone pulling together.

Introduction

This chapter contains jokes related to the game of golf. The word Golf is an acronym for Gentlemen Only/Ladies Forbidden. It started in Scotland many years back. The author used to play in a golf league once a week and got awarded for the "highest" score in school. One editor is very fond of playing golf. Ever since Mr. Tiger Woods got involved in the game, it has become very popular. If you enjoy golf, you will surely enjoy this chapter.

382 A man staggers into an emergency room with two black eyes and a five iron wrapped tightly around his throat. Naturally, the doctor asks him what happened.
"Well, I was having a quiet round of golf with my wife when she sliced her ball into a pasture of cows. We went to look for it and while I was looking around I noticed one of the cows had something white in its butt. I walked over and lifted up the tail and sure enough, there was my wife's golf ball, stuck right in the middle of the cow's butt. That's when I made my mistake."
"What did you do?" asks the doctor.
"Well, I lifted the tail and yelled to my wife, "Hey, this looks like yours!""

383 A guy out on the golf course takes a high speedball right in the crotch. Writhing in agony, he falls to the ground.
When he finally gets himself to the doctor, he asks, "How bad is it doc? I'm going on my honeymoon next week and my fiancée is still a virgin in every way."
The doc says, "I'll have to put your penis in a splint to let it heal and keep it straight. It should be okay next week."
So the doc takes four tongue depressors and forms a neat little four-sided bandage and wires it altogether; an impressive work of art.
The guy mentions none of this to his girl, marries, and on his honeymoon night in the motel room, she rips open her blouse to reveal a gorgeous set of breasts.
This was the first time he saw them. She says, "You'll be the first, no one has ever touched these breasts."
He whips down his pants and says, "Look at this, it's still in the crate!"

384   Three young men went to play golf and were looking for a fourth person. They saw an old man and asked him if he would like to play with them since their friend did not show up. The old man agreed to play and he played very well. Then he joined the young men for a beer. One of the young golfers asked, "Sir, have you noticed any sign of old age?" The old man replied, "Yes, last night I asked my wife if she would make love." Then she replied, "George, we made love just a few minutes back." The old man told the young golfers, "That was the first time when I felt that I was losing my memory."

385   Wife asked her husband, "If I die, would you remarry?" Her husband said, "Yes, since we had a very good marriage." This wife then asked, "Would you share our bed with your new wife?" Her husband said, "Yes, because it would remind me of you." She then asked, "Would you share my clothes with her?" Her husband said, "Yes." The wife continued, "Would you share my golf set with her?" Her husband said, "No. She's a lefty."

386   "I'll have to wear my golf socks today," grumbled Tom to his wife as he rummaged through the drawer.
"What golf socks?" she asked. "The old ones with the eighteen holes in them."

387   To put is to place a thing where you want it. To putt is a vain attempt to do the same thing.

388   The preacher was having pains in his knee and went to see an orthopedic surgeon. After an exam and X-rays, the doctor asked, "Reverend, do your church services require that you kneel quite often?"
"Well, not really," replied the clergyman, "But I always kneel on the green before I putt."

389   A husband and wife were out enjoying a round of golf and were about to tee off on the third hole, which was lined by beautiful homes. The wife hit her shot and the ball began to slice. Her shot was headed directly at a very large glass window. Much to their surprise, the ball smashed through the window and shattered it into a million pieces. They felt compelled to see what damage was done and went to see what happened.

When they peeked inside the home, they couldn't find anywhere there. Upon further investigation, they saw a gentleman sitting on the couch with a turban on his head. The wife said, "Do you live here?"

"No, someone just hit a ball through the window, knocked over the vase you see there, and freed me from that little bottle. I am so grateful," he answered.

The wife said, "Are you a genie?"

"Oh why yes, I am. In fact, I am so grateful, I will grant you two wishes and the third one I will keep it for myself." the genie replied. The husband and wife agreed on two wishes: one was for a scratch handicap for the husband, to which the wife readily agreed. The other was an income of $1,000,000 per year forever. The genie nodded and said, "Done!" "For my wish I would like to have my way with your wife. I have not been with a woman for many years and after all, I have made you a scratch golfer and millionaire."

The husband and wife agreed. After the genie and wife finished, the genie asked the wife "How long have you been married?"

She replied, "Three years."

The genie then asked, "How old is your husband?"

She responded, "31 years old."

The genie then asked, "How long has he believed in this genie stuff?"

390   A guy is stranded on a desert island for ten years. One day he sees a speck in the horizon. He thinks to himself, "It's not a ship." The speck gets a little closer, and he thinks, "It's not a boat." The speck gets even closer and he thinks, "It's not a raft."

Then out of the surf comes this thin gorgeous blonde woman, wearing a wet suit and scuba gear. She comes up to the guy and she says, "How long has it been since you have had a cigarette?" "Man, oh man! Is that good!"

Then she asked, "How long has it been since you have had a drink of whiskey?"

He replies, "Ten years!" She reaches over, unzips her waterproof pocket on the right and pulls out a flask and gives it to him. He takes a long swig and says, "Wow, that's fantastic!"

Then she starts slowly unzipping the zipper that runs down the front of her wet suit and she says to him, "And how long has it been since you have played any games?"

And the man replies, "My God, don't tell me that you've got golf clubs in there!"

391   Three retirees, each with a hearing problem, were playing golf one day. One remarked, "Windy, isn't it?" "No," the second man replied, "It's Thursday." And the third man chimed in, "So am I. Let's have a beer."

392   "I just got a new set of golf clubs for my wife!" a man exclaimed. "Great trade!"

393   A married man was having an affair with his secretary. One day, their passions overcame them and they took off for her house, where they made passionate love all afternoon. Exhausted from the wild sex, they fell asleep and awoke at around 8 p.m. As the man threw on his clothes, he told the woman to take his shoes outside and rub them through the grass and dirt. Mystified, she nonetheless complied and he slipped into his shoes and drove home.
"Where have you been?" demanded his wife when he entered the house.
"Darling," replied the man, "I can't lie to you. I've been having an affair with my secretary and we've been having sex all afternoon. I fell asleep and didn't wake up until eight o'clock."
The wife glanced down at his shoes and said, "You lying bastard! You've been playing golf!"

394   One day a man and his wife went golfing, as they frequently did together. They arrived at the 12th hole where the husband promptly hit a tremendous slice that ended up behind an old barn.
"I guess I'll just have to play it safe and chip it onto the fairway," said the man.
"No wait," said his wife. "You can hit the ball through the barn."
The man decided to give it a try. But he sliced the ball, which ricocheted off the barn and struck his wife in the head, killing her instantly. The man was distraught and wallowed in his misery for many weeks, depriving himself of golf the whole time.
A year later, he went to the same resort with a new friend.
On the 12th hole, he hit the same shot and his friend suggested he hit it through the barn.
He said, "No, last year it turned into a disaster."
His friend said, "What happened?"
He said, "I shot an 8 on this hole."

395   There was a room full of pregnant women and their partners in a Lamaze class. The instructor is teaching the women how to breathe properly and informing the men how to give the necessary assistance.

The teacher then announces, "Ladies, exercise is good for you. Walking is especially beneficial. And, gentlemen, it wouldn't hurt you to take the time to go walking with your partner."

The room gets really quiet. Finally, a man in the middle of the group raises his hand.

"Yes?" the teacher inquires.

"Is it alright if she carries a golf bag during the walk?"

396   To celebrate 50 years of marriage, a couple books a weekend at St. Andrews.

On the third tee, the husband says, "Darling, I have to confess something. Twenty years ago I had a brief affair. It meant nothing. I hope that you can forgive me."

His wife is hurt but says, "Dearest, those days are long gone. What we have now is far more valuable. I forgive you." They embrace and kiss, then continue the golf game.

On the 17th tee, the wife says to her husband, "Darling, since we're being honest with each other, I have something to tell you. Fifty-two years ago, I had a sex change operation. I was a man before we met."

The husband throws a fit. He curses, throws his driver, breaks his favorite clubs one by one, tears at his clothes, rants, and sobs. Finally, he screams at his wife: "You liar, you despicable cheat. I trusted you, and all these years you've been playing from the ladies tees?"

397   A woman goes to the local newspaper office to see that the obituary for her recently deceased husband is published. The obituary editor informs her that there is a charge of 50 cents per word.

She pauses, reflects, and then she says, "Well then, let it read 'Fred Brown dies.'"

Amused at the woman's thriftiness, the editor tells her that there is a seven-word minimum for all obituaries.

She thinks it over and in a few seconds says, "In that case, let it read, 'Fred Brown died: golf clubs for sale.'"

398   A 75-year-old woman goes to the doctor for a check up. The doctor tells her she needs more cardiovascular activity and recommends that she engage in sexual activity three times a week.

A bit embarrassed, she says to the doctor, "Please tell my husband."

The doctor goes out into the waiting room and tells the husband that his wife needs to have sex three times a week.

The 78-year-old husband replies, "Which days?"

The doctor answers, "Monday, Tuesday and Friday would be ideal."

The husband says, "I can bring her on Monday, but on Tuesdays and Fridays I golf, so she'll have to take the bus."

399   A husband and wife love to golf together, but neither of them is playing as well as they want to, so they decide to take private lessons. The husband has his lesson first. After the pro sees his swing, he says, "No, no, no. You are gripping the club way too hard."
"Well, what should I do?" he asks the man.
"Hold the club gently," the pro replies, "Just like you'd hold your wife's breasts." The man takes the advice, takes a swing, and POW! He hits the ball 250 yards straight down the fairway.
The next day the wife went for her lesson. After the pro watches her swing, he says, "No, no, no. You're gripping the club way too hard."
"What can I do?" asks the wife.
"Hold the club gently, just like you'd hold your husband's penis." The wife listens carefully to the pro's advice, takes a swing, and THUMP! The ball goes straight down the fairway, about 35 feet.
"That was great," the pro says. "Nice and gentle. Now take the club out of your mouth and swing it like you're supposed to."

400   A foursome finishes its Sunday morning round and gets to talking about how lucky they are that their wives let them play 18 holes every week. The discussion turns to their secrets for getting permission to play.
"I take my wife out to dinner every Friday night," says Tom. "We have a nice meal, a bottle of wine, and she's happy to let me play golf."
"My wife loves to shop," says Dick. "I just give her the Nordstrom's and Nieman-Marcus credit cards and she shops to her heart's content. She's happy to let me play golf."
"My wife likes to ski," says Harry. "So every winter I take her to Vail or Aspen for two weeks of skiing. When summer comes, she's happy to let me play golf."
"My wife doesn't care about going out for dinner," George says. "She doesn't shop much and she doesn't like to ski."
"So how do you get her to let you play golf?"
"That's easy. Every Sunday morning I wake her up at 5:30 and say 'Intercourse or golf course?' and she says, 'Don't forget your sweater.'"

401   A bride is walking down the aisle and when she reaches the altar, the groom is standing there with his golf bag and clubs at his side.

She says, "What are your golf clubs doing here?"

He looks at her and says, "This isn't going to take all day is it?"

402   A man arrives home from his Saturday afternoon round of golf looking particularly tired. His wife greets him at the door and asks how the round went.

"I played horribly and to top it off, Harry had a heart attack on the third hole," he says.

"My goodness!" his wife says. "That must have been very depressing."

"Yeah, at every hole it was — hit the ball, drag Harry, hit the ball, drag Harry."

403   First Time With Tiger

A couple was on their honeymoon, lying in bed, about ready to consummate their marriage, when the new bride says to the husband, "I have a confession to make. I'm not a virgin."

The husband replies, "That's no big thing in this day and age."

The wife continues, "Yeah, I've been with one guy."

"Oh yeah? Who was the guy?"

"Tiger Woods."

"Tiger Woods, the golfer?"

"Yeah."

"Well, he's rich, famous and handsome. I can see why you went to bed with him."

The husband and wife then make passionate love.

When they are done, the husband gets up and walks to the telephone.

"What are you doing?" asks the wife.

The husband says, "I'm hungry, I was going to call room service and get something to eat."

"Tiger wouldn't do that," she says

"Oh yeah? What would Tiger do?"

"He'd come back to bed and do it a second time."

The husband puts down the phone and goes back to bed to make love a second time.

When they finish, he gets up and goes over to the phone. "Now what are you doing?" she asks. The husband says, "I'm still hungry so I was going to get room service to get something to eat."

"Tiger wouldn't do that."

"Oh yeah? What would Tiger do?"

"He'd come back to bed and do it again."

The guy slams down the phone, goes back to bed, and makes love one more time.

When they finish he's tired and beat. He drags himself over to the phone and starts to dial.

The wife asks, "Are you calling room service?"

"No! I'm calling Tiger Woods to find out what the par is for this damn hole."

404 A husband and wife came for marriage counseling after 20 years of marriage. When asked what the problem was, the wife went into a passionate, painful tirade listing every problem they had ever had in the 20 years they had been married. She went on and on and on: neglect, lack of intimacy, emptiness, loneliness, feeling unloved and unlovable, an entire laundry list of unmet needs she had endured over the course of their marriage.

Finally, after allowing this to go on for a sufficient length of time, the male therapist got up, walked around the desk, and after asking the wife to stand, embraced her and kissed her passionately as her husband watched with a raised eyebrow. The woman shut up and quietly sat down as though in a daze.

The therapist turned to the husband and said, 'This is what your wife needs at least three times a week. Can you do this?'

The husband thought for a moment and replied, "Well, I can drop her off here on Mondays and Wednesdays, but on Fridays, I golf."

405 A male golfer hurt his penis. A lady doctor checked his penis. While holding his penis the lady doctor asked him to cough and say "88". The golfer took his time saying, "1,2,3,...to 88" since he was enjoying the lady doctor holding his penis.

406 Three ladies were talking about their children. The first one said, "I have three boys." The second one said, "I have four girls." The third one said, "I have a golf course, including myself."

407 A man goes to a doctor and asks for medicine to make him laugh. Since no medicine worked, the doctor suggests he go to a local circus and perhaps the clown would make him laugh. The man says, "Doctor, I am the clown."

408 A wife goes to her psychiatrist and complains about her husband and how he has an inferiority complex. For example, when somebody tells him he is handsome he says, "No, Tom Cruise is more handsome." The psychiatrist says, "Let me examine him." The wife brings in her husband. Not long after being in the room, the psychiatrist comes out and tells the wife, "I have good news and bad news. The good news is your husband does not have an inferiority complex, and the bad news is that he is simply inferior."

409 A lady goes to the urologist and asks what she can do to make her son's penis grow. The doctor suggests that feeding her child pancakes should make it grow. After hearing this, the lady goes home and prepares a stack of pancakes. The son asks her, "Are all those pancakes for me?" The mom replies, "No, two are for you and the rest are for your father."

410 A foreigner sends home a new kind of pill to make people younger. When he returns to his country at the airport, his mother comes with a small child in her arms. He asks his mom where his father is. She said, "I am holding him in my arms. I gave him too many pills."

411 A psychiatrist and a surgeon see a patient in the hospital with his pants down and his finger in his rectum so that a fly will not get in his body. The surgeon argues it is a surgical problem and the psychiatrist argues it is a mental problem.
The surgeon operates on the patient to get the fly out. However, even after the operation, the patient keeps his finger in his rectum saying, "I want to make sure another fly does not go in my body." Mental problem cannot be solved by surgical procedure.

412 The Good Doctor
A beautiful, voluptuous woman goes to a gynecologist. The doctor takes one look at this woman and all his professionalism goes out the window. He immediately tells her to undress. After she has disrobed he begins to stroke her thigh.
As he does this he says to the woman, "Do you know what I'm doing?"
"Yes," she says, "You're checking for any abrasions or dermatological abnormalities."
"That is correct," says the doctor. He then begins to fondle her breasts.
"Do you know what I'm doing now?" he asks.
"Yes," says the woman, "You're checking for any lumps or breast cancer."
"That's right," replies the doctor. He then begins to have sexual intercourse with the woman.
He says to her, "Do you know what I'm doing now?"
"Yes," she says. "You're getting herpes."

413 The Dentist

A guy and a girl meet at a bar. They get along so well that they decide to go to the girl's place. A few drinks later, the guy takes off his shirt and then washes his hands.

He then takes of his trousers and washes his hands again.

The girl has been watching him and says, "You must be a dentist."

The guy, surprised, says, "Yes! How did you figure that out?"

"Easy," she replied, "You keep washing your hands."

One thing led to another and they made love.

After they were done, the girl says, "You must be a good dentist."

The guy, now with a boosted ego says, "Sure, I'm a good dentist. How did you figure that out?"

 "I didn't feel a thing!"

414 A foreigner having a headache asked some local people for a doctor's name. The local guys suggested that he take Tylenol or aspirin but would not give the doctor's name. India has free advice and free prescription but no doctors.

415 The fee for the first visit to a doctor's office was $60 and the second visit was $35. One day, a patient walked into the doctor's office and walks right back out. "What are you doing?" the receptionist asked. "Just trying to save $25."

416 A couple visited a psychiatrist and to seek advice about their dull sex life. The psychiatrist advised ways to get in the mood like going to a movie or out to dinner in a nice restaurant. At the next week's session, the psychiatrist asked, "So, how did it go?" "Well," the wife said, "The sex was amazing, but the restaurant manager wasn't too pleased."

417 Why our health insurance is so expensive:

Bubba had shingles.

He walked into a doctor's office and the receptionist asked him what he had. Bubba said, "Shingles." So she wrote down his name, address, medical insurance number and told him to have a seat.

Fifteen minutes later a nurse's aide came out and asked Bubba what he had.

Bubba said, "Shingles." So she wrote down his height, weight, complete medical history and told Bubba to wait in the examining room.

A half hour later a nurse came in and asked Bubba what he had.

Bubba said, "Shingles." So the nurse gave Bubba a blood test, a blood pressure test, an electrocardiogram, and told Bubba to take off all his

clothes and wait for the doctor.

An hour later the doctor came in and asked Bubba what he had. Bubba said, "Shingles." The doctor asked, "Where?" Bubba said, "Outside on the truck. Where do you want them?"

418 Mr. Singh goes to see a doctor for stomach pain and the doctor says, "Tonight you should sleep on an empty stomach." Later that evening, Mr. and Mrs. Singh go to a party. He eats but tells his wife, "Don't eat. The doctor said I had to sleep on an empty stomach."

419 A man went to see a doctor. "I've been misbehaving, Doc, and my conscience is troubling me," he complained.
"And you want something that will strengthen your willpower?" asked the doctor.
"Well, no," said the fellow. "I was thinking of something that would weaken my conscience."

420 A patient was required by the doctor to drink fresh milk after an operation. He went to his neighbor who just had a baby and asks her to help him. She cooperated and let him drink milk from her breasts. As he was drinking she asked, "And would you like some cookies, too?"

421 A female patient asks her OB, "When can I have sex?" The doctor replies, "Not right now, I have more patients to see."

422 A man went into surgery to have one of his legs removed. After the surgery, the doctor said, "I have good news and bad news. The good news is that the operation was successful. The bad news is that I removed the wrong leg."

423 A Texas oil man goes to the dentist. The dentist says, "Good news! No cavities." The Texan says, "Keep drilling. This is obviously my lucky day."

424 Mr. Singh had a bad cough. A friend suggested that he drink prune juice, which would not cure the cough but make him think twice before coughing.

425 A doctor asks his patient, "Would you pay for an operation if I told you it was necessary?" The patient replied, "If I said no, would you still find it necessary to operate?"

426 A man quit his gynecology job due to frustration. He explained, "It's like a diamond miner. You can see it but can't use it."

427 A patient worries and tells the surgeon that it was his first operation. The surgeon said, "Don't worry, this is my first operation too."

428 Patients were waiting in the doctor's office. They were asked to go into the examination rooms and remove their clothes. The patients were asking each other what their problems were. "Headache," said one patient. "Backache," said another. "I am the electrician and just came to fix the circuit."

429   A dentist fee was $100 but a patient was charged $300. "Why the increase?" the patient asked. The doctor said, "You shouted so loud that two patients walked out."

430   An intern is someone who knows nothing and does nothing. A surgeon is someone who knows nothing and does everything. A psychiatrist is someone who knows everything and does nothing. A pathologist is someone who knows everything and does everything too late.

431   A surgeon and an internist were running for an elevator that was just about to close. The surgeon stuck his head through the door to keep the door open. Confused, the internist said, "What was that all about?" The surgeon replied, "I cannot afford to injure my hand."

432   An overweight man went to a health spa. The first day he paid $10 and lost 10 pounds by chasing a pretty girl. Second day he paid $20 and lost 20 pounds by chasing a nude girl. Third day he paid $30 and lost 50 pounds because a naked man was chasing him.

433   My family keeps my chair, hot water and slippers ready when I enter into my house. My friend says, "You are lucky to have such an affectionate family." Reply: "The truth is, they don't want me to clean the dishes in cold water."

434   The day after surgery a patient asks the doctor if she can have sex. The doctor replied, "Only with your husband. I don't want you to have too much excitement."

435   Three stages of sickness: ill, pill and bill.

436   A psychiatrist draws a line and asks a patient what he sees. The patient replies, "A couple making love." The doctor says, "You are a sex maniac." The patient says, "Doctor, you're the sex maniac. You're the one who drew the picture."

437   What's the difference between a PPO and an HMO? With the PPO, sperm samples are collected by the nurses. With an HMO, it's self-serve.

438   A man went to a mental hospital and asked if any patients had run away. "Why do you ask" said the hospital administrator. "My wife has been kidnapped and only a crazy person would do that."

439   A woman was discussing her recent nose job. "My friends used to laugh at me because of my nose. Now they laugh at the doctor for doing such a bad job."

440 Mr. Singh thinks that there are monsters under his bed. He visits a psychiatrist so that he hopefully can get a good night's sleep. The psychiatrist recommends that he come for counseling services, which would cost only $120 per visit. After not hearing back from Mr. Singh, the doctor calls him to see what's up. "My problem is solved," Mr. Singh says. "I just had a carpenter shorten the legs of my bed."

441 A man asked the doctor if he could make a home visit to see his mom. The fee was $100. The taxi would have cost him $125. So he asked to ride with the doctor and saved $25.

442 A lady went for a check up and the doctor says, "Everything is OK except for a lot of wax in your belly button." Her husband likes to do everything by candlelight.

443 The psychiatrist helped me get over the fear of answering phone. Now I answer the phone whether it rings or not.

444 A husband went for a physical and asked the doctor to tell his wife that he needs sex every day or he will die. His wife told her husband, "Well, it was nice knowing you."

445 A man was worried about getting a serious disease. The doctor said, "Only two things can happen to you; either you will live or you will die. If you die two things can happen. Either you go to heaven or to hell. If you go to hell you will meet all your friends. So why worry?" The patient replied, "You're right. Please send my bill to hell. Why worry?"

446 A patient collapsed near the door while leaving the doctor's office. "Quick!" the doctor said to the nurse. "Turn him around so it looks like he fell while coming in."

447 A doctor said to his patient, "I have good news. My son got admission at Columbia University. The bad news is my fees will be higher from now on."

448 A doctor asked a new patient, "Do you have any vices?" The patient answered, "No." The doctor asked, "Then why do you want to live for 50 years?"

449 Chief Minister's brain surgery. The neurosurgeon forgot to put the brain back in after the operation. The minister said, "No problem. I never used it much anyway, I just sign papers."

450 A doctor gave a prescription to his patient and told him to take it three times a day. There was no improvement because the patient swallowed the paper three times a day.

451 Genealogists look at the family tree. Gynecologists look at the family bush.

452   A receptionist at a very busy doctor's office told a persistent would-be patient, "Sorry. We don't have any appointments for three months." The patient said, "What? I may die within three months." The receptionist said, "Well in that case, can you ask your wife to cancel the appointment if you die?"

453   One patient gave a piece of art in the form of an eye to an ophthalmologist. Another patient gave a tooth to his dentist. Mr. Singh wondered what gift to give to a gynecologist.

454   Three men were asked to give money or get AIDS infection. Americans and Germans gave money but Mr. Singh refused to give money because he uses condoms.

455   A urologist gave a shot for an erection which was good for 2 hours. He was delayed in the taxi and his wife was not at home. He called the doctor and asked what to do. "I still have an erection." Reply: "Find a neighbor, babysitter or someone." Patient says, "Dr., I do not have a problem with them."

456   A doctor told his patient, "You have 6 months to live." The patient asked, "Is there anything I can do to extend my life?" The doctor said, "Call your mother-in-law. Six months will seem like six years."

457   "Doctor, I need something that will put me in a fighting mood," a patient said. The doctor replied, "Wait until you get my bill."

458   There are two patients in a mental hospital: One acts like a light bulb and the other sweeps the floor. The bulb guy is moved to another room. The second patient says, "How am I supposed to sweep in the dark?"

459   Mr. Singh tells his doctor, "I have a problem when I fart. It has no smell and no sound. The doctor replied, "The real problems are your sinuses and your hearing."

460   Four ladies went to a psychiatrist with their kids. The psychiatrist asked the first lady what the name of her child was. She says, "Candy." The psychiatrist replied, "You must be obsessed with candies and sweets." The second mother said her child's name was Penny. He said, "You must be obsessed with money." The third lady said her child's name was Brandy. He said, "You must be obsessed with alcohol." At this point the fourth lady walked out of the office and the psychiatrist stopped her and asked why she was leaving. "My son's name is Dick."

461   Some relatives gathered in the waiting room, where their family member lay
gravely ill.

Finally, the doctor came in looking tired and somber.

"I'm afraid I'm the bearer of bad news," he said as he surveyed the worried faces.

"The only hope left for your loved one at this time is a brain transplant.

It's an experimental procedure, very risky but it's the only hope. Insurance will cover it, but
you will have to pay for the brain yourselves."

The family members sat silently as they absorbed the news. After a great length of time,
someone asked, "Well, how much does a brain cost?"

The doctor quickly responded, "$5,000 for a male brain, and $200 for a female brain."

The moment turned awkward. Men in the room tried not to smile, avoiding eye contact with
the women, but some actually smirked.

A man unable to control his curiosity, blurted out the question everyone wanted to ask, "Why
is the male brain so much more?"

The doctor smiled at the childish innocence and explained to the entire group, "It's just
standard pricing procedure. We have to mark down the price of the female brains, because
they've actually been used."

462. Neurosis is a patient who builds castles in the air. Psychosis is a patient who believes he
lives in these castles, and psychiatrists are the ones who collect the rent from these castles.

463   A man goes to a mental hospital and takes a guided tour. One patient was shouting
"Yashmeen!" The visitor asked the doctor what happened to him. The doctor explained, "His
problem is that he was in love with Yashmeen and she got married to very wealthy man."
Then the visitor saw another patient who was shouting "Yashmeen." The doctor explained,
"He married Yashmeen and is not happy."

464   Osama Bin Ladin's dad was very stressed after the 9/11 attack on the world trade
center. As a result he developed a heart problem. A cardiologist said, heart surgery is needed
but we must find a matching blood donor as you have a rare type of blood." After a long
search they found Kanti Patel whose blood matched his father's blood. An operation was
planned and Mr. Patel gave blood to Osama's dad. His Dad was so pleased with Mr. Patel's
generosity that he sent him a Rolls Royce car, $1,000,000 and a five carat diamond. After a
few months Osama's dad developed health issues again and needed blood so Mr. Patel was
contacted and happily donated blood. This time Mr. Ladin sent a box of sweets, chocolates
and $100. Mr. Patel was disappointed and asked, "How come you were so generous the first
time and this time not so generous?" Mr. Ladin responded, "Now I have Gujju blood."

465 Mr. Singh went to a hospital and was very impressed with the high tech features: a THEATER to see movies, a LABOR ROOM where employees can rest, and a RADIOLOGY room to get radios repaired.

466 A medical student was asked to remove a kidney from a dead body. He also removed his penis and wrapped it in a handkerchief. He went to a party and put it in a lady's purse. The lady was scared to see the penis and threw it out the window. It fell on Mr. Singh's head. He wondered how his penis got from top to bottom. His wife said, "God is very happy with you so he has sent you a spare."

467 Charles G. Tennent, former president of Rotary International, was in the hospital recovering from major surgery. It irked him to know his name was misspelled on every report, food tray, and door plaque. The correct spelling is Tennant, not Tennent. He protested loud and long. Finally, his nurse, a Mrs. Hall, could take it no longer.
"What possible difference does it make?" she asked "Whether they spell it with an "e" or an "a"?
"Nurse Hell," he snorted back, "It makes a hall of a difference!"

468 Doctor: "Is your cough better this morning?"
Patient: "Yes, it is. I've been practicing all night."

469 An expectant couple's obstetrician was out of town, so the dad-to-be called another doctor.
"My wife is beginning to have labor pains," he said.
"Is this her first child?" asked the doctor.
"No" said the man. "This is her husband."

470 A doctor, making his rounds in the hospital, visited a patient who had a hernia operation three days before. He asked how the patient was doing.
"I'm still very sore, doctor. You don't know how bad it feels."
Trying to show compassion, the doctor replied, "I know exactly how it feels – I had the very same operation a few months ago."
The irritated patient answered, "Yes, but you had a different surgeon!"

471   It's your first time. As you lie back your muscles tighten. You put him off for a while searching for some excuse, but he refuses to be swayed as he approaches you. He asks if you're afraid and you shake your head bravely. He has had more experience but it the first time his finger has found the right place. He probes deeply and you shiver, your body tenses; but he's gentle like he promised he'd be. He looks deeply within your eyes and tells you to trust him – he's done this many times before. His cool smile relaxes you and you open wider to give him more room for an easy entrance. You begin to plead and beg him to hurry, but he slowly takes his time, wanting to cause you as little pain as possible. As he presses closer, going deeper, you feel the tissue give way; pain surges throughout your body and you feel a slight trickle of blood as he continues. He looks at you concerned and asks you if it's too painful. Your eyes are filled with tears but you shake your head and nod for him to go on. He begins moving in and out with skill but you are too numb to feel him within you. After a few frenzied moments you feel something bursting within you and he pulls it out of you, you lay panting, glad to have it over. He looks at you and smiling warmly, tells you, with a chuckle that you have been the most stubborn yet most rewarding experience. You smile and thank your dentist. After all it was your first time to have your tooth pulled.

472   A man walks into a psychiatrist's office wearing only Saran Wrap.
The psychiatrist says, "Well, I can clearly see you're nuts."

473   Mr. Singh went to the doctor and said, "Doc, I ache all over. Everywhere I touch it hurts." The doc said, "OK, touch your elbow."
Mr. Singh touched his elbow and winced in genuine pain. The doc, surprised, said, "Touch your head." Mr. Singh touched his head and jumped in agony. The doctor asked him to touch his knee and the same thing happened. Everywhere Mr. Singh touched, it hurt like hell. The doctor was stumped and ordered a complete examination with x-rays, etc. He told Mr. Singh to come back in two days. Two days later Mr. Singh came back and the doctor said, "We have found the problem."
"Oh yeah? What is it?"
Doc says, "You have a broken finger."

474   An old country doctor was called out to deliver a baby. It was really far away and there was no electricity. When the doctor arrived, no one was home except for the laboring mother and her five-year-old child. The doctor instructed the child to hold a lantern high so that he could see while he helped the woman deliver the baby. The child did so, the mother pushed, and after a little while, the doctor lifted the newborn baby by the feet and spanked him on the bottom to get him to take his first breath. "Hit him again, Doc! Hit him again!" the five-year-old said. "He shouldn't have crawled up there in the first place!"

475　Mr. Singh had some health problems and was advised by the doctor to take a Urine Test. In the morning he put urine in a bottle and kept it in the bathroom. His wife went to the toilet and accidentally spilled the urine. She was scared that Mr. Singh would scold her so she decided to put her own urine in the bottle.

After some time Mr. Singh took the bottle to the Lab for testing. In the evening he went to collect the report and was shocked to see the results that he was pregnant. He came home and shouted at his wife, "I told you so many times not to sit on me while making love. Look what happened now. See the report: I have become pregnant."

476　A man walked into a pharmacy and wandered up and down the aisles. He asked the salesgirl for a box of tampons for his wife. She directed him down the correct aisle.

A few minutes later, he placed a huge bag of cotton balls and a ball of string on the counter. The salesgirl was confused and said, "Sir, I thought you were looking for tampons for your wife?" He answers, "You see, it's like this. Yesterday, I sent my wife to the store to get me a carton of cigarettes and she came home with a tin of tobacco and some rolling paper. So I figure that if I have to roll my own, so does she."

477　Two men are in the urologist's office. Both of them are there to get a vasectomy. The nurse comes into the room and tells both men, "Strip and put on these gowns before going in to see the doctor to have your procedure done."

A few minutes later she returns and reaches into one man's gown and proceeds to fondle and ultimately begins to masturbate him. Shocked as he was, he asks, "Why are you doing that?" To which she replies, "We have to vacate the sperm from your system to have a clean procedure." The man, not wanting to be a problem and enjoying it, allows her to complete her task.

After she is through, she proceeds to the next man. She starts to fondle the man as she did to the previous man, but then drops to her knees and proceeds to give him oral sex. The first man, seeing this, quickly responds, "Hey! Why is it that I get masturbated and he gets a blowjob?"

The nurse simply replies, "That, sir, is the difference between an HMO and PPO.

478　Mr. Singh had two red ears so he went to his doctor. The doctor asked him what had happened to his ears. He answered, "I was ironing a shirt and the phone rang. But instead of picking up the phone I accidentally picked up the iron and stuck it to my ear." The doctor exclaimed in disbelief, "Oh dear, but what happened to the other ear?"

479　Mr. I am so depressed that my doctor refused to write me a prescription for Viagra. He said it would be like putting a flagpole on a condemned building.

480 A cardiologist married a gynecologist and they were blessed with twin girls, Angina and Vagina.

481 A mother was telling her teenage daughter that she didn't like her boyfriend. "I don't like the guy you are going out with. He's too dumb."
"No, mamma," the girl said. "He is going to be a doctor. He's already cured me of that illness that I used to get every month."

482 A man was eager to have sex with his girlfriend, but she was reluctant. "Don't you know that sex is good for arthritis?" he asked her.
"I don't have arthritis," she replied. He retorted, "Don't you believe in preventive medicine?"

483 An eminent surgeon attended the unveiling of a bust of himself at a renowned university. After the ceremony, a well-developed young lady came up to remark, "Doctor, I hope you appreciate that I have come more than 500 miles to see your bust unveiled." The doctor replied, "Madam, I would gladly return the compliment."

484 Sign posted in a psychiatrist's office: "Amnesia patients must pay in advance."

485 A son takes his father to a doctor. The doctor gives them the bad news that the father is dying of cancer. Father tells the son that he has had a long life and wants to stop at the bar to celebrate.
While at the bar, the father sees several of his friends and tells them that he is dying of AIDS. When the friends leave the son asks, "Dad, you are dying of cancer. Why did you tell them that you are dying of AIDS?
The father replies, "I don't want them to have sex with your mother after I'm gone."

486 A man is lying in bed in a Catholic hospital with an oxygen mask over his mouth. A young auxiliary nurse comes to sponge his face and hands.
"Nurse," he mumbles from behind the mask, "Are my testicles black?" Embarrassed, the young nurse replies, "I don't know, I'm only here to wash your face and hands."
He struggles again to ask, "Nurse, are my testicles black?"
Again the nurse replies, "I can't tell. I'm only here to wash your face and hands."
The ward sister was passing and saw the man getting a little frustrated so she marched over to inquire what was wrong.
"Sister," he mumbled, "Are my testicles black?"
Being a nurse of long-standing, the sister was undaunted. She whipped back the bedclothes, pulled down his pajama trousers, moved his penis out of the way, had a right good look, pulled up the pajamas, replaced the bedclothes and announced, "Nothing's wrong with them!"
Frustrated, the man pulled off his oxygen mask and asked again, "Are my test results back?!"

487   Steve had been suffering from blinding headaches for many years. He decided to try one last time to remedy his situation, and went to see a neurologist.

The doctor said, "The good news is that I can cure your headaches. The bad news is that it will require castration. You have a very rare condition that causes your testicles to press up against the base of your spine and the pressure creates one hell of a headache. The only way to relieve the pressure is to remove your testicles."

Steve was shocked and depressed. He wondered if he had anything to live for. He couldn't concentrate enough to answer, but decided he had no choice but to go under the knife.

When he left the hospital he was without a headache for the first time in 20 years, but he felt like he was missing an important part of himself. As he walked down the street, he realized that he felt like a different person. He could make a new beginning and live a new life.

He saw a men's clothing store and thought, "That's what I need, a new suit." Steve entered the shop and told the salesman, "I'd like a new suit."

The elderly tailor eyed him briefly and said, "Let's see...size 44 long."

Steve laughed, "That's right. How did you know?"

The salesman replied, "'I've been in the business for 60 years!" Steve tried on the suit. It fit perfectly. As Steve admired himself in the mirror, the salesman asked, "How about a new shirt?"

Steve thought for a moment and then said, "Sure."

The salesman eyed Steve and said, "Let's see. 34 sleeve and 16 and a half neck."

Steve was surprised, "That's right. How did you know?"

"Been in the business for 60 years!"

Steve tried on the shirt, and it fit perfectly. As Steve adjusted the collar in the mirror, the salesman asked, "How about new shoes?"

Steve was on a roll and said, "Sure."

The salesman eyed Steve's feet and said, "Let's see. 9-1/2 E."

Steve was astonished, "That's right. How did you know?"

"Been in the business 60 for years!"

Steve tried on the shoes and they fit perfectly. As Steve walked comfortably around the shop the salesman asked, "How about some new underwear?"

Steve thought for a second and said, "Sure."

The salesman stepped back, eyed Steve's waist and said, "Let's see, size 36."

Steve laughed, "Ah ha! I got you! I've worn size 32 since I was 18 years old."

The salesman shook his head, "You can't wear a size 32. A size 32 underwear would press your testicles up against the base of your spine and give you one hell of a headache."

488   A lady walked into a drug store and told the pharmacist she needed some cyanide poison. The pharmacist said, "Why in the world do you need cyanide?" The lady then explained she needed it to poison her husband. The pharmacist's eyes got big and he said, "Lord have mercy, I can't give you cyanide to kill your husband! That's against the law! They'll throw both of us in jail and I'll lose my license." Then the lady reached into her purse and pulled out a picture of her husband in bed with the pharmacist's wife and handed it to the pharmacist. The pharmacist looked at it and replied, "Well now, you didn't tell me you had a prescription."

489   A girl asks her boyfriend to come over on Friday night and have dinner with her parents. Since this is such a big event, the girl announces to her boyfriend that after dinner, she would like to go out and make love for the first time.
Well, the boy is ecstatic, but he has never had sex before, so he takes a trip to the pharmacist to get some condoms. The pharmacist helps the boy for about an hour. He tells the boy everything there is to know about condoms and sex.
At the register, the pharmacist asks the boy how many condoms he'd like to buy, a 3-pack, 10-pack, or family pack. The boy insists on the family pack because he thinks he will be rather busy, it being his first time and all.
That night, the boy shows up at the girl's parents' house and meets his girlfriend at the door. "Oh, I'm so excited for you to meet my parents, come on in!"
The boy goes inside and is taken to the dinner table where the girl's parents are seated. The boy quickly offers to say grace and bows his head.
A minute passes, and the boy is still deep in prayer, with his head down.
10 minutes pass, and still no movement from the boy.
Finally, after 20 minutes with his head down, the girlfriend leans over and whispers to the boyfriend, "I had no idea you were this religious."
The boy turns, and whispers back, "I had no idea your father was a pharmacist."

490   A dentist noticed that his next patient, a little old lady, was nervous so he decided to tell her a little joke as he put on his gloves. "Do you know how they make these gloves?" he asked. "No, I don't." "Well," he spoofed, "There's a building in Mexico with a big tank of latex and workers of all hand sizes walk up to the tank, dip in their hands, let them dry, then peel off the gloves and throw them into boxes of the right size."
She didn't crack a smile. "Oh, well. I tried," he thought.
But five minutes later, during a delicate portion of the procedure, she burst out laughing. "What's so funny?" he asked.
"I was just envisioning how condoms are made!"

491   Mr. Singh goes to a psychologist and says, "Doc, I got a real problem. I can't stop thinking about sex."

The psychologist says, "Well, let's see what we can find out," and pulls out his ink blots.

"What is this a picture of?" he asks.

Mr. Singh turns the picture upside down then turns it around and states, "That's a man and a woman on a bed making love."

The psychologist says, "Very interesting," and shows the next picture. "And what is this a picture of?"

Mr. Singh looks and turns it in different directions and says, "That's a man and a woman on a bed making love."

The psychologist tries again with the third ink blot and asks the same question, "What is this picture of?"

Mr. Singh again turns it in all directions and replies, "That's a man and a woman on a bed making love."

The psychologist states, "Well, yes, you do seem to be obsessed with sex."

"Me!?" says Mr. Singh. "You're the one who keeps showing me these dirty pictures!"

492   An Italian was in a bad car accident and after months of recovery he still had a problem. He had to have his penis amputated. He went to see the doctor and the doctor reassured him that he could help him.

"First of all you have to pick a new penis," says the doctor. The doctor picks up a box from his table and says, "This is our six-inch standard model. It is dependable and will cost you only $6,000. It comes with a lifetime guarantee."

The man says, "OK. What's in the other box?"

"This is our 10-inch super model. 10 inches of muscle to please any woman.

But for this you have to pay $10,000!!"

The man says, "Oh yea, that's the one I want. My wife will love me forever. Well, what's in that other box?"

The doctor picks up yet another box from his table. "This is our super deluxe model. It's 12 inches of all beef and will drive all the ladies wild. But if you want this much power you gotta pay $12,000!"

The man is really on a roll and is tickled pink, "Doc, that's it, that's the one for me. I'll be the envy of everyone I know. But does it have a lifetime guarantee?"

"Yes sir."

Then the man says he has just one more question. "Does it come in white?"

493 A cowboy with a toothache goes to the dentist's office. The dentist examines him and says, "That tooth has to come out. I'm going to give you a shot of Novocain and I'll be back in a few minutes."
The man grabs the dentist's arm, "No way. I hate needles I'm not having any shot!"
So the dentist says, "OK, then we will have to go with gas." The man replies, "Absolutely not. It makes me very sick and it lasts a few days. I'm not having gas."
So the dentist steps out and comes back with a glass of water. "Here," he says. "Take this pill."
The man asks "What is it?" The doc replies, "Viagra."
The man looks surprised. "Will that reduce the pain?" he asks.
"No," replies the dentist, "But it will sure give you something to hang on to while I pull your tooth."

494 A man comes running to the doctor shouting and screaming in pain, "Please doctor you've got to help me. I've been stung by a bee."
DOCTOR: "Don't worry; I'll put some cream on it." MAN: "You will never find that bee. It must be miles away by now."
DOCTOR: "No, you don't understand. I'll put some cream on the place you were stung."
MAN: "Oh! It happened in the garden where I was sitting under a tree."
DOCTOR (in anger): "No, no, you IDIOT! I mean on which part of your body did that bee sting you?"
MAN (still screaming in pain): "On my finger! The bee stung me on my finger and it really hurts!" DOCTOR (banging his fist and shouting): "Which one?"
MAN (innocently): "How am I to know? All bees look the same to me."

495 Hospital Humor
Two little kids are in a hospital, lying on stretchers next to each other, outside the operating room. The first kid leans over and asks, "What are you in here for?" The second kid says, "I'm in here to get my tonsils out and I'm a little nervous."
The first kid says, "You've got nothing to worry about. I had that done when I was four. They put you to sleep, and when you wake up they give you lots of Jell-O and ice cream. It's a breeze."
The second kid then asks, "What are you here for?" The first kid says, "A circumcision." The second kid says, "Whoa, good luck buddy, I had that done when I was born. Couldn't walk for a year."

496   There is a new study just released by the American Psychiatric Association about women and how they feel about their asses. The results are pretty interesting:

1. 85% of women surveyed feel their ass is too big.

2. 10% of women surveyed feel their ass is too small.

3. The remaining 5% say they don't care; they love him; he's a good man and they would have married him anyway.

497   Only at Wal-Mart:

One day, in line at the company cafeteria, Joe says to Mike behind him, "My elbow hurts like hell. I guess I better see a doctor."

"Listen, you don't have to spend that kind of money," Mike replies.

"There's a diagnostic computer down at Wal-Mart. Just give it a urine sample and the computer will tell you what's wrong and what to do about it. It takes ten seconds and costs $10…a lot cheaper than a doctor."

So Joe deposits a urine sample in a small jar and takes it to Wal-Mart. He deposits $10 and the computer lights up and asks for the urine sample. He pours the sample into the slot and waits. Ten seconds later, the computer ejects a printout: "You have tennis elbow. Soak your arm in warm water and avoid heavy activity. It will improve in two weeks." Thank you for shopping at Wal-Mart.

That evening while thinking about how amazing this new technology is, Joe began wondering if the computer could be fooled. He mixed some tap water, a stool sample from his dog, urine samples from his wife and daughter, and a sperm sample for good measure. Joe hurries back to Wal-Mart, eager to check the results. He deposits $10, pours in his concoction, and awaits the results.

The computer prints the following:

Your tap water is too hard. Get a water softener. (Aisle 9)

Your dog has ringworm. Bathe him with anti-fungal shampoo. (Aisle 7)

Your daughter has a cocaine habit. Get her into rehab.

Your wife is pregnant. Twins. They aren't yours. Get a lawyer.

If you don't stop playing with yourself, your elbow will never get better.

Thank you for shopping at Wal-Mart.

498 A mild-mannered man was tired of being bossed around by his wife so he went to a psychiatrist. The psychiatrist said he needed to build his self-esteem and gave him a book on assertiveness, which he read on the way home.

He had finished the book by the time he reached his house. The man stormed into the house and walked up to his wife. Pointing a finger in her face, he said, "From now on, I want you to know that I am the man of this house, and my word is the law! I want you to prepare me a gourmet meal tonight, and when I'm finished eating my meal, I expect a sumptuous dessert afterward. Then, after dinner, you're going to draw me my bath so I can relax. And, when I'm finished with my bath, guess who's going to dress me and comb my hair?"

"The goddamn funeral director," said his wife.

499 A woman and a baby were in the doctor's examining room, waiting for the doctor to come in. The doctor arrived, examined the baby, checked his weight, found it somewhat below normal, and asked if the baby was breast fed or bottle fed.

"Breast fed," she replied. "Well, strip down to your waist," the doctor ordered. She did. He pressed, kneaded, rolled, cupped, and pinched both breasts for a while in a detailed, rigorously thorough examination. Requesting her to get dressed, he said, "No wonder this baby is underweight. You don't have any milk."

"I know," she said, "I'm his grandma, but I'm glad I came."

500 Q: Who is a gynecologist?
A: He is the only fool on the earth who looks for problems in a place where most people find pleasure.

501 A doctor exclaimed to his patient, "You look so weak and exhausted! Are you having your meals three times a day as I advised?"

"Doctor," replied the female patient, "I thought you said three males a day!!"

502   One December day, we found an old straggly cat at our door. She was a sorry sight. Starving, dirty, smelly, skinny and her hair was all matted down. We felt sorry for her, put her in a carrier, and took her to the vet.

We didn't know what to call her, so we named her "Pussycat." The vet decided to keep her for a day or so. He said he would let us know when we could pick her up. My husband said, "OK, but don't forget to wash her, she stinks." He reminded the vet, "It was my wife that wanted the dirty cat, not me." My husband and the vet don't see eye to eye. The vet calls my husband "El-Cheap-O," and my husband calls the vet "El-Charge-O." They hate each other and constantly "snipe" at one another.

The next day my husband had an appointment with his doctor, who is located in the same building, next-door to the vet. The MD's waiting room and office was full of people waiting to see the doctor. A side door opened and the vet leaned in. He had seen my husband arrive. He looked straight at my husband and in a loud voice said, "Your wife's pussy doesn't stink anymore and it's finally clean and shaved, so she now smells like a rose. Oh, and, by the way, | I think she's pregnant. God only knows who the father is!"

503   Mr. Singh was amazed at the high cost of hearing aids. So one day he wrapped a copper wire around his ear. He doesn't hear better, but people sure do talk louder.

504   Mr. Singh had to go for B.M. (Bowel Movement) and could not find a toilet in the London hotel room so he shat in his socks and tried to throw it through the ventilation window. The sock got stuck in the fan and the shit spread all over the wall. Mr. Singh was worried that he would have to pay a 200 pound penalty for cleaning up. The janitor said, "I will give you the 200 pounds, if you tell me how you managed to shit on all the walls."

505   A pig and a chicken went to a restaurant for a breakfast of ham and eggs. The pig said, "For us pigs it is a full commitment but for you chickens it's just a contribution."

506   Mr. Singh was eating at a cheap restaurant. After eating his food he gargled some water. In the process of gargling, he sprayed water on the other customers. The customers complained to the manager about his inappropriate behavior. The manager came to Mr. Singh and asked him if he had ever eaten in a nice restaurant. His response was, "Yesterday I ate at a five-star restaurant." The manager inquired if he sprayed water on the customers there as well. Mr. Singh replied, "Yes." The manager asked, "Did the five-star manager approach you like I am doing now?" Mr. Singh replied, "Yes, and he also said that the next time I want to eat and spray water that I should go to your restaurant. So I guess you could say I am here with a recommendation."

507   Mr. Singh goes to a tea shop. While looking at the menu he realizes that there are three kinds of tea. There is special tea, regular tea, and public tea. The special tea costs $5 per cup. The regular tea costs $1 per cup. The public tea costs 25 cents per cup. Mr. Singh, being a miser person, orders the popular tea, which tastes very good. Mr. Singh calls for the manager. He asks, "What is the logic behind the price difference of the tea?" The manager replies, "Well, the special tea is made with the highest quality of ingredients. The regular tea is made in a percolator. The public tea is the leftover tea collected by the waiter."

508   A blind man walks into a restaurant and sits down. The owner walks up to him and hands him a menu.

"I'm sorry, sir, but I am blind and can't read the menu. Just bring me a fork used by a previous customer. I'll smell it and order from there."

A little confused, the owner walks over to the dirty dish pile and picks up a greasy fork. He returns to the man's table and hands it to him.

The blind man puts the fork to his nose and takes in a deep breath.

"Ah, yes. That's what I'll have — meatloaf and mashed potatoes."

Unbelievable, the owner thinks as he walks toward the kitchen and tells his wife, Gladys, the cook, what just happened.

The blind man eats and leaves. Several days later, the blind man returns and the owner mistakenly brings him a menu again. "Sir, remember me? I'm the blind man." "I'm sorry! I didn't recognize you. I'll go get you a fork."

The owner retrieves a dirty fork and brings it to the blind man. After another deep breath, the blind man says, "That smells great. I'll take the macaroni and cheese with broccoli."

Walking away in disbelief, the owner thinks the blind man is screwing around with him and tells his wife Gladys that the next time the blind man comes in he is going to test him.

He returns the following week, but this time the owner sees him coming and runs to the kitchen. He tells his wife, "Gladys, rub this fork on your panties before I take it to the blind man."

Gladys complies and hands her husband the fork.

As the blind man walks in and sits down, the owner is ready and waiting.

Good afternoon, sir, this time I remembered you, and I have your fork ready for you."

The blind man puts the fork to his nose, sniffs, and says "Hey, I didn't know Gladys worked here!"

509   A Pakistani, Bangladeshi and Mr. Singh are in a bar one night having a beer. The Pakistani drinks his beer and suddenly throws his glass in the air, pulls out a gun and shoots the glass to pieces.

He says "In Islamabad, our glasses are so cheap that we don't need to drink from the same one twice."

The Bangladeshi, impressed by this, drinks his beer, throws his glass into the air, pulls out his gun and shoots the glass to pieces.

He says "In Dhaka, we have so much sand to make the glasses that we don't need to drink out of the same glass twice either."

Mr. Singh, cool as a cucumber, picks up his beer and drinks it, throws his glass into the air, pulls out his gun and shoots the Pakistani and Bangladeshi.

He says "In India, we have so many Pakistanis and Bangladeshi that we don't need to drink with the same ones twice."

510   Mr. Singh went to a café one day. He asked the waiter, "How much does a cup of coffee cost?" The waiter replied, "Hot coffee is $1 and iced coffee is $2." Mr. Singh ordered a cup of hot coffee and drank it very fast, so it would not get cold.

511   Mr. Singh goes to a café and orders a hot dog which he has never seen before. The waitress comes with the hot dog and Mr. Singh asks, "Don't you have another part of the dog?"

512   An old couple went to the restaurant. The waiter noticed that they took turns eating. When he asked why, they replied, "We only have one set of dentures."

513   A lawyer couple went on their honeymoon and stayed in a hotel. They were billed food that they did not order. The manager said, "The food was prepared. It was your choice not to eat it." The lawyer then handed a bill to the manager for flirting with his wife and said, "She was well-dressed and ready. If you did not touch it was not my problem."

514   A coupled walked into a restaurant and asked, "Do you serve Chinese food?" The hostess replied, "We serve to all nationalities."

515   Mr. Singh was angry in a hotel room because it was too small, had no T.V. and no telephone. Finally he realized he was in an elevator.

516   A waiter puts his thumb in the salad but avoids putting his thumb in the ice cream because he has a cut on it. He avoids cold. A customer asks, "Why don't you put your thumb in your asshole since it is not cold?" Reply: "That is what I did in the kitchen."

517   Mr. Singh went for a vacation and a burglar stole $100 from his house. The next time they went for a vacation he turned on the AC and put all the lights on. The electricity bill was $400.

518   A customer, who was very hungry and had been waiting awhile for his food, yelled at the waiter, "Do I have to starve all night?" "No, sir. We close at 9 p.m."

519   A man gave three pennies to a waitress as a tip. She was angry and said, "This first penny shows you are miser. This second shows you are a bachelor. And, this third penny shows your father was also a bachelor.

520   An Italian in a hotel asked for a sheet but pronounced it "shit." The manager said, "Go to the toilet, no shit on the bed." Then, sitting at the table, he asked for a fork but pronounced it "fuck." The manager answered, "Go to bed."

521   A restaurant had a new marketing person who advised them to put up a sign saying, "Eat as much as you want and your grandchildren will pay." Some college students thought they could eat and not pay. They ordered a lot of food and as they were walking out of the restaurant, the manager stopped them and handed them a bill. The students argued that the sign said, "Your grandkids will pay." The manager said, "You are right, but the bill is for the food your grandfather ate here before you were born."

522   A man was fond of bread. The first night that he had dinner at the town's finest restaurant, he was served two slices. He asked for more and got more. The waitress took note of the fact and the next evening served him four slices of bread. Again the man asked for more. Every evening he was given more bread than the evening before. Finally in desperation, the waitress took a giant loaf of French bread, cut it lengthwise, and served it on a huge platter. As the man was paying his check, the manager asked if the meal was satisfactory.

"Everything was fine," said the man, "Except the bread. I noticed you are back to two slices."

523   The clock in a restaurant window had stopped a few minutes past noon. One day, one of the restaurant owner's friends asked him if he knew that the clock did not work.

"Yes," replied the owner. "But you would be surprised to know how many people look at that clock, think they are hungry, then come in and get something to eat."

524   Getting married is like going to a restaurant with friends. You order what you want, and then when you see what other fellow has, and you wish you had ordered that.

525   A millionaire was asked how he got rich. "Well," he said, "I began by buying peanuts for five cents a bag and selling them for ten cents. I worked long hours and all holidays. However, I did not become a millionaire for five years." "What happened after that?" the interviewer asked. "Well, my father died and left me a chain of hotels."

526   We are irrational creatures: We are always looking for a homey atmosphere in a hotel and hotel service at home.

527   A customer at a restaurant was unhappy with the way his meat was cooked. He summoned the waiter. "Didn't I say well done?"

The waiter replied, "Yes, you did, thank you. I very seldom get a compliment."

528   A traveler ordered breakfast at a diner in a small town. When the waiter brought his order, he noticed the toast was extremely well done.

"Isn't that toast a little too dark?" the customer asked.

"Well," said the waitress, "That way you can scrape it to any shade you want."

529   Two men went to a bar and after ordering two beers took some sandwiches out of their pockets and started to eat them. "You cannot eat your own sandwiches in here," complained the owner.
The two men swapped their sandwiches.

530   A group of girlfriends went on vacation. They saw a five-story hotel with a sign that read, "For Women Only." Since they were without their boyfriends, they decided to go in. The doorman, a very attractive guy, explained to them how it worked. "We have 5 floors. Go up floor by floor, and once you find what you are looking for, you can stay there. It's easy to decide, since each floor has signs telling you what's inside." So they went up. On the first floor the sign read, "All the men here are horrible lovers, but they are sensitive and kind…" The friends laughed and without hesitation moved on to the next floor. The sign on the second floor read, "All the men here are wonderful lovers, but they generally treat women badly." This wouldn't do. So the friends moved up to the third floor where the sign read, "All the men here are great lovers and sensitive to the needs of women." This was good but there were still two more floors. On the fourth floor, the sign was perfect. "All the men here have perfect builds; are sensitive and attentive to women; are perfect lovers; they are also single, rich and straight."
The women seemed pleased but they decide that they would rather see what the fifth floor had to offer before they settled for the fourth. When they reached the fifth floor, there was only a sign that read, "There are no men here. This floor was built only to prove that there is no way to please women."

531   Mr. Singh goes to the bar and orders three glasses of cold beer. He takes one sip from each glass and continues until he is done. He repeats this for several weeks. The bartender says, "Why don't you just order one at a time and I'll give you a cold one each time?" Mr. Singh says, "I have a brother in California and a brother in New York, and we vowed to always drink together." The bartender says, "That makes sense." A few months go by. Mr. Singh comes in and orders only two beers. The bartender says, "I'm sorry for your loss." Mr. Singh says, "What do you mean?" The bartender says, "I'm assuming you lost one of your brothers?" Mr. Singh says, "Oh that's not the case. I have just decided to quit drinking."

Chapter 10
Indian

YOU KNOW YOU'RE AN INDIAN IF...

YOU ASK YOUR PARENTS FOR HELP WITH ONE
MATH PROBLEM AND TWO HOURS LATER THEY
ARE STILL LECTURING

532   Mr. Singh meets a girl for an engagement and tells her that his salary is $5,000 but he also makes $10,000 under the table (ooper ki kamai/bribes). She tells him that her salary is $2,000 but she also makes $20,000 under the skirt (neeche ki kamai/prostitution).

533   At a dance show in Chennai (Madras), only South Indians were permitted to attend. Four students from north India wanted to see the show as they were visiting the town and a famous dancer was there. When they entered, the bouncer asked their names and denied them entry. The students went to a hotel and dressed in South Indian clothes. Now when they were asked their names they said, Subranmanium, Harmonium, Aluminum, Titenium…

534   Height of patriotism – wearing a Khadi (linen) condom on October 2.

535   Dilemma for Marwari Jain: free meat.

536   Festival of Nag Panchami (the day many Indians worship snakes): A friend stops by and the hostess offers milk. The guest is surprised because normally the lady does not offer even water or tea. Her reasoning was, "Today is Nag Panchami and we offer milk to snakes."

537   About the Indian surnames, some may find this offensive or insulting and that is the way it should be.

A man from Uttar Pradesh (a state in India) was away from his
wife for four years while his wife was in Saharanpur (UP).

At the end of the four years, he distributed sweets to his
colleagues in the office, saying that his wife had given birth to a son.

His colleagues were quite shocked and they asked how this "happy event" happened when
he had not seen his wife for four years.

The man said it is common in U.P. for neighbors to take care of the wives when their husbands
are away.

The colleagues asked him, "What name will you give to the son?"

The man explained, "If it's the second neighbor who
has taken care, then the name would be DWIVEDI.

If it's the third neighbor, then it would be TRIVEDI.

If it's the fourth neighbor then, it would be CHATURVEDI.

If it's the fifth neighbor, then it would be PANDEY…

After listening to this, questions followed.

What if it is a mixture of neighbors? "Then the boy
would be named MISHRA."

And what if the wife is too shy to tell the name of the neighbor? "Then it would
be SHARMA."

But what if she refuses to divulge the name of the neighbor? "Then the name of the child
would be GUPTA."

If she does not remember the name then? "It is YAAD-AV."

But who knows whether the child resulted from a rape? "Then it will be named DOSHI."

Finally, if the child was conceived because of the wife's burning desire for sex? "Then
he will be named JOSHI."

And if the whole country had made efforts for the happy arrival? "DESHPANDEY."

If the son was born in a motel, then he would be called Patel.

If the boss was found responsible for the birth of the child, then the young
child would be named Sheth.

If the son was born with unusually large genitals,
he would be called Mahalingam.

538   Gujarati playing flash (3 card poker), asked for "so" (show) and said, "I have three "asses" (aces)."

539   A doorkeeper was watching Indians saying, "Happy Diwali (festival of lights)." Not understanding the word "diwali" he started saying, "Happy Diwala (bankruptcy)." The Indian replied, "Same to you."

540   What is it that travels and changes its name. Reply: hair – from head, mustache, beard. Teacher says, "Stop because my name is Jaal" (pubic hair).

541   Indian GNP: Gross Number of Patels.

542   Trying to teach English in a village: The teachers used A for apple, B for boy and C for cat. After six months the inspector found that villagers were not learning English. A new teacher taught A for Amariya's wife, B for Bhanvariya's wife, M for Mohan's wife, etc. When the inspector came after a few months, the villagers had learned the alphabet much faster. When inspector asked for W one of the villagers replied, "Mohan's wife is hanging upside down."

543   An impotent man goes to see a snake charmer. When the snake charmer plays the flute, a rope rises up. The man borrows the flute and starts to play. His pajama string rises up.

544   Mr. Singh got a blood infusion from a Gujarati so now he talks about business rather than wars.

545   Mahatma Gandhi's statue saying to Indira Gandhi: "I am tired of a car, you bring a horse." She brings Mr. Singh as a bodyguard and a voice comes from the statue, "I asked for a horse and you brought a donkey."

546   A man goes to the restroom frequently and a friend asks, "Don't you have CHAIN (peace)?" He replies, "I have chain (zipper) but it does not open."

547   A man asked Mr. Singh what a husband is. Mr. Singh replies, "A person who stops laughing after marriage" (Jiski Hasi Band).

548 Mr. Singh forces a Bihari to tell a joke and he says, "There was a Bihari…" Mr. Singh says, "Are all Singhs dead?"

549 One man lost his job so he and his wife decided to start a small café. The wife cooked inside and the husband sold standing outside the window, but he was not successful. Then the wife said, "You cook and I will sell." The husband was surprised that his wife was selling items very quickly. He came out and noticed that her blouse buttons were open and customers could see her cleavage. He asked his wife, "Why are you showing your breasts?" She said, "Jab dikhta hai to bikta hai." (When something shows, then things sell fast.)

550 Mr. Singh and his family visit a girl and her parents describe her qualities. She is kalavati (an artist), she is padamavati (like a goddess), she is saraswati (learned), and leelavati (an actress). Mr. Singh is impressed and agrees to marry her. Within a month after the engagement he tells the girl's parents, "I cannot marry her because you did not tell me that she is garbhvati" (pregnant).

551 A juice shop in Jodhpur, India, had a sign which had the words Mr. Amitabh Bachhan Rs. 50, Jaya Bhaduri Rs. 25. A visitor asked the salesman the reason for the difference. Reply, "Amitabh represents large glass and Jaya represents small glass."

552 One day, a cruise ship carrying people from all over the world was going on an around-the-world tour when it came to a halt. The captain of the ship called an emergency meeting and told the passengers, "Friends, we are in trouble. The Gods are angry with us. We need to give a sacrifice and I need three people to sacrifice their lives so that rest of us can be saved."
All of them moved toward the deck, where a Japanese man came forward and shouted "Long Live Japan" and jumped into the sea. Then an Israeli Jew stepped forward and said, "Hallelujah" and dived into the sea. After that, no one came forward and everyone stared at each other.
Suddenly, out of nowhere, Mr. Singh from India came forward near the railing and chanted, "Bharat mata ki Jai (victory to India)!" and kicked the Pakistani standing next to him into the sea.

553 After making a trip to South India, Mr. Singh, his wife and his son were on their way back to Delhi. Mr. Singh was in the lower berth, his wife the middle berth and his son the top most berth in the train. When the train stopped, the son asked his dad to bring him some ice cream, to which Mr. Singh agreed. When Mr. Singh returned, he saw that a South Indian, who could not understand Hindi, had climbed into his son's berth.

Outraged, Mr. Singh called the ticket collector and asked him to help. The ticket collector asked Mr. Singh to explain to problem. Mr. Singh explained, "That man sleeping on top of my wife is not giving birth to my child."

554 A man was lying nude on the beach. A sexy woman started playing tabla (drum) on his butt.

Man: what are you doing?

Girl: Playing tabla (drum).

The man turned over and said, "Can you play the flute?"

555 All couples pass through the different phases of sex life:

20-25 years	Dinraat (Day and Night)
25-30	Rojraat (Daily night)
30+	Jummerat (Weekly)\
40+	Chandraat (Bi-weekly)
50+	Jazzbat (emotional)
60+	Khayalat (in dreams)

556 You know you're an Indian if…

Your parents are never on time for anything.

Your dad is some sort of engineer or doctor.

Your parents still try to get you into places half price saying you are 12 when you are really 18.

You ask your parents for help with one math problem and two hours later they are still lecturing.

You have a 25-pound bag of basmati rice in your pantry.

557   Letter from his mother...

Pyaarey Puttar,

Namaste. I'm writing this letter slowly, because I know you cannot read fast. We don't live where we did when you left home. Your dad read in the paper that most accidents happen 20 miles from home, so we moved 20 miles away. I won't be able to send the address as the last owner who stayed here took the house numbers with him for his new house so he wouldn't have to change his address.

This place is really nice. It even has a washing machine, situated right above the commode. I'm not sure it works too well. Last week I put in three shirts, pulled the chain and haven't seen them since. The weather here isn't too bad. It rained only twice last week. The first time it rained for three days and the second time for four days. The coat you wanted me to send you, your Aunt said it would be a little too heavy to send in the mail with all the metal buttons, so we cut them off and put them in the pocket.

Your father has another job. He has 500 men under him. He is cutting the grass at the cemetery. Your sister had a baby this morning. I haven't found out whether it's a girl or a boy, so I don't know whether you are an aunt or an uncle.

Your uncle, Jatinder, fell in the nearby well. Some men tried to pull him out, but he fought them off bravely and drowned. We cremated him and he burned for three days.

Your best friend, Balwinder, is no more. He died trying to fill his father's last wishes. His father had wished to be buried in the sea after he died. And your friend died while in the process of digging a grave for his father. There isn't much more news this time. Nothing much has happened.

Love,

Mom.

PS: I was going to send you some money but the envelope was already sealed.

558   Flag hosting explanation: "Orange, white and green color cloth, pull a string and say, "Jai Hind." Mr. Singh sees a woman with tricolor clothes and pulls her pajama string and says, "Jai Hind" (Victory to India).

559   One day, Mr. Singh is talking with his friend…

Mr. Singh: We have to learn Chinese within 6 months or we will not be able to communicate with my child.

Friend: Why is that?

Mr. Singh: We have adopted a Chinese child and it will start to speak in 6 months.

Chapter 11
Marriage

560 Man: Doctor, what's the secret to a long life?
Dr: Get married.
Man: Will it help?
Dr: No, but the thought of having a long life will never come.

Why do couples hold hands during their wedding?
It's a formality, just like two boxers shaking hands before the fight begins.

Wife: Darling, today is our anniversary. What should we do?
Husband: Let's stand in silence for two minutes.

It's funny when people discuss marrying for love vs. an arranged marriage.
It's like asking someone if suicide is better than being murdered.

It is difficult to understand God. He makes beautiful people such as women and then he turns them into wives.

If you are married, please ignore this message.
For everyone else: Happy Independence Day.

Before marriage, a man will lie awake all night thinking about something you said. After marriage, he'll fall asleep before you finish.

Girlfriends are like chocolate: they taste good anytime.
Lovers are like pizzas: hot, saucy, and eaten frequently.
Husbands are like leftovers: eaten when there's no choice.

Husband receives telegram: Wife dead; should she be buried or cremated?
Husband: Don't take chances. Burn the body and bury the ashes.

Fact of life: One woman brings you into this world crying and the other woman ensures you continue to do so for the rest of your life.

Q: Why doesn't the law permit a man to have a second wife?
A: Because you can't be punished twice for the same offense.

A prospective husband goes to a bookstore and asks the saleslady, "Do you have a book called, Man, The Master of Women?
The salesgirl replies, "The fiction department is over there."

561   A boy goes to meet a girl's parents with his friend. The parents ask the friend to describe the boy's qualities. He says that he is a great guy except sometimes he smokes, but only when he's drunk; he drinks only when he steals money from his parents; he steals only when he gambles; and he gambles only when he goes to a night club.

562   A wife says that she makes all the major decisions and her husband makes all the minor decisions. The husband clarifies, "What is major and what is minor is a minor decision." Therefore, he decides.

563   A man sees a marriage ad that reads, "Seeking eligible man for ugly, overweight, and short girl. A 5-story building will be given in the dowry." The man replies, "I am interested in your matrimonial offer. Please send a picture of the building."

564   A rich man has three unmarried daughters; he put a matrimonial ad in the newspaper which stated, "The man who marries my oldest daughter who is 50 years old will get 50 ounces of gold in the dowry. The one who marries my second daughter, who is 40 years old, will get 40 ounces of gold in the dowry. The one who marries the 20-year-old will receive one hundred ounces of gold in the dowry." A young man who responds to the ad asks the father of the bride what the rationale is for giving a large dowry for the youngest girl. The father responds, "Young man, there is a reason for everything; the youngest daughter is pregnant."

565   A man goes to a barbershop and asks him if he is busy. The barber says that it will take at least half an hour before he can cut his hair. After hearing this, the customer leaves the shop and goes away. The next day he comes in and asks the same question. The barber's response is the same. The same thing happens every day for a week. The next time the man comes in, the barber asks his assistant to follow the customer and find out where he goes. The assistant reports back, "He goes to your house."

566   A father-in-law asks his son-in-law, "What have you done to my million-dollar daughter to make her lose so much weight?" The son-in-law replied, "Why don't you take your daughter back and give me $500,000?"

567   A wife asks her husband to install a curtain to cover the bathroom window because the neighbors watch her and she doesn't like it. The miser husband says, "Why don't you show your face once and nobody will bother you again?"

568   On the first night of their marriage, Mr. Singh told his wife that it takes nine months to conceive and deliver a child. He asks how long it takes her. The wife, knowing that she was three months pregnant, replies, "It takes six months in my town."

569 A white mother delivered a black baby. Her husband commented to his wife that, just like toast, she has a habit of burning everything.

570 Two friends where talking about contraceptives. One lady said that they use the Atlantic Ocean as a contraceptive. The other lady was very confused. The lady explained, "My husband lives in Germany."

571 A newlywed couple had a problem. Every night the wife would come to the husband's room very late after doing all the household chores. The husband was very impatient. As soon as he saw her he started touching her profoundly. The wife did not like his lack of self-control. One day she told him, "You have no self control, and no willpower. Our neighbor Mr. Singh has strong will power. Yesterday he quit smoking after many years. You have no self-control, shame on you." This hurt the husband, and he got upset. He took his sleeping bag and went into the next room. The wife was thinking the husband would come back to her after a couple hours. Two days later he was still sleeping in the next room. The wife got impatient and went to her husband and knocked on the door and said, "Dear, Mr. Singh has started smoking again."

572 Mr. Singh gave $20 to his wife the first night after marriage, based on his habit of going to prostitutes. Mrs. Singh returned $10 and told him, "My fee is only $10."

573 Mr. Singh had a fire in his house. The insurance company told him that they would not pay cash for his home, but would replace the house. Immediately Mr. Singh told his agent to cancel the life insurance on his wife, because he didn't want another lady if his wife died.

574 An absent-minded husband, Mr. Singh, goes to the shopping mall and meets his wife. Mr. Singh tells her, "Sister I've seen you somewhere before."

575 A couple seeking a divorce went to court. Each asked the judge for custody of two out of their three children. The judge said, "Why don't you have a fourth child and then each one can get custody of two?" The wife said, "My husband is impotent and if I waited for him to have the fourth one we would not have had the first three kids."

576 Mr. Singh went to join the Indian Army and he asked his landlord to take care of his wife. Upon his return he found his wife was pregnant. He was very upset with his landlord and asked for the compensation of $10,000 if his wife gave birth to a girl to cover her dowry, and if his wife gave birth to a boy he asked for $30,000 for his education. The landlord agreed to his conditions. Then Mr. Singh thought for a minute, "If there is a miscarriage then I will lose everything." The landlord asked, "What do you want in that case?" Mr. Singh said, "Repeat the process again."

577   A husband removed his moustache and came home late one night. He crawled into bed with his wife. She said, "Young man, you better make it fast before my husband comes home."

578   A young man went to his future in-laws for dinner. Everything was made of squash because she was told by a common friend that the young man loved squash. During the dinner, the host kept on offering squash again and again. While serving dinner the host asked the young man how many siblings he had. The young man replied, "If I survive from this overdose of squash, four brothers; otherwise we are three brothers."

579   A husband agreed to put a $1 bill in a piggy bank each time he had sex with his wife. After one month they opened the piggy bank and the husband saw a $5 bill. He asked his wife, "How did this bill get in the piggy bank?" The wife replied, "Not everyone is a miser like you."

580   A man sold his wife for a bottle of scotch. After a month he wanted her back because he ran out of scotch.

581   A father blamed his son for stealing some money from his coat pocket. His wife said that she stole the money. The husband replied, "I know it's not you. If you stole it, nothing would have been left in my pocket."

582   A wife tells her husband, "Sometimes you appear to be very manly and other times you are not." The husband replies, "It is hereditary; half of my ancestors were men and other half were women."

583   She did not marry me because I told her I have a rich uncle. Now she is my aunt.

584   A judge asked a woman appearing before him in court, "Why did you hit your husband with a chair?" She replied, "Because I could not lift the table."

585   Mr. Singh distributed half of each sweet to his friends because the engagement was not yet confirmed by the girl.

586   To create excitement, the man cuts out his pants pockets and tells his wife that he exchanged his penis with his friend. His wife puts her hands in his pockets and feels around for a while. The husband is getting excited.
She says, "That is impossible, your friend's penis is much bigger."

587   A couple's son got married and all four are sleeping in the same room. Every time the newlyweds make love the father gets inspired and makes love with his wife. After the 5th time, the father tells his son to stop because his mother is getting tired.

588   A mother and her three daughters told about their honeymoon using a code word – "good morning" - for each time they made love. The first daughter said good morning once, the second said good morning two times and the third one said good morning till morning.

589   Three girls on their honeymoon explained their experience using code words: Coca Cola (cold and refreshing), hot chocolate (hot and exciting), and Delta Airlines (in and out every five minutes).

590   Three college friends meet and are talking about their lives. One man works in the Minnesota twin cities and has twins. Another man works for 3M and has triplets. The last man who works for 7 Up is worried in anticipation that his wife might give birth to seven children.

591   A young man planned to propose to his girlfriend in a hot air balloon. He brought a basketful of wine and cheese. In all the excitement, he forgot to take a bottle opener so he asks the pilot if he could borrow the bottle opener. A few minutes later he realized he forgot to bring a knife to cut the cheese so he again asks the pilot if he could borrow his knife. The pilot, getting irritated, replies, "Yes, I will lend you my knife but don't ask if I have the engagement ring for your girlfriend."

592   A dad tells his son, "The girl you want to marry is your sister but your mom does not know it." His son is frustrated and goes to his mom who says, "You can marry this girl because you are not your dad's son but he does not know it."

593   Difference between first honeymoon and second honeymoon. First one we talked about Niagara Falls. Second one we talked about Viagra pills.

594   Mr. Singh met a person with beard and asked, "Why do you have a beard? Did your father have a beard?" "Yes." "Are you married?" "No." "Was your father married?" "No." "Was your grandfather married?" "No." "So you are all bastards."

595   A wife can tell what type of liquor her husband has been drinking. If he greets her with "Hi, Darling," that means he has had imported liquor. If he says, "Hi, Rani," then that means he has had Indian liquor. If he says, "Hi, Bitch," that means he has had no liquor.

596   A wife told her husband, "You should do something so that people will remember you after you die." He said, "Yes, I have bought a diamond for $50,000 and have not paid for it yet. The shopkeeper will remember me forever."

597   A man tells his friend to listen to his wife because she will always give advice. The friend says, "My wife gives 90% sound and 10% advice."

598 A family planner shows how to use condoms by putting one on a stick. A few months later, the villagers were getting pregnant. Turns out they were putting their condoms on a stick.

599 A family was visiting friends with a 4 bedroom house. While taking a tour, the owner said, "One room is for me and the other one is my wife's room and so on." The curious visitor asked, "How is your married life working out this way?" "We like our independence but if I want her I blow the whistle." The visitor asked, "How about if your wife wants you?" "Then she asks, 'did you blow the whistle?'"

600 A husband asks his wife upon his death – would she remarry? Reply: "No I will stay with my widow sister." A wife asks her husband if he would remarry when she dies. Reply: "No, I will also stay with your widow sister."

601 A lady was not satisfied after marriage because her first husband was a psychiatrist and he talked too much in bed. Her second husband was a gynecologist who stared at her vagina in bed. Finally she decided to marry a chef who licked everything in bed.

602 Three husbands were joking about their wives' weight. The first one says, "When my wife sits, she breaks the bed." The second one says, "When my wife walks through the door, it breaks." The third one says, "When I take my wife's skirt to the drycleaners, they say, 'We don't wash tents.'"

603 A son tells his mom, "Our female servant is flirting with our male servant." He then says, "April fools! The male servant isn't flirting with her, but dad is."

604 A couple used a code word about "eating sugar" for love making. A servant watched the couple through the keyhole. One day when the couple went out their teenage daughter was at home. The servant took her in the bedroom and asked if she wanted to "eat sugar" and followed the routine. When the couple came back and found out what happened to their daughter the man said, "If you wanted to eat sugar why did you open a new bag? Why not use the old sugar bag that is already open?"

605 A matrimonial ad had a lot of responses but from rental companies, florists, band groups, etc.

606 A newly married man went to the store to buy lingerie for his new wife. The shopkeeper asked for her size. The inexperienced husband did not know. So he responded by using sign language and showed the size of her breasts using his hands.

607   A daughter asks her father, "Should I marry Ron?" "Ask your mom since she made a good decision to marry me."

608   A wife did not come to the airport for the honeymoon trip to Kashmir because she had already been there before.

609   A lady, who married 7 times, was asked, "What is your opinion about men?" Reply: "All men are different, but husbands are all the same."

610   A man tells his girlfriend, "I cannot marry you because my family does not approve of non-arranged marriages." When asked, "Who in your family doesn't approve?" the man replies, "My wife and children."

611   A wife asks her husband, "Do you remember when you held my hand for the first time?" The husband holds her hand. "Do you remember how you used to kiss me?" The husband kisses his wife. The wife asks, "Do you remember how you used to bite my neck?" The husband goes to the bathroom. The wife is disturbed that her husband walks to the bathroom in the middle of the conversation. The husband explains, "I have to get my dentures."

612   After dissolving the marriage, a husband asks his ex-wife, "Why is our sixth child a blonde?" The wife answers, "The first five kids aren't yours."

613   Two pick pocketers get married and have a baby. Their child is born with his fist closed…with the doctor's ring in it.

614   Into 40 years of marriage the husband says, "I will trade you for 2 -20 years of marriage." The wife responds, "You are not wired for 220."

615   Code word for making love was playing the flute. Wife came late to the room after fulfilling all the household duties. When asked for love making the husband replied, "I played the flute by hand."

616   Some ladies in a club decided to wear dresses according to the color of their husband's hair. One woman wore a black dress, another wore a brown dress, and another wore a silver dress. When one of the ladies showed up naked, she remarked, "My husband is bald."

617   Purpose of 5 fingers: 1.) hitchhike 2.) itch ear, 3.) itch eye, 4.) itch nose, and the 5th one is to hit your head when frustrated with your wife on a golden night when she is not able to make love due to her period. Grandpa says, "I will explain the meaning of the 5th finger at the time of your wedding."

618   A husband says to his wife, "Did you know that you eat one lb. of lipstick each month?" The wife replied, "Well then you eat a half a pound each month by kissing me."

619   When does life begin: at conception, at birth or when the last kid leaves the house?

620   Independence Day is when your wife goes to her parents' house without you.

621   A husband goes to a doctor to find out how much it would cost to treat his wife. The doctor replies, "About Rs.100,000." The husband says, "That's stupid to spend that kind of money on my wife. I can get a new one for half that amount."

622   There was no time to get married when a father was raising three sons. They refused to give a loan to their father when he asked. The father says, "You guys are not only illegitimate but you are also cheap."

623   Those guys, who were beaten by their wives with a stick, please stand up. Everyone stood up except one person who could not get up because he was beaten up too badly.

624   A man tells his wife, "Balwant Singh, our neighbor's wife, serves him well with a massage, hot food and goodbye kisses every morning." The wife says, "If I do all this, would Balwant Singh accept me?"

625   A man asks for a fat, ugly, short prostitute for $200 per night. When asked why, he replies, "She would remind me of my wife."

626   A wife hears a noise coming from the basement and asks her husband to go and find out what it is. Her husband finds a man and asks him who he is. Reply: "I am a rapist." The husband calls his wife and says, "There is a man who is asking for you."

627   A son asked his mom her age, date of birth and why his dad divorced her. She did not give any reply. After a few days the son tells his mom, "I found your driver's license and know all the answers. You are 34 years old, your birthday is May 10 and dad divorced you because you got an F grade in Sex."

628   A young man goes to a marriage interview. A friend suggests that when asked what he likes, to respond always one level higher. For example, "Do you like motorcycles?" Say you like cars. "Do you like a flat?" Then say bungalow. At the end of the interview, the young man is asked if he likes the daughter. He responds, "No, I like her mother."

629   A man says, "I feel 10 years younger after shaving my beard." The wife says, "Why don't you shave every night before going to bed?"

630   A mother disapproved of her son's new girlfriend because she didn't cook like her, dress like her or dance like her. After being introduced to different girlfriends, she finally met a girl who cooked like her, dressed like her and danced like her. She asked her husband if he would approve of a marriage between their son and the girl. The father said, "No way. She is too much like you."

631   A wife is in bed with a friend; her husband enters the room and asks, "What are you doing?" She tells her friend, "Didn't I tell you my husband is stupid and blind?"

632   A band master charges Rs. 100 per uniformed performer and Rs. 25 per performer wearing ordinary clothes. Mr. Singh says, "Can I get naked people for free?"

633   A newlywed couple on a train was sleeping on the upper berth and an old bald headed man was sitting on the lower berth and he told his wife, "I feel a drip of honey on my head."

634   A priest tells a bridegroom that there are three vows which will keep your marriage happy: trust, confidence and harmony. After a year the groom tells the priest that his marriage is falling apart. The priest says, "Did you not follow all 3 vows that I told you? Do you understand what "harmony" is? 1.) her money, 2.) accept defeat (haar maani).

635   Why do men become smarter during sex? Because they are plugged into a genius.
Why don't women blink before foreplay? They don't have enough time.
Why does it take a million sperm to fertilize one egg? They don't stop to ask for directions.
Why did God put men on earth? Because a vibrator can't mow the lawn.
What do electric trains and breasts have in common? They are intended for children, but men end up playing with them.
Why did God make men before women? Because you need a rough draft before you make a final copy.

636   A son brings home an ugly and fat girl to meet his parents. The Dad says quietly, "Son, she is fat and ugly." The son replies, "Dad, you can speak up. She is also deaf."

637   A wife tells her husband, "I need sex twice a week." The husband says, "I can give you a ride once a week but you have to take the bus the second time."

638   Thomas Edison tells his wife one night about his discovery of the light bulb. He says, "I am very excited!" His wife says, "Put your bulb down and you come to bed and make love."

639   A thief tells a man, "I am going to kidnap your wife." The man replies "Go ahead. I took her from her parents 20 years ago and I'm still regretting it."

640 Two men were talking about a new product that is said to reduce a man's sexual desire. One of the men says, "I married such a product 25 years ago."

641 You have been drinking again:
An Irishman had been drinking at a pub all night. The bartender finally said that the pub was closing. The Irishman stood up to leave and fell flat on his face. He tried to stand up again and had the same result. He figured he'd crawl outside, get some fresh air and maybe that would sober him up.
Once outside, he stood up and fell on his face again. So he decided to crawl the four blocks home. He crawled through the door and into his bedroom. When he reached his bed he tried once more to stand up. He managed to pull himself upright, but he quickly fell right into the bed and fell sound asleep as soon as his head hit the pillow. He was awakened the next morning by his wife standing over him, shouting, "So, you've been drinking again!"
Putting on an innocent look, he said, "What makes you say that?"
"The pub just called. You left your wheelchair there again."

642 Wife says to husband, "What right do you have?" Reply: "I have drilling rights."

643 A wife complains to her husband, "You are not affectionate. Our neighbor Mr. Singh kisses his wife every morning." The husband replies, "I don't really know her or I would kiss her, too."

644 "You look so young without your glasses," a wife told her husband. The husband replied, "You also look young when I don't have my glasses."

645 A husband calls from the basement three times for his wife to prepare him some coffee. Hearing no answer, he thinks she has a hearing problem. His wife says that she replied each time saying that the coffee was ready.

646 A beggar, who is getting married, is riding a horse and throwing coins for the poor people. He gets down and collects the coins.

647 A man brings his mother on his honeymoon and the three of them take a boat ride. His mother asks him, "If the boat sinks, who would you save, me or your wife?" The son is not sure how to reply. His wife realizes his dilemma and says, "Mom, your son would definitely save you because there are a lot of young men who would jump to save me, but not to save an old lady."

648 One couple goes to Kashmir for their honeymoon costing $1000. Another couple goes to Agra for $900. Mr. Singh sends his wife with a friend to Europe and it cost nothing to him.

649 There is a husband who drinks a lot. His wife is reading him an article in the newspaper that talks about the dangers of drinking. The husband comments, "You convinced me. We'll stop getting the paper tomorrow."

650 A husband tells his wife that she should have an affair to create some excitement in their marriage. She replies, "I already tried and it didn't work."

651 Two men met at heaven's door. One died due to hypothermia because he was hiding in the freezer from his beloved's husband who committed suicide for accusing his wife of having an affair. The first guy told the second one, "If you had checked the freezer we both would be alive."

652 A man says, "I don't understand women two times in life – before marriage and after marriage."

653 Marriage is a three-ring circus: engagement ring, wedding ring and suffering.

654 A friend asks, "Why do you have your wedding ring on the wrong finger?" "Because I am married to the wrong girl."

655 Mr. Smith went next door to Mrs. Conner's house and said, "I will give you $100 if you show me your breasts and $300 for showing the rest of your body." As he walked back to his house, Mr. Smith thought, "That's one way to pay back the $400 I owed Mr. Conner."

656 A wife asks her husband to hold her and he gets excited. She says, "I cannot do anything tonight, you don't understand my emotional needs." The man takes his wife shopping; she picks out some expensive clothes, cosmetics, etc. and puts them in the shopping cart. When he reaches the cashier he removes everything from the cart and tells his wife, "You do not understand my financial situation just like I don't understand your emotional needs."

657 A lady was checking her marital status in an application form and checked single, married and divorced in that order.

658 In an apartment building, parents asked their son to stand on the balcony so that they could have some privacy and asked him to write a report on people coming and going. The report said, "Uncle A was bringing groceries, Uncle B went to the temple with flowers and Uncle C was making love because his son was also standing in the balcony writing a report."

659 There was a survey asking how many times a man makes love to his wife. Conclusion: 50% said once a day, 25% said twice a week, 10% said once a week. One man said once a year and he seemed to be the happiest in the crowd. Upon asking the secret of his happiness he responded, "Tonight is my night."

660 Three husbands describe the personalities of their wives. The first one says, "My wife is very cold when she sleeps with me at home." The second one says, "My wife is hot when we stay in a 5 star hotel." The third husband says, "My wife is cold when she sleeps with me but very hot when she sleeps with my friend."

661 A husband asks his new wife to go on their honeymoon. The wife responds, "I am tired. Take your mother."

662 A couple is fighting for custody of their child after their divorce went to court. The judge asks the lady her reason for wanting custody of the child. Reply: "I carried the child in my stomach and suffered labor pain." The judge asks the husband for his reason and his reply is, "Judge, if a thirsty person goes to a vending machine and puts a quarter in the machine, a can of pop comes out. Does the can belong to the vending machine or the person who put the money in the machine?" The Judge says, "I get the point" and tells the man, "OK, you get custody."

663 Four ways to spread news quickly: telephone, telegram, television and tell a woman not to tell.

664 Husband pulled his underwear from the drawer and powder came out of it. His wife asked, "What is the powder?" His reply, "Miracle growth powder."

665 A wife with small breasts asked her husband for $10,000 for breast implants. Her husband asked, "Why do you want to spend so much money? Instead, just rub toilet paper between your cleavage every day and your breasts will grow just like your butt has grown over the years."

666 After marriage a wife changed her husband's wardrobe, shoes, eyeglasses, etc., and after several years complained, "You have changed a lot since I got married to you."

667 A wife asked her husband, "When are you going to build The Taj Mahal for me?" He replied, "I have bought land in Agra and I will build it after you die."

668   Mr. Singh lost his job and bought a cow for Rs. 5,000 so that he could sell the milk and raise calves. However, the cow never gave milk or a calf. His friend suggested that he buy a bull to make her pregnant. The cow ran away from the bull. His friend asked, "Did you get the cow from Dayton?"   "Yes, but how did you know?" He replied, "My wife is also from Dayton and she also runs away from me."

669   A college student says to a girl on their first date, "I am interested in your geography, not in your history."

670   Widows were happy at a party because they knew where their husbands were. The married women were not happy because they didn't know where their husbands were.

671   Two men were talking one day. One of them said, "I'm depressed. My wife keeps talking about her first husband." The other man replied, "You have it easy. My wife talks about her next husband."

672   "Dad," the young drama student bragged, "I got my first part in a play. I'm a man who's been married for 20 years."
"That's nice," replied his dad. "Maybe next time you'll get a speaking part."

673   "My dear," said the young man, "Tomorrow is your birthday, and to think that one year ago I didn't even know you."
His girlfriend replied in the same tone of voice, "Let's not discuss our past, darling. Let's talk about our present."

674   A man neglected to report that his wife had lost her credit card. Two weeks later, he received the bill from the bank for charges that were not made by his wife. Upon seeing that the bill was much lower than when his wife used it, he decided to ignore the whole thing.

675   A worried-looking man in a florist shop asked for three potted geraniums.
"I'm sorry," said the clerk. "We're out of geraniums just now but we have nice potted chrysanthemums." "No, they won't do," replied the man. "I promised my wife I'd water her geraniums while she was away."

676   Overheard in an elevator: "My wife says I only listen to 25 percent of what she says, so she tells me everything four times."

677   When the husband exclaimed, "I've just discovered oil on our property!" his wife exclaimed, "Wonderful! Now we can get a new car!"
"No," he responded, "We'd better get the old one fixed. That's where the oil is coming from."

678 A businessman had finally retired after some 40 years of catching the 7:30 a.m. train. The first morning at breakfast, when his wife placed his plate in front of him, he said he wished she would not make the toast that dark. He did not like that way.

"My dear," she exclaimed, "why didn't you ever tell me?"

"I never had time before," he replied.

679 Within a year after marrying one of a set of identical twins, the executive found himself in court, asking for a divorce. When the judge asked for his reasons, the executive replied, "My wife's sister visits us a lot and I sometimes come home and make love to her by mistake."

"But surely there's some difference between the two women" the judge said.

"You bet there is," responded the executive. "That's why I want a divorce."

680 On their way to get married, a loving couple dies in a car accident. The couple is sitting outside Heaven's Gate waiting on St. Peter to finish the paperwork so they can enter. While waiting, they wonder if they could possibly get married in Heaven. St. Peter finally shows up and they ask him. St. Peter replies, "I don't know, this is the first time anyone has ever asked. Let me go find out," and he leaves.

The couple sits for a couple of months and begins to wonder if they really should get married in Heaven, what with the eternal aspect of it all. "What if it doesn't work out?" They wonder, "Are we stuck together forever?" St. Peter returns after yet another month, looking somewhat bedraggled. "Yes," he informs the couple, "You can get married in Heaven."

"Great," says the couple, "But what if things don't work out? Could we also get a divorce in Heaven?"

St. Peter, red-faced, slams his clipboard onto the ground.

"What's wrong?" exclaims the frightened couple.

"Geez!" St. Peter exclaims, "It took me three months to find a priest up here! Do you have any idea how long it's going to take for me to find a lawyer?"

681 Did you hear about the man who heard his wife was running around with his best friend? He got a gun, went out in the back yard and shot his dog.

682 Have you heard of the credit card for wives? It self-destructs after $100.

683 Before a man is married, he is incomplete. When he is married, he is completely finished.

684 Marriage is an institution in which a man loses his bachelor's status and the woman gets her master's status.

685 A little boy asked his father, "Daddy, how much does it cost to get married?" And the father replied, "I don't know son, I am still paying for it."

686 Young son: "Is it true, Dad? I heard that in some parts of Africa, a man doesn't know his wife until he marries her?"
Dad, "That happens in most countries, son."

687 There was a man who said, "I never knew what real happiness was until I got married, and then it was too late."

688 A happy marriage is give and take. The husband gives and wife takes.

689 When a newly married man looks happy, we know why. But when a 10-year married man looks happy, we wonder why.

690 Married life is very frustrating. In the first year of marriage, the man speaks and the woman listens. In the second year, the wife speaks and man listens. After five years they both speak and the neighbors listen.

691 After a quarrel, a wife said to her husband, "You know, I was a fool when I married you."
And the husband replied, "Yes, dear, I was in love and did not notice it."

692 A man placed an ad in the classifieds: "Wife wanted." The next day he received 100 letters. They all said the same thing: "You can have mine."

693 When a man opens the car door for his wife, you can be sure of one thing: Either the car is new or his wife is new.

694 A woman was telling her friend, "I made my husband a millionaire."
"And what was he before you married him?" the friend asked. The woman replied, "A multimillionaire."

695 A judge was interviewing a woman regarding her pending divorce, and asked "What are your grounds for your divorce?"
She replied, "About four acres and a nice little home in the middle of the property with a stream running by."
"No," he said, "I mean, what is the foundation of this case?"
"It is made of concrete, brick and mortar," she responded.
"I mean," he continued, "What are your relations like?"
"I have an aunt and uncle living here in town, and so do my husband's parents."

He said, "Do you have a real grudge?"

"No," she replied, "We have two-car carport and have really never needed one."

"Please," he tried again, "Is there any infidelity in your marriage?"

"Yes, both my son and daughter have stereo sets. We don't necessarily like the music, but the answer to your question is yes."

"Ma'am, does your husband ever beat you up?"

"Yes," she responded. "About twice a week he gets up earlier than I do."

Finally in frustration, the judge asked, "Lady, why do you want a divorce?"

"Oh, I don't want a divorce" She replied. "I have never wanted a divorce. My husband does. He said he cannot communicate with me."

696 The most effective way to remember your wife's birthday? Forget it once.

697 I married Miss Right. I just didn't know her first name was Always.

698 I have not spoken to my wife for 18 months. I don't like to interrupt her.

699 A husband is someone who, after taking the trash out, acts like he just cleaned the whole house.

700 Smart man, smart woman = Romance
Smart man, dumb woman = Affair
Dumb man, smart woman = Marriage
Dumb man, Dumb woman = Pregnancy

701 A man will pay $20 for a $10 item he needs.
A woman will pay $10 for a $20 item she does not need.

702 A woman worries about the future until she gets a husband.
A man never worries about the future until he gets a wife.
A successful man is the one who can make more money than his wife can spend.
A successful woman is the one who can find such a man.

703 To be happy with a man, you must understand him a lot and love him a little.
To be happy with a woman, you must love her a lot and not try to understand her at all.

704 Married men live longer than single men do, but married men are a lot more willing to die.

705 A woman marries a man hoping that he will change.
A man marries a woman hoping that she will not.

706 A woman has the last word in any argument. Anything a man says after that is the beginning of a new argument.

707 Two deaf people get married. During the first week of marriage, they find that they are unable to communicate in the bedroom when the lights are off because they cannot see each other using sign language. After several nights of fumbling around and misunderstandings, the wife decides to find a solution.

"Honey," she signs, "Why don't we agree on some simple signals? For instance, at night, if you want to have sex with me reach over and squeeze my left breast one time. If you do not want to have sex, reach over and squeeze my right breast one time."

The husband thinks this is a great idea and signs back to his wife, "Great idea. Now if you want to have sex with me, reach over and pull on my penis one time. If you don't want to have sex, reach over and pull on my penis 50 times."

708 Why men are happier people:

Your last name stays put. The garage is all yours. Wedding plans take care of themselves. Chocolate is just another snack. You can never be pregnant. You can wear a white T-shirt to a water park. You can wear no shirt to a water park. Car mechanics tell you the truth. The world is your urinal. You never have to drive to another gas station restroom because this one is just too icky. You don't have to stop and think of which way to turn a nut on a bolt. Same work, more pay. Wrinkles add character. Wedding dress - $10,000. Tux rental - $100. People never stare at your chest when you're talking to them. New shoes don't cut, blister, or mangle your feet. One mood, all the time.

Phone conversations are over in 30 seconds flat. You know stuff about tanks. A five-day vacation requires only one suitcase. You can open all your own jars. You get extra credit for the slightest act of thoughtfulness. If someone forgets to invite you, he or she can still be your friend.

Your underwear is $8.95 for a three-pack. Three pairs of shoes are more than enough. You almost never have strap problems in public. You are unable to see wrinkles in your clothes. Everything on your face stays its original color. The same hairstyle lasts for years, maybe decades. You only have to shave your face and neck.

You can play with toys all your life. One wallet and one pair of shoes — one color for all seasons. You can wear shorts no matter how your legs look. You can "do" your nails with a pocketknife. You have freedom of choice concerning growing a mustache.

You can do Christmas shopping for 25 relatives on December 24 in 25 minutes.

No wonder men are happier.

709 A couple came upon a wishing well. The husband leaned over, made a wish and threw in a penny. The wife decided to make a wish, too. But she leaned over too much, fell into the well, and drowned. The husband was stunned for a while but smiled and said, "It really works."

710 A man rushed home from work and exclaimed to his wife, "Pack your bags, I've won the lottery!!!" The wife excitedly asked, "Should I pack clothes for cold or warm weather? "Pack them all — you're leaving!"

711 A woman went to a party without her husband. While at the party, she overheard another man saying to his wife, "Pass the sugar, sugar," and "Pass the honey, honey" She thought that sort of sweet talk was a good idea, so she decided to try it on her husband the next morning at the breakfast table. "Pass the bacon, pig."

712 A woman accompanied her husband to the doctor's office. After the check-up, the doctor called the wife into his office alone. He said, "If you don't do the following, your husband surely will die:
Each morning, fix him a healthy breakfast.
Be pleasant and make sure he is in good mood.
For lunch, make him a nutritious meal.
For dinner, prepare him an especially nice meal.
Don't burden him with chores as he probably had a hard day.
Don't discuss your problems with him.
And most importantly, have sex with him several times a week and satisfy his every whim."
On the way home, the husband asked his wife what the doctor said to her.
"He said you're going to die."

713 A woman's husband had been slipping in and out of a coma for several months, yet she stayed by his bedside every single day. When he finally regained consciousness, he motioned for her to come nearer.
As she sat by him, he said, "You know what? You have been with me all through the bad times. When I got fired, you were there to support me. When my business failed, you were there. When we lost our house you were by my side. You know what?"
"What dear?" she asked gently.
"I think you bring me bad luck."

714   Three men were sitting in a bar, drinking and talking about how stupid their wives were.

The first one says, "My wife is so stupid. Last week she went to the supermarket and bought $300 worth of meat because it was on sale and we do not even have a freezer."

The second one says, "Just last week, my wife went out and spent $20,000 on a car and she doesn't even know how to drive."

The third one nods and agrees that these two women sound like they both fell out of a tree and got hit by every branch on the way down. However, he thinks his wife is dumber. He chuckles and says, "My wife just left to go on a holiday in Greece. I watched her packing her bag and she must have put about 100 condoms in there. And she does not even have a penis."

715   One day, a girl proposed to her boyfriend and he turned her down, saying, "In our family we marry only our relatives."

The girlfriend asked, "What do you mean?"

He responded, "My mom married my dad, my brother married my sister-in-law and my uncle married my aunt."

716   Mr. Singh says to a girl. "I want to marry you."

Girl: "But I am one year older than you."

Mr. Singh: "No problem, then I will marry you next year."

717   A woman was having an affair while her husband was at work. One rainy day, she is in bed with her boyfriend when, to her horror, she hears her husband's car pull into the driveway.

"Oh my God. Hurry! Grab your clothes and jump out the window. My husband's home early!"

"I can't jump out the window. It's raining out there!"

"If my husband catches us in here, he'll kill us both!" she replied."He's got a hot temper and a gun, so the rain is the least of your problems!"

The boyfriend scoots out of bed, grabs his clothes and jumps out the window. As he runs down the street in the pouring rain, he quickly discovers he has run right into the middle of the town's annual marathon, so he starts running along beside the 300 other runners. Being naked, with his clothes tucked under his arm, he tries to blend in as best as he can. After a little while, a small group of runners who have been watching him with some curiosity jog closer.

"Do you always run in the nude?" one asks.

"Oh yes!" he replies, gasping in air. "It feels so wonderfully free!"

Another runner moves alongside him. "Do you always run carrying your clothes with you under your arm?"

"Oh, yes" he answers breathlessly. "That way I can get dressed right at the end of the run and get in my car to go home!

Then a third runner casts his eyes a little lower and queries,
"Do you always wear a condom when you run?"
"Only when it's raining."

718   A boy goes to meet a future wife and takes his friend with him and asks him to exaggerate whatever he says to the girl and her family. The boy says he came from a small village. The friend corrects him and says he came from a big city. Then the boy says he came riding a scooter. The friend corrects him and says he came riding a big car. The boy coughs a little and he says he got a little cold and his friend says he has been suffering from tuberculosis (TB) for the last 5 years.

719   A wife tells her husband, "I was born beautiful so that you could marry me." He replied, "I was born stupid so that I could marry you."

720   A lady asked her neighbor if she could borrow a matchbox. The neighbor asked, "Why do you need a matchbox?" Reply: "I want to start a fire in my house." The neighbor said: "You can borrow my mother-in-law; she can start a fire without a matchbox."

721   A couple is lying in bed. The man says, "I am going to make you the happiest woman in the world." The woman says, "I'll miss you."

722   "It's just too hot to wear clothes today," Jack says as he steps out of the shower. "Honey, what do you think the neighbors would think if I mowed the lawn like this?" "Probably that I married you for your money," she replies.

723   A man told his girlfriend, "Since I first laid eyes on you, I have wanted to make love to you really badly." She said, "Well, you succeeded."

724   Q: What do you call an intelligent, good looking, sensitive man?
A: A rumor.

725   A businessman sends an email to his wife:

To My Dear Wife,

You will surely understand that I have certain needs that you with your 54 years can no longer satisfy. I am very happy with you and I value you as a good wife. Therefore after reading this email, I hope that you will not wrongly interpret the fact that I will be spending the evening with my 18-year-old secretary at the Comfort Inn Hotel. Please don't be mad. I shall be home before midnight.

When the man came home, he found the following letter on the dining room table.

My Dear Husband,

I received your email and thank you for your honesty. I would like to take this opportunity to remind you that you are also 54 years old. At the same time I would like to inform you that while you read this, I will be at the Hotel Fiesta with Michael my tennis coach, who, like your secretary, is also 18 years old. As a successful businessman and with your excellent knowledge of math, you will understand that we are in the same situation, although with one small difference.

Eighteen goes into 54 a lot more times than 54 goes into 18. Therefore I will not be back before dinner tomorrow.

726   **Types of sex:**

Social Security sex:

You get a little each month, but not enough to live on!

Loud sex:

A wife went in to see a therapist and said, "I've got a big problem, doctor.

Every time we're in bed and my husband climaxes, he lets out this ear-splitting yell."

"My dear," the shrink said, "That's completely natural.

I don't see what the problem is."

"The problem is," she complained, "It wakes me up!"

Quiet sex:

Tired of a listless sex life, the man came right out and asked his wife during a recent lovemaking session, "How come you never tell me when you have an orgasm?" She glanced at him casually and replied, "You're never home."

Wedding anniversary sex:

A husband and his wife had a bitter quarrel on the day of their 40th wedding anniversary. The husband yelled, "When you die, I'm getting you a headstone that reads:

'Here Lies My Wife - Cold As Ever.'"

"Yeah," she replied, "When you die, I'm getting you a headstone that reads:

'Here Lies My Husband — Stiff At Last.'"

OLYMPIC SEX:

Once in four years.

727   There was this couple that had been married for 20 years. Every time they made love the husband always insisted on shutting off the lights. Well, after 20 years the wife felt this was ridiculous. She figured she would break him out of this crazy habit.
So one night, while they were in the middle of a wild, screaming, romantic session, she turned on the lights. She looked down...and saw her husband was holding a battery-operated pleasure device...a vibrator! Soft, wonderful and larger than a "real one."
She went completely ballistic. "You impotent bastard," she screamed at him, "How could you be lying to me all of these years? You better explain yourself!"
The husband looked her straight in the eyes and says calmly, "I'll explain the toy... you explain the kids."

728   W.I.F.E.
Worries Invited For-Ever
Wisdom Invited For-Ever
Wealth Inherited For-Ever
Wonderful Instrument For Enjoyment

729   Two men are talking about their wives.
The first one says, "My wife is an angel."
The second one says, "You're lucky. Mine is still alive."

730   A boy went to see a girl and told his parents, "I don't like her because she is too fat." Reply: "Girls are like a T.V. screen; some are 12" wide and some are 16" wide but you control the channels with your 8" remote control."

731   A husband asks his wife to prepare an omelet. While she is making it, he keeps nagging her: "There is only one egg, be careful; don't burn it, be careful; put less salt and pepper, be careful." The wife gets upset and says, "What is wrong with you?" He replies, "Now you know how I feel when I drive."

732   A host catches one of his guests stealing a silver spoon and putting it in his coat pocket. He thinks, "How can I get that expensive spoon back without embarrassing the guest?" So he announces that he will do a magic trick for his guests. He takes his own silver spoon and puts it in his own pocket and claims to make it disappear. He then walks over to the mischievous guest, reaches into his pocket and exclaims, "Magic!"

733   A mother took her young child to a birthday party. While at the party the child came up to the mother and said, "Mom, I have to pee." The mom, being, very embarrassed took the child into the hallway and said, "I don't like it when you scream that loud. Let us use a code word. When you need to pee, say, 'I want to sing.'" One night, the mother went out and the dad watched the child. That night the child told his father that he needed to sing. The father replied, "OK, son, sing slowly in my ear."

734   A wife asks her husband if she can use silver spoons at their anniversary party. The husband says no. The wife says, "Do you think the guests will steal the spoons?" The husband replies, "No, the guests will recognize the items that I have stolen from their parties."

735   It was the king's birthday party and a farmer brought vegetables and fruits as gifts. The king was disappointed to see that a farmer brought cucumbers as a gift so he told his minister to shove them up the farmer's butt. The next farmer, staring down at the watermelons he had brought, ran away.

736   A husband celebrated when his wife became an American citizen because when he came to the USA he had a cherished dream to sleep with an American citizen.

737   A man ate a lot of beans at his wedding anniversary. A surprise party was planned at home. A friend blindfolded him and took him to the party planned at his house. The man released air loudly as he was walking. He felt embarrassed when he found all the guests were sitting in the room.

738   At their silver wedding anniversary, a wife asked for a photo of husband's penis. She heard that Kodak was able to enlarge things.

739   A man used highly polished shoes and went to a party. He put his shoes under the women's skirts or dresses so he could tell the color of the ladies undergarments. He was baffled when he saw a crack and no panties.

740   A couple, who was married in July, always celebrates their anniversary on December 21. When asked why, they say, "It's the longest night of the year!"

741   There are three types of men: those who believe in Santa Claus, those who don't believe in Santa Claus, and those who become Santa Claus to entertain the kids.

742   A son asks for a sling shot (Gulel) on his birthday every year as gift. One year his mom said, "Ask for something else." The boy asked for a girl so that he could remove her panties and use the elastic to make a sling shot.

743   Mr. Singh gave a slap to his friend on Christmas Day. One year back his friend had said that he looked like a pig. Today he saw a pig eating shit and it reminded him of the statement made by his friend.

744   There are two kinds of partygoers: one who wants to leave early and one who wants to leave late. Unfortunately, they're usually married to each other.

745   A married couple was invited to go to a Halloween party. As they were getting ready to go, the wife said she had developed a migraine headache and had to stay home. She told her husband to go to the party without her. "Don't let me spoil a good time for you," she said. The husband put on his costume and went to the party. The wife took some aspirin and went to bed.
After sleeping for a while, she woke up feeling much better and decided to go to the party to surprise her husband. As she was getting ready, she thought, "I wonder what my husband really does when I am not around." She then got into a different costume so her husband would not recognize her. After arriving, she stood and watched.
There was her husband dancing with one girl after another and getting very physical with them. She decided to see just how far he would go. She went up and started dancing with him and got very close. She whispered that they should go outside. Going to one of the cars, they made love. Prior to the midnight unmasking, she went home to wait for her husband so she could confront him.
He arrived home about 1:00 a.m. and climbed into bed. She sat up and asked, "Well, how was the party? He replied, "It was no fun without you honey." She said, "I don't believe you. You had lots of fun!" He replied, "Really, honey, when I got to the party some of the guys and I got bored and we went downstairs and played poker all night. But you know, that guy I loaned my costume to had one hell of a great time."

746   On Christmas morning, a cop on horseback was sitting at a traffic light. Next to him was a kid on his shiny new bike. The cop says, "Nice bike you got there. Did Santa bring that to you?" The kid says, "Yeah." The cop says, "Next year tell Santa to put a tail light on that bike." The cop then proceeds to issue a $20 ticket for bicycle safety violation. The kid takes the ticket and before he rides off says, "By the way, that's a nice horse you got there. Did Santa bring that to you?" Humoring the kid, the cop says, "Yeah, he sure did." The kid says, "Well next year, tell Santa to put the dick underneath the horse, instead of on top."

A LITTLE OLD LADY CALLS 911...

HELP, SEND THE POLICE TO MY HOUSE RIGHT AWAY... THERE'S A DAMN REPUBLICAN ON MY FRONT PORCH AND HE'S PLAYING WITH HIMSELF!

WHAT?

I SAID THERE IS A DAMN REPUBLICAN ON MY FRONT PORCH PLAYING WITH HIMSELF AND HE'S WEIRD. I DON'T KNOW HIM AND I'M AFRAID! PLEASE SEND THE POLICE!!

WELL, NOW, HOW DO YOU KNOW HE'S A REPUBLICAN?

BECAUSE, YOU DAMN FOOL, IF IT WAS A DEMOCRAT, HE'D BE SCREWING SOMEBODY ELSE!

747   What is politics? Dad is a capitalist since he earns the bread. Mom is the government as she runs the house. The maid servant is the masses and the younger brother is the future. At night mother is sleeping, father is sleeping with the maid servant, and the younger brother is in shit. Conclusion: When a capitalist is screwing the masses, the government is sleeping and the future is in shit.

748   The German neurosurgeon bragged that they can transplant a brain in a patient and have him working within a day. The English surgeon says they can transplant a brain and the patient starts working in 4 hours. The US surgeon says they can transplant a brain and an asshole from Texas to Washington and have half the country looking for jobs the next day.

749   An information minister was asked by the king to find out who was the head of the household for families in the city: the husband or the wife. If the husband was the head of the household, the minister gave the husband a horse. If the wife was the head, the minister gave the wife a white egg. Upon reaching one house, which belonged to a wrestler, the minister asked him, "Who dominates your house?" The wrestler said, "Me, of course." The minister said, "I want to give you a horse. What color would you like, black or white?" The wrestler replied, "I want a black horse." His wife shouted from the other room, "No, I want a white horse." The minister reached into his pocket and said to the wrestler, "OK. Here is your white egg."

750   Mr. Singh was asked to explain the meaning of word OBAMA. Reply: Originally born in Africa to manage Americans.

751   The Mexican President was visiting the White House. President Kennedy kept admiring his ring so the Mexican president gave it to him. The next year President Kennedy went to Mexico and the Mexican President said, "Your wife Jacqueline Kennedy is very beautiful." After hearing this several times Kennedy returned the ring to the Mexican President.

752   Prime Minister Churchill gave some very embarrassing numbers to the House of Commonwealth. An aide asked how he prepared these numbers in one day; normally it took 6 months. He replied, "It will take 6 months for the opposition to understand these numbers."

753 A man wrote on a public building, "Mr. Richard Nixon is a fool." The man was sentenced for six months for insulting a political figure and an additional three months for leaking a secret.

754 Hitler chopped off the ears of a soldier and asked if he had any pain. "No, because I belong to the German Army." Then he chopped off his big nose – no pain. Then he chopped off his penis – no pain because it belongs to the person standing behind him.

755 A politician and a clergyman went to heaven. The politician was treated much better than the clergyman because only 1% of politicians reach heaven.

756 Why did it take the politician 30 minutes to read a 15-minute speech? The speech writer gave him two copies.

757 USA is a free country; you can criticize President Bush, no problem. Gorbachev says, "You can criticize Bush in Russia too, no problem."

758 A man brings his son to church and asks a priest, "What will my son be when he grows up?" The priest puts down a $1 bill, a Bible and a bottle of whiskey. The priest explains that if the boy reaches for the $1 bill, he'll be a banker. If he picks the Bible, he'll be a priest. And if he picks the whiskey, he'll be a bartender. The boy grabbed all three items. "Uh-oh," the priest said. "That means he'll be a politician."

759 Mr. Singh comes to the USA to learn English from President Reagan who says, "After a month I failed to teach English but Mr. Singh taught me Hindi."

760 A husband asks his wife, "Why do you spend money to dye your hair? Let your hair grow grey like Barbara Bush's hair." The wife says, "Yes. As soon as you are inaugurated as the president."

761 Why was Mahatma Gandhi lean and thin? Because he was the father of a poor nation.

762 Why did M. Gandhi wear long clothes? (dhoti) Because he believed in freedom of movement.

763 Elizabeth's passion, Calvin Klein's obsession, Bush's recession and Gorbachev's depression.

764 Kissinger to Bush: "Who is my dad's son, who is not my brother?" Bush could not answer so Kissinger replied, "It is me." Bush asks the same question to Cheney and tells Bush, "It is me, Cheney." Bush says, "No it is Kissinger."

765 Mom is an alarmist. One cough and she thinks bronchitis. A headache equals a brain tumor. And one lie means her kid is destined to be a politician.

766 Titanic ship: Reagan says, "The ship is sinking!" Nixon says, "Screw it!" And Clinton says, "Do we have time?"

767 Mr. Singh was the president of his Rotary Club when he met Clinton and asked, "Who are you?" Reply, "I am the President and the husband of Hillary." Mr. Singh replied, "Me too."

768 The Bush-Clinton-Bush era is known as the period of sex between two bushes.

769 An astrologer predicted that Osama Bin Laden will die on America's national holiday. Any day he dies will be a national holiday in America.

770 Bush watching Indian Idol program on Indian TV observed that people were asked to send SMS. The next day he asked India's prime minister what SMS meant. Reply: Sardar Manmohan Singh.

771 Bob Hope tells the story of a gala event in Washington, D.C. at the Kennedy Center. He was invited to sit in the box of President Ronald Reagan.
When Hope and the president arrived, there were two vacant seats left. One was labeled "America's No. 1 Man" and the other, "Worn-out Actor." They had a wrestling match to see who got which seat.

772 Q: If an honest politician, an intelligent woman, and a tooth fairy walked in the room at the same time and there was $100 bill on the floor, who would pick it up?
A: The intelligent woman. The other two do not exist.

773   Once upon a time, the government had a vast scrap yard in the middle of a desert. Parliament said, "That's very valuable metal. Someone might be tempted to steal it and exchange it for cash."

So they hired a night watchman. Then parliament said, "How can the watchman do his job without a job description and instructions?"

So they created a planning department and hired two people, one person to write instructions, and one person do time studies.

The parliament said, "How are these people going to get paid?"

So they created the following positions: A time keeper and a payroll officer.

Then parliament said, "Who will be accountable for all of these people?"

So they created an administrative section and hired three people, an administrative officer, assistant administrative officer and a legal secretary.

Then parliament said, "We have had this command in operation for one year and we are $18,000 over our budget. We must cutback the overall cost of this operation."

So they laid off the night watchman.

774   The UN had a question for the countries of the world:

"Please give your honest opinion about solutions to the shortage of food in rest of the world."

The survey was a huge failure.

* In Africa, they didn't know what "food" meant.
* In India, they didn't know what "honest"' meant.
* In Europe, they didn't know what "shortage" meant.
* In China, they didn't know what "opinion" meant.
* In the Middle East, they didn't know what "solution" meant.
* In South America, they didn't know what "please" meant.
* And in the U.S., they didn't know what "the rest of the world" meant.

775   New bonds are being issued:

Lewinsky bond: Has no maturity.

McCain bond: Has no interest.

Clinton bond: Has no principle.

776   The Chinese government announced that it is changing its emblem to a condom because it more clearly reflects the government's political stance. A condom stands up to inflation, halts production, destroys the next generation, protects a bunch of pricks and gives you a sense of security while you are actually getting screwed.

777   Can you imagine working for a company that has a little more than 500 employees and has the following statistics:

36 have been accused of spousal abuse

7 have been arrested for fraud

19 have been accused of writing bad checks

117 have directly or indirectly bankrupted at least two businesses

3 have done time for assault

71, repeat 71, cannot get a credit card due to bad credit

14 have been arrested on drug-related charges

8 have been arrested for shoplifting

21 currently are defendants in lawsuits

And 84 have been arrested for drunk driving in the recent year.

Can you guess which organization this is?

Give up yet?

It's the 535 members of the United States Congress.
The same group of people that crank out hundreds of new laws each year designed to keep the rest of us in line.

778   Letters to the editor we wish we had written:

Replace all female flight attendants with good- looking strippers.

The attendants have gotten old and haggard looking.

They don't even serve food anymore, so what's the loss?

The strippers would double, triple, perhaps quadruple the alcohol consumption and get a "party atmosphere" going in the cabin.

Muslims would be afraid to get on the planes for fear of seeing naked women. And, of course, every heterosexual businessman in this country would start flying economy again hoping to see naked women.

Hijackings would come to a screeching halt and the airline industry would see record revenue.

Why didn't Bush think of this?

Why do I still have to do everything myself?

Sincerely,

Bill Clinton

779   A little old lady calls 911.

When the operator answers, she yells, "Help, send the police to my house right away. There's a damn Republican on my front porch and he's playing with himself."

"What?" the operator exclaimed.

"I said, there is a damn Republican on my front porch playing with himself and he's weird. I don't know him and I'm afraid! Please send the police," the little old lady repeated.

"Well, now, how do you know he's a Republican?"

"Because, you damn fool, if it was a Democrat, he'd be screwing somebody else!"

780   One day President George Bush was out jogging and accidentally fell from a ridge into a very cold river. Three boys, playing along the river, saw the accident. Without a second thought, they jumped in the water and dragged the wet president out of the river.

After cleaning up, he said, "Boys, you saved the president of the United States today. You deserve a reward. You name it; I'll give it to you."

The first boy said, "Please, I'd like a ticket to Disneyland!"

"I'll personally hand it to you," said Bush.

"I'd like a pair of Nike Air Jordan's," the second boy said.

"I'll buy them myself and give them to you," said the grateful president.

"And I'd like a wheelchair with a stereo in it," said the third boy.

"I'll personally…wait a second, son, you're not handicapped!"

"No – but I will be when my dad finds out I saved your sorry ass from drowning."

781   A farmer, a lawyer and a politician went to God. The farmer was ordered to run around hell four times because he committed four sins. The lawyer was told to do 17 laps because he committed 17 sins. When it came time to sentence the politician, God said, "Why don't you go home and get your bike?"

782   A man is praying to God and says, "Whatever I ask for, give twice to my neighbor." God is impressed with his consideration for the neighbor. Then he says, "I want to be blind in one eye."

783   A junior priest tells a church member, "You have to pay $10 for three offenses. Normally we charge $10 for five offenses. If you wish you can commit two more additional offenses and pay no additional charges."

784   A priest asks all church members during confessions for the names of the women in town who had committed adultery, so that he could add them to his black book and have fun with these ladies later on.

785   A neighbor borrows 18 brass plates for a party. The next day he returns 20. The owner asks, "How come there are two more brass plates then what you borrowed from me?" The neighbor replies, "The brass plates had two kids." Another party comes around and the neighbor asks to borrow 20 silver plates. The owner thinks, "Well, he did give me two more last time, so why not?" After the party the neighbor returns 18 sliver plates. The owner asks, "Where are the other two?" The neighbor says, "They died." The owner asks, "How can plates die?" The neighbor replies, "If they can give birth to kids, they can also die."

786   Catholic Mothers:
Four Catholic ladies are having coffee together, discussing how important their sons are. The first one tells her friend, "My son is a priest. When he walks into a room, everyone calls him 'Father.'"
The second Catholic woman chirps, "Well, my son is a Bishop. Whenever he walks into a room, people say, 'Your Grace.'"
The third Catholic woman says smugly, "Well not to put you down, but my son is a Cardinal. Whenever he walks into a room, people say, 'Your Eminence.'"
The fourth Catholic woman sips her coffee in silence. The first three women give her this subtle, "Well...?"
She replies "My son is a gorgeous, 6'2", hard-bodied, well-developed male stripper. Whenever he walks into a room, women say, 'My God.'"

787   Three pretty ladies went to heaven after an accident. God interviewed all of them and told the first lady, "Since you committed adultery once, you can sleep in the sliver room." God told the second lady, "Since you committed adultery twice, you can sleep in the gold room." God then interviewed the third lady, "Since you committed adultery 10 times, you can sleep in my room."

788   Mr. Singh shot his secretary's lover out of jealously. His friend said, "Things could have been worse. If Mr. Singh would have come two days earlier, I would have been shot."

789 Four religious leaders agreed to discuss their own weaknesses. The first one said, "My weakness is money." The second one said, "My weakness is ego." The third one said, "My weakness is women." The fourth leader, after listening to other three, ran away because his weakness was to criticize others.

790 A long-haired astrologer says he can predict the future because his ponytail acts like an antenna that connects him with God. Mr. Singh tells the astrologer, "I also have a long ponytail but I don't get any messages from God." The astrologer says, "But you also have a long beard and that grounds out the signal."

791 A preacher told the members of the church one day, "All members will die." Mr. Singh laughed and said, "Good thing I'm not a member."

792 Three priests decide to go to Pittsburgh. They approach the ticket window, where a beautiful clerk wearing a low-cut blouse showing cleavage is working. The first priest gets excited and accidentally says, "Give me three tickets to Tittsburg." The lady is offended by the priest's language and the way he is staring at her breasts. Then the second priest goes to pay for tickets and tells the lady, "I'd like my change in dimes and nipples." The third priest comes to the clerk to apologize for his colleagues' behavior and says, "I apologize for my fellow priests acting like such savage breasts."

793 A young boy asked the preacher for the time. The preacher wouldn't tell him the time because the boy then asked, "What is your address? How many kids do you have? Is your daughter married? Can I come to see her? Can I marry her?" The preacher thought, "I don't want my daughter to marry a boy who can't even afford a watch."

794 A man is sleeping with someone else's wife and hears the garage door open and hides himself in the closet. He hears a voice, "Wow, it's too dark in here." The man notices a little boy and gives him $40 to stay quiet. Later, the mother asks her son where he got the $40. He doesn't answer so she takes him to the church for confession. The boy goes into the confession booth and says, "Wow, it's too dark in here." The priest says, "Hey, don't even try to blackmail me again."

795 A nun is traveling in the desert with a priest and is dying of thirst. The priest proposes that he can put life in her body by having sex. The nun sees that a camel is dying and requests the priest put life in the camel first.

796 A liberated woman mentioned to God that husbands should have labor pain…A lady delivered and her chauffeur had labor pains.

797 A few women challenged a priest to see if he would get excited. Seeing nude women, the priest got excited but to hide his excitement, he covered his penis with his hat. When he removed his hands, his hat was still there hanging on his penis.

798 A poor boy writes a letter to God and asks for $500. The post office workers open the letter and send him $300 so the boy would not lose faith in God. The boy replies to God, "Thanks God, next time don't send money through the post office – those guys kept $200."

799 A father tells his son to think about all girls as his sisters. Reply: "That will improve my character but what about your character, Dad?"

800 Mr. Singh repents for sins he did not commit. In his next life he wants to start committing sins at a younger age.

801 A man had a dream where he saw God with a pegboard with different size holes. The smaller the hole the less lucky you are. His wife, sleeping next to him, slapped him because he was putting his finger in her nostril and trying to make it bigger.

802 Animal Trade Market:
Cow for $100 gives 2 Kg. of milk every day.
Second cow is $2000, gives 4 kg milk every day and 2 calves per year.
Third cow is $3500, gives no milk and no calves but has good character.

803 One man tells the Pope, "You are great, give me a plate." Second one says, "Pope you are divine, give me wine." Mr. Singh says, "Pope you are a bastard and give me custard."

804 The people in hell did not have AC so they made a hole in the wall connecting to heaven. The people in heaven were very upset at this and threatened to sue the people in hell. The people in hell said, "Where are you gonna find a lawyer? They're all down here."

805 God distributed 40 years of age to animals. A man comes to God and gets 40 years. He says, "It is not enough, please increase my age." God says, "I cannot give you more years but you can ask the animals to give you more years."
He begs a donkey, "What would you do with 40 years of life? Please give me some years of your life." So the donkey gives him 20 years. Then he goes to a dog who gives him 20 years. Then he goes to an owl who gives him another 20 years. Now the man has 100 years. For 40 years he enjoys life then he works like a donkey. Then comes the next 20 years; from 60-80, he barks like a dog. The remaining 20 years he has trouble sleeping at night.

806 Three men went to heaven. The first one was given a compact car because he had committed adultery three times. The second man was given a midsize car because he committed adultery one time while the third man got a BMW, but he was unhappy and crying when he saw his wife riding a bike.

807 A man was approached for a charitable donation and the fundraiser said, "Our records show that you have never donated any money." The man replied, "Do your records show that my mother is in the hospital, my sister is a widow, my father is in a mental hospital and my brother is disabled? If I have not given them a penny, why should I donate money now?"

808 A Russian told a visitor, "Things are very good; the potato harvest is so good that we can make a pile that reaches to God." The visitor said, "In Russia there is no God." "True, but we don't have potatoes either."

809 A beggar asks for a donation outside the temple and gets a small amount of money. Then he goes to a bar and gets a bigger donation and says, "God, you live somewhere, but give a different address."

810 A woodcutter lost his axe in a river and was crying. A monk came along and found a silver axe and asked the woodcutter if it was his. He said no. Then the monk went and got a gold axe. The woodcutter said, "No, this is not mine." Then the monk got a wooden axe. He said, "Yes." God was so impressed he gave all three axes to him.
The next day his wife drowned in the river and he was crying. The monk came and pulled one actress, Ashwarya Rai, out of the river and asked if she was his wife. He said yes. The monk was surprised that the woodcutter turned out to be dishonest so soon. Asked why he told lies, he said, "If I told the truth, you would have pulled out another woman, and then my wife. Then you would have said, 'Take them all.' I can't even handle one woman, let alone three."

811 A clock, one for each person in heaven, ticks for each sin committed by the person. God uses Mr. Singh's clock as a fan.

812 A fat lady's skirt got stuck in her partition. A man sitting behind her in a church tried to take the skirt out to make her comfortable. The lady slapped him. The next week he pushed the skirt in the partition thinking that was the way the lady liked it. The lady got upset and gave him a slap.

813 A man walks home from church and his wife says, "He is used to walking in his sleep."

814   A man invites monks to his house. His wife gets tired of cooking food with such short notice. The husband goes for a bath and his wife starts to cry. The monks ask, "Why are you crying?" "Because my husband uses a baseball bat to beat monks." They all run away. The husband asks his wife what happened and where the monks are. "They left because I refused to give the baseball bat to them." The husband takes the bat and runs after the monks, who seeing him with the bat, run even faster.

815   A middle-aged man got a facelift, a new hair piece and started working out with a young girl. A few months later he got into a car accident and went up to heaven. He asked God, "Why did you pick me up so early? I am your devotee." God replied, "I couldn't recognize you."

816   A boy studies religion and believes God will provide everything in his life. The boy's dad asks his wife, "So, does our son think I am God?"

817   International conference of Nigeria, Kenya and India. A genie appeared and told them to ask for one wish each. The Nigerian said, "I have a nice house, a nice car and a beautiful wife. The only thing that I want is a fair complexion." The Kenyan also asked for the same. The Indian didn't feel so unique looking anymore so he wished the other two were black again.

818   Three men's desires if they went back to earth: The first one says he wants to be a successful doctor. The second wants to be a successful diamond dealer. The third says, "Give me their addresses so I can be a successful thief."

819   A bus driver goes to heaven because when he drives, passengers pray to God for a safe trip.
A priest goes to hell because when he delivers sermons, people sleep.

820   A Sunday school teacher asks her class, "Where does Jesus live?" A kid answers, "He lives in the bathroom, because every morning my dad bangs on the bathroom door and says, 'Jesus Christ, are you still in there?'"

821   A man requested that God make him a woman because women have a great time shopping, going out for lunches with friends, watching TV, and don't have to work. God made his devotee a woman. A few months later he realized that a woman has to cook, wash laundry, change diapers, etc. He got tired of the chores and requested God to change him back to a man. God said, "It is too late because you're pregnant now."

822   King Henry was very angry drinking his soup. His grandson said, "Grandpa, I want to say something." The king got very angry at his grandson for interfering. After drinking his soup he asked his grandson, "What did you want to say?" He said, "Grandpa, there was a cockroach in your soup."

823   After a morning of church, a dad criticized the sermon. The mother thought the organist made a lot of mistakes. The sister didn't like the choir's singing. But they had second thoughts when the youngest piped up, "Still, it was a pretty good show for a dollar."

824   When God was making the world, he created man and bestowed upon him 20 years of a normal sex life. Man was horrified, "Only 20 years?!" But the Lord was very adamant. That was all man could have. Then the Lord called the monkey and gave him 20 years. "But I don't need 20 years," he said, "Ten is plenty for me." Man spoke up eagerly and asked, "Can I have the other 10?" The monkey graciously agreed. The Lord called the lion and gave him 20 years, and the lion, like the monkey said, "I do not need 20 years, 10 is plenty." Again the man spoke up, "Can I have the other 10?" The lion said, "Of course." Then came the donkey and he was given 20 years, and, like the others, 10 was sufficient and again man pleaded, "Can I have the other 10?" This explains why man has 20 years of a normal sex life, 10 years of monkeying around, 10 years of lying around and 10 years of making an ass of himself.

825   A Sunday school teacher asked her little children, as they were on the way to church service, "And why is it necessary to be quiet in church?"
A little girl replied, "Because people are sleeping."

826   There are two nuns walking. One of them is known as Sister Mathematical (SM) and the other is known as Sister Logical (SL).
It is getting dark and they are still far away from the convent.
SM: Have you noticed that a man has been following us for the past 38.5 minutes? I wonder what he wants.
SL: It's logical. He wants to rape us.
SM: Oh, no! At this rate he will reach us in 15 minutes at the most. What can we do?
SL: The only logical thing to do of course is to walk faster.
SM: It is not working.
SL: Of course, it is not working. The man did the only logical thing. He started to walk faster too.
SM: So, what shall we do? At this rate he will reach us in one minute.
SL: The only logical thing to do is we can split up. You go that way and I'll go this way. He can't follow both of us.
So the man decided to follow Sister Logical. Sister Mathematical arrives at the convent and is worried about what has happened to Sister Logical. Then Sister Logical arrives.
SM: Sister Logical! Thank God you are here! Tell me what happened!

SL: The only logical thing happened. He could not follow both of us, so he followed me.

SM: Yes, yes! But what happened then?

SL: The only logical thing happened. I started to run as fast as I could and he started to run as fast as he could.

SM: And?

SL: The only logical thing to do was I lifted my dress up.

SM: Oh, sister what did that man do?

SL: The only logical thing to do. He pulled down his pants.

SM: Oh, no! What happened then?

SL: Isn't it logical, Sister? A nun with her dress up can run faster than a man with his pants down.

827 There are only two things in life to worry about:

Whether you are well or whether you are sick.

If you are well, then there is nothing to worry about. But if you are sick, there are only two things to worry about:

Whether you are going to live or whether you are going to die.

If you live, then there is nothing to worry about. But if you die, then there are only two things to worry about:

Whether you are going to heaven or whether you are going to hell. If you go to heaven, then you have nothing to worry about.

But if you go to hell, you'll be so busy shaking hands with all your friends that you won't have time to worry!

828 Having lost his donkey, Mr. Singh got down to his knees and started thanking God. A passerby saw him and asked, "Your donkey is missing. What are you thanking God for?" Mr. Singh replied, "I am thanking God for seeing to it that I was not riding the donkey at that time, otherwise, I would be missing too."

829 Three couples were on their way to a party in a minivan one winter evening. As they were rounding the turn, the driver lost control of the vehicle, which ran off the road and down a hillside, bursting into flame and killing everyone inside.

Very shortly thereafter, the three couples appeared before St. Peter.

Peter pointed an accusing finger at one of the men and said, "You? All you ever thought about in life was drinking! You drank every morning, every evening, on the weekends, at lunch. You even married a girl named Sherry!"

He pointed at the second man and said, "AND YOU! You thought of nothing but money! Everything in your life had to do with greed, money, making money, keeping money, making more money. You even married a girl named Penny!"

The third man took his wife's hand and began walking away. "Come on, Fanny, I don't want to hear what he has to say to us."

830   One day while walking down the street, a highly successful woman executive was tragically hit by a bus and died. Her soul arrived up to heaven where she was met at the Pearly Gates by St. Peter himself.

"Welcome to heaven," said St. Peter. "Before you get settled in though, it seems we have a problem. You see, strangely enough, we've never had an executive make it this far and we're not really sure what to do with you."

"No problem, just let me in," said the woman.

"Well, I'd like to, but I have high orders. What we are going to do is let you have a day in hell and a day in heaven and then you can choose whichever one you want to spend in eternity in."

"Actually, I think I've made up my mind. I prefer to stay in Heaven," said the woman.

"Sorry, we have rules." And with that, St. Peter put the executive in an elevator and it went down-down-down to hell. The doors opened and she found herself out on the putting green of a beautiful golf course. In the distance was a country club and standing in front of her were all her friends and fellow executives that she had worked with. They were all dressed in evening gowns and cheering for her. They talked about old times. They played an excellent round of golf and at night went to a country club where she enjoyed an excellent dinner. She met the Devil who was actually a really nice guy and kinda cute. She had a great time telling jokes and dancing. She was having such a good time that before she knew it was time to leave.

Everyone shook her hand and waved goodbye as she got on the elevator.

The elevator went up and up and up and opened at the Pearly Gate and she found St. Peter waiting for her.

"Now it's time to spend a day in heaven. So she spent the next 24 hours lounging around on clouds and playing the harp and singing. She had a great time and before she knew it her 24 hours were up and St. Peter came and got her.

"So you've spent a day in hell and you've spent a day in heaven. Now you must choose eternity," he said.

The woman paused for a second and then replied, "Well, I never thought I'd say this, I mean heaven has really been nice and all but I think I had a better time in hell."

So St. Peter escorted her to the elevator and again she went down-down-down back to hell. When the doors of the elevator opened she found herself standing in a desolate wasteland covered in garbage and filth. She saw her friends were dressed in rags and were picking up the garbage and putting it in the sacks.

The Devil came up to her and put his arm around her.

"I don't understand," stammered the woman, "Yesterday I was here and there was a golf course and a country club and we had nice dinner and dance. Now all there is a wasteland of garbage and all my friends look miserable."

The Devil looked at her and smiled.

"Yesterday we were recruiting you; today you are staff."

831   We have all learned to live with voicemail as a necessary part of modern life. But have you wondered, what if God decided to install voicemail?"

Imagine praying and hearing this:

Hi! Thank you for calling God

Please select one of the following options:

Press 1 for Requests

Press 2 for Thanksgiving.

Press 3 for Complaints.

Press 4 for All Other Inquiries.

Or else wait for our customer support executive.

What if God used the familiar excuse, "I'm sorry, all of our angels are busy helping other sinners right now. However, your prayer is important to us and will be answered in the order it was received, so please stay on the line."

Can you imagine getting these kinds of responses as you call God in Prayer:

If you would like to speak to Ganeshji, Press 1.

For Lord Hanuman, Press 2.

For Lord Krishna, Sorry He is on Annual Leave!

For Jesus, please call next week, he is at the CANNES FILM FESTIVAL promoting his passion.

For a directory of other Gods and Angels, Press 3.

If you would like to hear Narad sing a Bhajan while you are holding, please press 4.

To find out if a loved one has been assigned to Heaven, Press 5, Enter his or her PAN number, then press the 0 key.

If you get a negative response, try area code 420 for (Hell). Our computers show that you have already prayed once today. Please hang up and try again tomorrow.

Please pray again Monday after 9:30 a.m. If you need emergency assistance when this office is closed, contact your local priest at your neighborhood temple.

832   President Clinton and the Pope died on the same day, and due to an administrative foul up, Clinton was sent to heaven and the Pope was sent to hell. The Pope explained the situation to the devil, he checked out all of the paperwork, and the error was acknowledged. The Pope was told, however, that it would take about 24 hours to fix the problem.

The next day, the Pope was called in and the devil said his goodbyes as the Pope went off to heaven. On his way up, he met Clinton who was on his way down, and they stop to chat.

Pope: Sorry about the mix up.

President Clinton: No problem.

Pope: Well, I'm really excited about going to heaven.

President Clinton: Why's that?

Pope: All my life I've wanted to meet the Virgin Mary.

President Clinton: You're a day late.

833   The daughter had not been to the house for over 5 years. Upon her return, her father cussed her out: "Where have you been all this time, you ingrate! Why didn't you write us, not even a line to let us know how you were doing? Why didn't you call? You little tramp! Don't you know what you put your Mom through?" The girl, crying, said "Dad. I became a prostitute."

"What? Out of here, you shameless harlot. You sinner! You're a disgrace to this family. I don't ever want to see you again!" "OK, dad, as you wish. I just came back to give mom this fur coat and the title to a mansion, a savings account certificate of $5 million for my little brother, and for you, daddy, this gold Rolex, the spanking new BMW that's parked outside and a lifetime membership to the country club...an invitation for you all to spend New Year's Eve on board my new yacht in the Riviera, and..."

"Now, what was it you said you had become?" the dad asked. The girl, crying again, replied, "A prostitute, Dad!"

"Oh! Gee, you scared me half to death, girl! I thought you said 'a Protestant.' Come here and give your old man a hug!"

834   A train hits a busload of school girls and they all perish. They are all in heaven trying to enter the Pearly Gates past St. Peter.

St. Peter asks the first girl, "Karen, have you ever had any contact with a penis?"

She giggles and shyly replies, "Well, I once touched the head of one with the tip of my finger."

St. Peter says, "OK, dip the tip of your finger in the Holy Water and pass through the gates."

St. Peter asks the next girl the same question, "Katrina, have you ever had any contact with a penis?"

The girl is a little reluctant but replies, "Well once I fondled and stroked one."

St. Peter says, "OK, dip your whole hand in the Holy Water and pass through the gate."

All of a sudden there is a lot of commotion in the line and one girl is pushing her way to the front of the line. When she reaches the front of the line St. Peter says, "Mary! What seems to be the rush?"

The girl replies, "If I'm going to have to gargle that Holy Water, I want to do it before Wendy sticks her ass in it."

835 The Pastor's Ass

The pastor entered his donkey in a race and it won. The pastor was so pleased with the donkey that he entered it in the race again, and it won again.

The local paper read:

PASTOR'S ASS OUT FRONT

The bishop was so upset with this kind of publicity that he ordered the pastor not to enter the donkey in another race.

The next day, the local paper headline read:

BISHOP SCRATCHES PASTOR'S ASS

This was too much for the bishop, so he ordered the pastor to get rid of the donkey.

The pastor decided to give it to a nun in a nearby convent.

The local paper, hearing of the news, posted the following headline the next day:

NUN HAS BEST ASS IN TOWN

The bishop fainted. He informed the nun that she would have to get rid of the donkey, so she sold it to a farmer for $10.

The next day the paper read:

NUN SELLS ASS FOR $10

This was too much for the bishop, so he ordered the nun to buy back the donkey and lead it to the plains where it could run wild.

The next day the headlines read:

NUN ANNOUNCES HER ASS IS WILD AND FREE.

The bishop was buried the next day.

836 A young man goes to a church for confession. The priest asks him to confess the sin. The man says he went on a date with a young girl. During the night he rubbed her private. The priest says your punishment is $100. The boy goes near a donation box and rubs it with $100 dollar bill but does not put in the box. He explains to the priest that rubbing the box and not putting money into it is similar to what he did with his girlfriend.

837 A little boy got on the bus, sat next to a man reading a book, and noticed he had his collar on backward. The little boy asked why he wore his collar backward. The man, who was a priest, said, "I am a father." The little boy replied, "My dad doesn't wear his collar like that." The priest looked up from his book and answered, "I am the father of many." The boy said, "My dad has four boys, four girls and two grandchildren and he doesn't wear his collar that way." The priest, getting impatient, said, "I am the father of hundreds" and went back to reading his book. The little boy sat quietly thinking for a while, then leaned over and said, "Maybe you should use a condom and wear your pants backward instead of your collar."

838   The inventor Arthur Davidson of the Harley Davidson Motorcycle Corporation died and went to heaven. At the gates, St. Peter told Arthur, "Since you've been such a good man and your motorcycles have changed the world, your reward is you can hangout with anyone you want in heaven."

Arthur thought about it for a minute and then said, "I want to hang out with God."

St. Peter took Arthur to the Throne Room, and introduced him to God.

Arthur then asked God, "Hey, aren't you the inventor of woman?"

God said, "Ah, yes,"

"Well," said Arthur, "Professional to professional, you have some major design flaws in your invention.

1. There's too much inconsistency in the front-end protrusion.

2. It chatters constantly at high speeds.

3. Most of the rear ends are too soft and wobble too much.

4. The intake is placed way to close to the exhaust. And finally,

5. The maintenance costs are outrageous."

"Hmmmm, you may have some good points there," replied God, "Hold on."

God went to his celestial super computer, typed in a few words and waited for the results. The computer printed out a slip of paper and God read it.

"Well, it may be true that my invention is flawed," God said to Arthur, "But according to these numbers, more men are riding my invention than yours."

839   A nun gets on a bus and sits behind the driver. She says to the bus driver, she needs someone to talk to. She lives in a convent and wants to experience sex before she dies. The bus driver agrees, but the nun explains she can't have sex with anyone who is married because it would be a sin. The bus driver says no problem and that he is not married. The nun says she also has to die a virgin, so she'll have to take it in the ass. The bus driver agrees again, and being the only people on the bus, they go to the back of the bus and take care of business. After they're done and he resumes driving, the bus driver says "Sister, I have a confession to make. I'm married and have three kids." The nun replies, "That's OK, I have a confession too. My name is Dave and I'm on my way to a costume party!"

Chapter 15
Sports

840 Mr. Singh, after coming back from the USA to India, built 3 swimming pools. One with cold water for the summertime, one with hot water for the wintertime, and one without water in case he didn't feel like swimming.

841 A country club member was walking naked with his face covered with a handkerchief. Four ladies playing bridge outside were very embarrassed. One lady said, "That's not my husband." The second lady said, "He is not from our club." The third lady said, "He is not from our office." And the fourth one said, "He is not from our town."

842 A hunter had licenses from 3 states. An inspector looked at the bottom of the turkeys, ducks and roosters to figure out the places where the hunter had been. He asked the hunter, "What place do you come from?" He pulled his pants down and told the inspector to figure it out.

843 The spirit of a dead baseball player tells his fellow player on earth – "I have good news and bad news." "It is a great feeling to be in heaven but unfortunately you are scheduled to pitch in heaven tomorrow."

844 A husband asks his wife, "Why do you cry at movies over people you're not related to?"The wife replies, "Why do you yell so loud when a man you don't know slides into second base?"

845 The only trouble with being a good sport is that you have to lose to prove it.

846 Two men went to a large lake and hired a fishing boat for the day. After settling into a particular spot, they proceeded to have a very bountiful day, catching dozens of fish. When they got back to shore, one of them said, "This is incredible! I hope you put a mark in the water where we caught all the fish, so we can go back there tomorrow."
"I did better than that," replied Mr. Singh. "I put an X on the side of the boat where we caught all the fish."
"How dumb you can be?" said his friend. "We may not get the same boat next time."

847 One day, a woman took her husband's small fishing boat out on the lake to read. She rowed out, anchored the boat, and started reading her book. Along came the coast guard in his boat. He pulled up alongside and said, "Good morning, Ma'am. What are you doing?"
"Reading my book," she replied as she thought to herself, "Is this guy blind or what?"
"You are in a restricted fishing area," he informed her.
"But officer, I'm not fishing. Can't you see that?"

"But you have all the equipment, Ma'am. I'll have to take you in and write you up."

"If you do that I will charge you for rape," she replies.

"I did not even touch you," says the agent.

"Yes, that is true. But you have all the equipment."

848 Softball vs. Sex

You can play softball as much or as little as you want; YOU get to decide.

After an unusually long and difficult softball game, you can still ride your bike home.

In softball, the other team pays attention throughout, even if they're done scoring.

If you have to take a piss during a softball game, you can say, "Excuse me, I gotta drain the swamp," and you don't lose style points.

In softball, nobody comments on the size of your bat, as long as you know what to do with it.

In softball, you don't feel guilty about winning the ugly ones.

The other team never has to forfeit a game because they're on their period.

In softball, you don't have to compliment the other team on how good they look in their new uniforms.

You don't have to buy the other team dinner to get a game.

If you get all scratched up in a softball game, you can brag about it to your wife.

In softball, if you go a couple of months without scoring, your balls don't hurt.

In softball, you can play the same team every day for a year and it's never the same twice.

You don't mind if your parents come to watch.

You can play three, maybe four softball games a day.

In softball, it's no concern of yours if the other team has had marital relations with diseased livestock.

Playing the wrong softball team won't get you shot.

You can be absolutely certain that, nine months after a softball game, the other team's lawyers won't call asking for half of your pre-tax income for the next 18 years.

During a softball game, you can spit tobacco juice all over the place.

Rest assured that the other team will not invite you to the ballet.

The other team doesn't demand that you shave before the game.

The other team can smell like road kill and you'll never know it.

If you don't score in a softball game, the other team doesn't ask you if you've had that problem before.

No matter how drunk the other team is, they never throw up in your bed.

849 Abbott: You know, strange as it may seem, they give ball players nowadays very peculiar names. Now, on the Cooperstown team we have Who's on first, What's on second, and I Don't Know is on third.

Costello: That's what I want to find out. I want you to tell me the names of the fellows on the Cooperstown team.

A: I'm telling you. Who's on first, What's on second, I Don't Know is on third.

C: You know the fellows' names?

A: Yes.

C: Well, then, who's playin' first?

A: Yes.

C: I mean the fellow's name on first base.

A: Who.

C: The fellow's name on first base for Cooperstown.

A: Who.

C: The guy on first base.

A: Who is on first base.

C: Well, what are you asking me for?

A: I'm not asking you. I'm telling you. Who is on first.

C: I'm asking you. Who's on first?

A: That's the man's name.

C: That's who's name?

A: Yes.

C: Well, go ahead, tell me!

A: Who.

C: The guy on first.

A: Who.

C: The first baseman.

A: Who is on first.

C: Have you got a first baseman on first?

A: Certainly.

C: Well, all I'm trying to find out is what's the guy's name on first base.

A: Oh, no, no. What is on second base.

C: I'm not asking you who's on second.

A: Who's on first.

C: That's what I'm trying to find out.

A: Well, don't change the players around.

C: I'm not changing anybody.

A: Now, take it easy.

C: What's the guy's name on first base?

A: What's the guy's name on second base.

C: I'm not askin' ya who's on second.

A: Who's on first.

C: I don't know.

A: He's on third. We're not talking about him.

C: How could I get on third base?

A: You mentioned his name.

C: If I mentioned the third baseman's name, who did I say is playing third?

A: No. Who's playing first.

C: Stay off a first, will you?

A: Please. Now what is it you want to know?

C: What is the fellow's name on third base?

A: What is the fellow's name on second base.

C: I'm not askin' ya who's on second.

A: Who's on first.

C: I don't know.

A & C: Third base.

C: (Makes noises) You got an outfield?

A: Oh, sure.

C: Cooperstown has got a good outfield?

A: Oh, absolutely.

C: The left fielder's name?

A: Why.

C: I don't know. I just thought I'd ask.

A: Well, I just thought I'd tell you.

C: Then tell me who's playing left field.

A: Who's playing first.

C: Stay out of the infield.

A: Don't mention any names out there.

C: I want to know what's the fellow's name in left field.

A: What is on second.

C: I'm not asking you who's on second.

A: Who's on first.

C: I don't know.

A & C: Third base.

C: (Makes noises)

A: Now take it easy, man.

C: And the left fielder's name?

A: Why.

C: Because.

A: Oh, he's center field.

C: Wait a minute. You got a pitcher on the team?

A: Wouldn't this be a fine team without a pitcher.

C: I don't know. Tell me the pitcher's name.

A: Tomorrow.

C: You don't want to tell me today?

A: I'm telling you, man.

C: Then go ahead.

A: Tomorrow.

C: What time?

A: What time what?

C: What time tomorrow are you gonna tell me who's pitching?

A: Now listen, Who is not pitching. Who is on –

C: I'll break your arm if you say who's on first.

A: Then why come up here and ask?

C: I want to know what's the pitcher's name.

A: What's on second.

C: I don't know.

A & C: Third base.

C: Ya gotta catcher?

A: Yes.

C: The catcher's name.

A: Today.

C: Today. And tomorrow's pitcher.

A: Now you've got it.

C: That's all. Cooperstown's got a couple of days on their team. That's all?

A: Well, I can't help that.

C: (Makes noises)

A: All right. What do you want me to do?

C: Gotta catcher?

A: Yes.

C: I'm a good catcher too, you know.

A: I know that.

C: I would like to play for the Cooperstown team.

A: Well, I might arrange that.

C: I would like to catch. Now, I'm being a good catcher. Tomorrow's pitching on the tea and I'm catching.

A: Yes.

C: Now, when he bunts the ball — me being a good catcher — I want to throw the guy out at first base, so I pick up the ball and throw it to who?

A: Now, that's the first thing you've said right.

C: (shouts) I don't even know what I'm talking about.

A: Well, that's all you have to do.

C: Is throw it to first base.

A: Yes.

C: Now, who's got it?

A: Naturally.

C: Who has it?

A: Naturally.

C: Naturally?

A: Naturally.

C: I throw the ball to Naturally?

A: You throw it to who.

C: Naturally…

A: Naturally. Well, say it that way.

C: That's what I'm saying.

A: Now don't get excited. Now don't get excited.

C: I throw the ball to first base.

A: Then Who gets it.

C: He better get it.

A: That's it. All right now, don't get excited. Take it easy.

C: Hmmmmmmmph.

A: Hmmmmmmmph.

C: Now, I throw the ball to first base, whoever it is grabs the ball, so the guy runs to second.

A: Uh-huh.

C: Who picks up the ball and throws it to What. What throws it to I Don't Know. I Don't Know throws it back to Tomorrow – a triple play.

A: Yeah. It could be.

C: Another guy gets up and it's a long fly ball to center. Who? I don't know. And I don't care.

A: What was that?

C: I said, I don't care.

A: Oh, that's our shortstop.

GROWING OLDER IS MANDATORY.
GROWING UP IS OPTIONAL.
LAUGHING AT YOURSELF IS THERAPEUTIC.

850 An elderly man made a bet with his friend that he could go to the salon and get his hair cut and a beggar's hair cut for free. The elderly man then walked with a young beggar to the hair salon. He told the barber to first cut his hair, then his "son's." After his haircut, the elderly man left the shop to buy a Coke while the barber cut his "son's" hair. After the barber was done cutting the "son's" hair, the beggar started to leave. The barber said, "Wait till your father comes back to pay." The young beggar replied, "I am sorry to tell you, but my father died a long time ago."

851 There are three stages of old age. First you forget your friends' names. Second you forget to close your zipper after urinating. Third, you forget to open your zipper before urinating.

852 The grandparents were listening through a keyhole to find out what young couples do on their first night. First they heard "You be up" then they heard "Me be down" and then they heard "We both will be up." The grandparents got confused with the last statement. The young couple was trying to close the suitcase.

853 A couple of old women wanted to get the attention of the some young men and went out without their clothes. One of the men said, "Ladies, you forgot to iron your clothes."

854 An old man asked, "Why are people running around so desperately? Are there terrorists around?" A man replied, "No. My wife is learning to drive."

855 A 60-year-old man says he is only 30 years because he does not count the nights.

856 An old man married a young girl. The doctor gave them sleeping pills. The old man thought that with the pills he could have sex with his young wife. The pills were for his wife so that she could sleep and not bother the old man.

857 A 90-year old man marries a young girl. She tells her husband she is pregnant. At the doctor's office, the doctor tells the man a story of a hunter who opened an umbrella and killed a lion. The old man says, "That's impossible. Someone must have shot the lion from the side." The doctor says, "Exactly. That is my point."

858   After the birth of his 10th grandchild, Joe was filming the baby with his camcorder. A friend exclaimed, "Aren't you just so excited?" The grandfather said, "Yes, it's a new camcorder."

859   An old man was crossing the street. He was hit by a 2 wheeler and was crying because the 2 wheeler had a sign that said, "We will meet again."

860   After heart surgery, Mr. Singh went to the doctor and said, "My wife does not make love with me because she thinks it may not be good for my health." He asked the doctor to write a letter saying that he was fit to have sex. The doctor sent a letter addressed to Mrs. Singh saying, "Your husband is fit to do anything, including sex." Mr. Singh, upon seeing the letter, asked the doctor to make a correction. "Instead of addressing it to Mrs. Singh, can you address it "To Whom It May Concern?"

861   After being married for 40 years, I took a careful look at my wife one day and said, "Honey, 40 years ago we had a cheap apartment, a cheap car, slept on a sofa bed and watched a 10-inch black and white TV, but I got to sleep every night with a hot 18-year old girl. Now, I have a $500,000 home, two $45,000-cars, a nice big bed and plasma screen TV, but I'm sleeping with a 58-year old woman. It seems to me that you're not holding up your side of things." She told me to go out and find a hot 18-year-old chick, and she would make sure that I would once again be living in a cheap apartment, driving a cheap car, sleeping on a sofa bed and watching a 10-inch black and white TV.

862   An old couple went out to a fine restaurant to celebrate their 50th wedding anniversary. The husband told his wife, "Mary, I am very proud of you even after 50 years of marriage." His wife, who was hard of hearing, said, "George, I am tired of you too."

863   An elderly man was looking at himself in the mirror and was visibly upset upon noticing his wrinkled face, gray hair and big belly. His wife tried to comfort him and said, "At least your eyesight is good."

864   Granddad bought a small, almost unnoticeable hearing aid and was so pleased he returned to the office to express his satisfaction.
"I imagine your family is very happy, too," said the salesman.
"Oh, they don't know I have it," chuckled the elderly man. "And am I having fun. In the past two weeks, I've changed my will four times."

865   The young photographer had just taken a portrait of an elderly gentleman on his 98th birthday. He thanked the old man, adding cheerfully, "I hope I'll be around to take your picture when you hit 100."
"Why not?" replied the patriarch. "You look reasonably healthy."

866   On a senior citizen bus tour, the driver was surprised. While the passengers were unloading to do some sightseeing, one elderly lady stopped and whispered in his ear, "Driver, I believe that I was sexually harassed!" The driver didn't think much of this complaint, but promised he would check into it soon.

Later that very same day, as the passengers were unloading again, a second little old lady bent down and whispered in his ear, "Sir, I believe I was sexually harassed!" This time, he knew it had to be taken care of soon. A few passengers had remained on the bus, and he decided to go back and question them, to see if they had any knowledge of what was going on.

He found one little old man crawling along the bus floor underneath the seats and stooped down to question him. "Excuse me, sir, could I help you?" The elderly man looked up and said, "Well, sonny, you sure can. I've lost my toupee and I'm trying to find it. I thought I'd located it twice, but they were parted in the middle, and mine's parted on the side."

867   Money can't buy happiness, but it sure helps you look for it in comfort. Wisdom does not automatically come with old age. Only wrinkles do.

868   An older couple, living apart, had been dating for a number of years. One day Elmer says to Betsy, "We should stop this nonsense. We are paying two rent payments, two car insurance payments, buying separate food and cooking separate meals. We should just move in together."
Betsy: Whose house would we live in?
Elmer: Mine, it is paid for.
Betsy: Whose car should we keep and pay insurance on?
Elmer: Yours, it is newer and runs better than mine.
Betsy: Who would do the cooking?
Elmer: You cook and I'll do the dishes.
Betsy: What about sex?
Elmer: Infrequently.
Betsy: Is that one word or two?

869   You know when you're getting old when:
Your little black book contains names ending in M.D.
Your children begin to look middle aged. You look forward to a dull evening.
You turn out the lights for economic reasons rather than romantic reasons.
A dripping faucet causes an uncontrollable urge.
Your back goes out more often than you do.
You burn the midnight oil until 9:00 p.m.
You have plenty of room in the house but not enough in the medicine cabinet.
The little old gray haired person you help across the street is your spouse.
It takes twice as long to rest and half as long to get tired.
Weight lifting consists solely of standing up.

870   An old man sitting in a doctor's waiting room finally gets called. He struggles to his feet and hobbles into the doctor's office, walking very slowly and in obvious pain.
Five minutes later, the man comes out of the examining room, standing tall and perfectly straight. Another patient in the waiting room is amazed: "Wow, this doctor must be wonderful! Five minutes ago you were walking all bent over," he said to the old man. "What did he do to you?"
"He gave me a longer cane," the old man answered.

871   How do senior people spend their time? According to one survey: 40% of the daily time in sleeping. 20% of the time in cooking and cleaning and 40% of the time looking for things they just had in their hands a few minutes ago.

872   A senior couple was talking to each other. The wife says, "Dear, do you know that over the last 50 years, I have been losing my dumb brain?" The husband comments, "Yes, dear. You have been giving it to me over the years."

873   A tour bus driver is driving with a bus full of seniors down a highway when he is tapped on his shoulder by a little old lady. She offers him a handful of peanuts that he promptly gobbled up.
After about 15 minutes, she taps him on his shoulder again and hands him another handful of peanuts. She repeats this gesture about five more times. When she is about to hand him another batch again he asks the little old lady why they don't eat the peanuts themselves.
"We cannot chew them because we have no teeth." She replied. The puzzled driver asks, "Why do you buy them then?"
The old lady replied, "We just love the chocolate-covered coating."

874   A couple in their 80's was having problems remembering things, so they decided to go to their doctor to get checked out.
After checking the couple out, the doctor told them that they were physically okay but might want to start writing things down to help them remember things. The couple thanked the doctor and left.
Later that night while watching TV, the old man got up from his chair and his wife asked, "Where are you going?"
He replied, "To the kitchen."
She asked, "Will you get me a bowl of ice cream?"
He replied, "Sure."
She then asked him, "Don't you think you should write it down so you can remember it?"
He said, "No, I can remember."
She then said, "Well, I also would like some strawberries on top. You had better write it down because I know you will forget that."
He said, "I can remember that, you want a bowl of ice cream with strawberries."

She replied, "Well, I also would like whip cream on top. I know you will forget, so write that down."

With irritation in his voice, he said, "I don't need to write that down. I can remember that."

After about 20 minutes he returned from the kitchen and handed her a bowl of cereal and milk.

She stared at the bowl for a moment and says, "You forgot my toast."

875   An elderly woman walked into the Bank of Canada one morning with a purse full of money. She wanted to open a savings account and insisted on talking to the president of the bank because she said she had a lot of money.

After a lengthy discussion, the employee took the elderly woman to the president's office. The president of the bank asked her how much she wanted to deposit. She placed her purse on his desk and replied, "$165,000." The president was curious and asked her how she had been able to save so much money. The elderly woman replied that she made bets.

The president was surprised and asked, "What kind of bets?"

The elderly woman replied, "Well, I will bet you $25,000 that your testicles are square."

The president started to laugh and told the woman that it was impossible to win a bet like that.

The woman looked at the president and said, "Would you like to take my bet?"

"Certainly," replied the president. "I bet you $25,000 that my testicles are not square."

"Done," the elderly woman answered. "But given the amount of money involved, if you don't mind I would like to come back at 10 o'clock tomorrow morning with my lawyer as a witness."

"No problem," said the president confidently.

That night, the president became very nervous about the bet and spent a long time in front of the mirror examining his testicles, turning them this way and that, checking them over and over again until he was positive that no one could consider that his testicles were square and that there was no way he could lose the bet.

The next morning at exactly 10 o'clock the elderly woman arrived at the president's office with her lawyer and acknowledged the $25,000 bet she made the day before.

The president confirmed the bet and proceeded to drop his pants. The elderly woman came closer so she could see better and asked the president if she could touch them. "Of course," said the president. "Given the amount of money involved, you should be 100% sure."

The elderly woman did so with a little smile. Suddenly, the president noticed that the lawyer was banging his head against the wall. He asked the elderly woman why he was doing that.

She replied, "Oh, it is probably because I bet him $100,000 that around 10 o'clock in the morning I would be holding the balls of the president of Bank of Canada."

876   Recently, I was diagnosed with A.A.A.D.D. - Age Activated Attention Deficit Disorder. This is how it manifests:

I decide to wash my car. As I head toward the garage, I notice that there is mail on the hall table. I decide to go through the mail before I wash the car. I lay my car keys down on the table, put the junk mail in the trash can under the table, and notice that the trash can is full. So, I decide to put the bills back on the table and take out the trash first.

But then I think, since I'm going to be near the mailbox when I take out the trash anyway, I may as well pay the bills first. I take my checkbook off the table and see that there is only one check left. My extra checks are in my desk in the study, so I go to my desk, where I find the can of Coke that I had been drinking. I look for my checks, but first I need to push the Coke aside so that I don't accidentally knock it over. I see that the Coke is getting warm, and I decide I should put it in the refrigerator.

As I head toward the kitchen with the Coke, a vase of flowers on the counter catches my eye. The flowers need to be watered. I set the Coke down on the counter and I notice my reading glasses that I've been searching for all morning. I decide I better put them back on my desk, but first I'm going to water the flowers. I set the glasses back down on the counter, fill a container with water and suddenly I spot the TV remote. Someone left it on the kitchen table. I realize that tonight when we go to watch TV, I will be looking for the remote, but I won't remember that it's on the kitchen table, so I decide to put it back in the den where it belongs. But first I'll water the flowers. I splash some water on the flowers, but most of it spills on the floor. So, I set the remote back down on the table, get some towels and wipe up the spill. Then I head down the hall trying to remember what I was planning to do.

At the end of the day: the car isn't washed, the bills aren't paid, there is a warm can of Coke sitting on the counter, the flowers aren't watered, there is still only one check in my checkbook, I can't find the remote, I can't find my glasses, and I don't remember what I did with the car keys.

Then when I try to figure out why nothing got done today, I'm really baffled because I know I was busy all day long, and I'm really tired.

I realize this is a serious problem, and I'll try to get some help for it, but first I'll check my e-mail.

877   Senior citizen to his 80-year-old buddy, "So I hear you are getting married?"

"Yep!"

"This woman, is she good looking?"

"Not really."

"Is she a good cook?"

"No, she can't cook too well."

"Does she have lots of money?"

"No, poor as a church mouse."

"Well then, is she good in bed?"

"I don't know."

"Why in the world do you want to marry her?"

"She can still drive."

878   An old man, a boy and a donkey were going to town. The boy rode on the donkey and the old man walked. As they went along, they passed some people who remarked it was a shame the old man was walking and the boy was riding. The old man and the boy thought that maybe the critics were right, so they changed places. Later, they passed some more people that remarked, "What a shame he makes that little boy walk." They then decided they both would walk. Soon they passed some more people who thought they were stupid to walk when they had a decent donkey to ride. So, they both rode the donkey. Later they passed some more people that shamed them by saying how awful it was to see such a load on a poor donkey. The boy and the man said they were probably right, so they decided to carry the donkey. As they crossed a bridge, they lost their grip on the animal and he fell into the river and drowned. The moral of the story?

If you try to please everyone, you might as well kiss your ass goodbye.

879   After retiring, I went to the Social Security office to apply for my benefits, and the woman behind the counter asked me for my driver's license to verify my age. I looked in my pockets and realized I had left my wallet at home. I told the woman that I was very sorry but I seemed to have left my wallet at home. "I will have to go home and come back later." The woman said, "Unbutton your shirt." So I opened my shirt, revealing my curly silver hair. She said, "That silver hair on your chest is proof enough for me" and she processed my Social Security application. When I got home, I excitedly told my wife about my experience at the Social Security office. She said, "You should have dropped your pants. You might have gotten disability too."

880   A little old lady was running up and down the halls in a nursing home. As she walked, she would flip up the hem of her nightgown and say, "Super sex!" She walked up to an elderly man in a wheelchair. Flipping her gown at him, she said, "Super sex!" He sat silently for a moment or two and finally answered, "I'll take the soup."

881   A Mexican family was considering putting their grandfather in a nursing home. All the Catholic facilities were completely full so they had to put him in a Jewish home. After a few weeks in the Jewish facility, they came to visit grandpa.

"How do you like it here?" asked the grandson.

"It's wonderful! Everyone here is so courteous and respectful," said grandpa.

"We're so happy for you. We were worried that this was the wrong place for you. You know, since you are a little different from everyone."

"Oh, no! Let me tell you about how wonderfully they treat the residents here," grandpa said with a big smile. "There's a musician here who is 85 years old. He hasn't played the violin in 20 years and everyone still calls him 'Maestro'! There is a judge in here – who is 95 years old. He hasn't been on the bench in 30 years and everyone still calls him 'Your Honor'!"

And there's a physician here –who is 90 years old. He hasn't been practicing medicine for 25 years and everyone still calls him 'Doctor'! And me, I haven't had sex in 35 years and they still call me 'The F+++++g Mexican'!!!"

882   A man and his wife, now in their 60's, were celebrating their 40th wedding anniversary. On their special day, a good fairy came to them and said that because they had been such a devoted couple, she would grant each of them a very special wish. The wife wished for a trip around the world with her husband.

Whoosh! Immediately she had airline and cruise tickets in her hands. The man wished for a female companion 30 years younger...

Whoosh! The man immediately turned 90.

883   Joe visits a nudist colony in Amsterdam. While wandering around naked, he spots a gorgeous blonde and immediately gets an erection. The woman notices his erection, comes over and says, "Sir, did you call for me?"

Joe replies, "No!"

She says, "Well, it's a rule here that if I give you an erection, it means you called for me." She then lays him down and starts making love to him.

Later that day Joe visits the sauna, but as he sits down he farts. A huge big hairy guy gets up, drops his towel to show a huge erection and says, "Sir, did you call for me?"

Joe replies, "No!"

The man says, "It's a rule that when you fart, it means you called for me."

The man then knocks Joe to the floor and has his way with him. As soon a he's finished, Joe rushes back to his room, grabs all his things and heads for the exit.

On his way out, he's stopped by the manager who asks, "Can I help you?"

Joe says, "Here are my room keys. I'm leaving early."

The manager asks why and Joe replies, "I'm 60 years old; I get an erection once a week but I fart 20 times a day."

884 There was a man who really took care of his body. He lifted weights and jogged 8 miles a day. One day, he took a look in the mirror and noticed that he was tan everywhere but on his "thingie." So he decided to do something about it. He went to the beach, completely undressed himself and buried himself in the sand, except for his "thingie," which he left sticking up. Two old ladies were strolling along the beach, one using a cane. Upon seeing the thingie" sticking up over the sand, one of the ladies began to move it around with her cane, remarking to the other lady, "There's no justice in the world."
The other lady asked what she meant.
She said, "When I was 20, I was curious about it. When I was 30, I enjoyed it. When I was 40, I begged for it. When I was 50, I paid for it. When I was 60, I prayed for it. When I was 70, I forgot about it. Now, I am 80 and the damn things are growing wild on the beach and I'm too old to squat."

885 Jacob, age 92, and Rebecca, age 89, are living in Florida and are excited about their decision to get married. They go for a stroll to discuss the wedding, and on the way they pass a drugstore. Jacob suggests they go in. Jacob addresses the man behind the counter: "Are you the owner?"
The pharmacist answers, "Yes."
Jacob: "We're about to get married. Do you sell heart medication?"
Pharmacist: "Of course we do."
Jacob: "How about medicine for circulation?"
Pharmacist: "All kinds."
Jacob: "Medicine for rheumatism, scoliosis?"
Pharmacist: "Definitely."
Jacob: "How about Viagra?"
Pharmacist: "Of course"
Jacob: "Medicine for memory problems, arthritis, jaundice?"
Pharmacist: "Yes, a large variety. The works."
Jacob: "What about vitamins, sleeping pills, Geritol, medicine for Parkinson's disease?"
Pharmacist: "Absolutely."
Jacob: "You sell wheelchairs and walkers?"
Pharmacist: "All speeds and sizes."
Jacob asks the pharmacist:
"Great. Can we use your store for our wedding registry?"

886   An old couple walking around a lake noticed a male and a female duck making love. The wife says to her husband, "You have never made so much love to me." The husband ignores her. They make a second loop around the lake and the ducks are still mating. The wife makes the same comment when the husband replies, "Did you notice it's a different female duck now?"

887   An old man was sitting on a bench at the mall.
A young man walked up to the bench and sat down. He had multi-colored spiked hair. The old man just stared.
The young man said, "What's the matter, old timer? Never done anything wild in your life?" The old man replied, "Got drunk once and had sex with a parrot. I was just wondering if you were my son."

888   After Christmas, a teacher asked her young pupils how they spent their holiday away from school. One child wrote the following: We always used to spend the holidays with grandma and grandpa.
They used to live in a big brick house but grandpa got retarded and they moved to Arizona. Now they live in a tin box and have rocks painted green to look like grass. They ride around on their bicycles and wear name tags because they don't know who they are anymore. They go to a building called a wrecked center, but they must have got it fixed because it is all OK now, and do exercises there, but they don't do them very well. There is a swimming pool too, but in it, they all jump up and down with hats on. At their gate, there is a doll house with a little old man sitting in it. He watches all day so nobody can escape. Sometimes they sneak out. They go cruising in their golf carts. Nobody there cooks, they just eat out. And, they eat the same thing every night: early birds. Some of the people can't get out past the man in the doll house.

889 The driver of a new car says to the owner, "I'm going to change gears." The owner asks, "Why are you changing the parts? It's a brand new car."

890 Mr. Singh is traveling for the first time on an airplane and is feeling very cold. He looks out the window and then walks up to the cockpit. He asks the pilots, "Can you turn those big fans outside off? It's getting really cold."

891 Mr. Singh tries to outsmart the train conductor by buying a return ticket even though he has no intention of returning.

892 Mr. Singh parked his scooter near a black car in a parking lot. Upon returning, he didn't see the scooter and was convinced that it was stolen. The black car had moved and Mr. Singh was looking for his scooter next to the black car.

893 Mr. Singh asked the bus conductor to hold the handle so that he could get the money from his pocket.

894 Mr. Singh goes to rent a flat and the landlord says, "A train passes by every night and makes noise but you will get used to it in a month." Mr. Singh quickly replies, "I will rent the flat after one month."

895 Mr. Singh was listening to the radio in Toronto which made an announcement that it was a New York radio station. He asked a local person, "Where is the Empire State building?"

896 Mr. Singh and his son are traveling on the train. He asks his son, "Where do you live?" His son replies, "In Dayton, Ohio." "What street?" "Washington Avenue." "Me too." "What apartment building?" "1309." "Me too." "What floor?" "22nd floor." "Me too.' "What apartment number?" "Number 5." "Me too." A third passenger is irritated and says, "Hey guys, you live in the same place and you don't know each other?" Mr. Singh says, "Yes, we do but we are just passing the time."

897 Four people are traveling on a train: 2 boys, a mother and her daughter. The train gets dark as it passes through a tunnel and suddenly there are two sounds: a kiss and a slap. No one is sure what happened.
The mother thinks a boy tried to kiss her daughter and she gave him a slap. The daughter thinks a boy kissed her mother and she gave him a slap. One boy thinks the other boy tried to kiss the girl and he got slapped.
The reality is that one boy kissed his own hand and slapped his friend for fun.

898 Mr. Singh was traveling on a train with a dog. He did not have a ticket for the dog. The conductor asked for a ticket for the dog. Mr. Singh asked, "If I have to buy a ticket for the dog how about the 100 lice in my hair?"

899 A pretty girl flying in a plane sat by a young man. The young man asked her not to disturb him during the flight. Later her dress went up and showed some of her privates. The young man instantly put a blanket on her thighs in order not to be disturbed.

900 A man and his wife are returning from vacation, where they decided to buy some pets. He bought a snake and the woman got a skunk.
As they pass through airport control, they notice a sign that says, "No animals will be allowed through without being quarantined"
Slightly distressed, the woman turns to her husband and asks what they should do. After thinking hard for a few minutes, the man says, "I'll tie the snake around my waist and try to pretend that it's a snake skin belt."
The woman asks, "But what about the skunk?"
"You'll just have to hide it up your skirt."
"But what about the smell?" she asks.
The man replies, "Look. If it dies, it dies."

901 Mr. Singh jumped into the ocean to save a child. The ship captain praised Mr. Singh and asked him to say a few words. Mr. Singh said, "Before I say a few words, I would like to know who pushed me in the water?"

902 A student is flying for the first time from Sri Lanka to the United States of America. While on the flight the student orders a cup of tea. The flight attendant brings out hot water, a tea bag, and a packet of sugar. The student opens the tea bag as oppose to just dropping it into the hot water. The flight attendant tells the student, "That is not the correct way to use the tea bag." She explains that in order to use the tea bag, you put it in as is. The student then proceeds in preparing his cup of tea. He drops the sugar packet into his cup of hot water. The flight attendant again approaches him and tells him, "That is not how you do it. The proper way is to open the sugar packet and pour it into the hot water."

903 Mr. Singh goes to a train track to kill himself. He carries a lunch bag with him just in case the train is late.

904 Mr. Singh entered a train and slept on the upper berth. At the railway station he complained to his friend that he could not sleep well on the upper berth. His friend said, "Why didn't you exchange the seat with the passenger sleeping on the lower berth?" Mr. Singh replied to his friend, "I couldn't ask him because no one was there."

905   A truck driver picks up a hitch hiker who asks the driver, "Aren't you going to ask me whether I'm a boy or a girl?" The driver says, "It doesn't matter. I'm going to screw you anyhow."

906   Mr. Singh wakes up in the hospital. He asks what happened. They say that he went to the toilet on the airplane and passed out. He says, "I was sitting there pushing the buttons to pass the time. Last thing I remember I was pushing a button labeled T.P." "Ah, that explains it. You pushed the Tampon Puller (T.P.) button. Your penis is under your pillow."

907   Mr. Singh went to the restroom at a train station and noticed lots of graffiti in the stall.   Inside the stall, someone wrote, "Turn your head to the right." Mr. Singh complied. On the right side of the stall, someone wrote, "Turn your head to the left." Again, Mr. Singh complied. On the right side, someone wrote, "Now look up." On the ceiling, someone wrote, "You idiot. Why are you looking all around? Finish your business because there is a line of people waiting."

908   A young man travels in a plane and looks at the beautiful air hostess and tells her that she looks like his wife – same figure, complexion, same features like cheeks and lips. She gets irritated and gives a bad look to the passenger, who comments that she not only resembles his wife, she has similar habits.

909   A driver asked the cop if he could park his car in the no parking zone. Reply- "No." "How come others have parked cars here?" Reply: "They never asked me."

910   A military man on a train asked a villager who has three brothers and one wife, "If a child does not resemble you what do you do?" Reply: "We send them to the military."

911   A boy applies for the job of a flagman at a Railway station. The interviewer asks, "If two trains come from opposite directions, what would you do?" Reply: "I will run home and call my brother."

912   A Bengali family of four and a Bihari were traveling on a train. The father was slapped by the Bihari for not giving him a seat. Then one by one all four members got slapped and then the Bengali gave a seat to the Bihari. The Bengali Dad did not want to be ridiculed by his family, kids and relatives at a wedding gathering in Delhi so he let all of them get slapped before giving a seat to the Bihari.

913   Four people died and a monkey survived in a car accident. The police asked the monkey what had happened. The monkey made a motion that dad was drunk, mom was talking on her cell and the kids were fighting. The police asked him what he was doing. He made a motion that he was driving.

914 An uneducated rowboat sailor was asked by an educated passenger: "Do you know Psychology?" Reply, "No." "Then 50% of your life is wasted." Again he asked, "Do you know sociology?" "No." "Then 75% of your life is wasted." Suddenly a big wave came and the sailor asked the passenger, "Do you know how to swim?" And the passenger says, "No." "Then 100% of your life is wasted."

915 Mr. Singh slept in a car which wouldn't go forward because there was no gas. Mr. Singh told his driver, "In that case, drive backwards."

916 Similarity between donkey and Mr. Singh - cute when they are born and they get into the transportation business when they grow up.

917 Three people were flying in an airplane. The American said, "We are flying over New York City because I saw the Statue of Liberty." The Arabian said, "We are flying over Kuwait because I smell oil." And an Indian said, "We are flying over Bombay because I lost my watch."

918 Mr. Singh sees a sign that says "Clean restrooms at every gas station." "It took a long time to reach my destination," says Mr. Singh. "I have been cleaning the restrooms at every gas station."

919 A lady bought a necklace with an airplane as a pendent. She asked her boyfriend, "How do you like my necklace?" Reply: "I like the airport more than the airplane."

920 The Police pulled a driver over and said, "You won $50 dollars for wearing your seat belt. What will you do with money?" The driver said, "Go to driving school and obtain a driver's license." His wife said, "My husband is much smarter when he is drunk so he will spend the money in a bar." A friend said, "I know he will be caught for a stolen car." A voice came from the trunk, "Have we crossed the boarder yet?"

921 A Texan, as usual, was trying to convince his friend that everything in his state was bigger, better, taller, hotter, colder, and more expensive, etc.
"Why, Texas is so big," he bragged to his Mexican friend, "that you can ride a train all day long, all night long, all day and night the next day and night – and still be in Texas."
"Yes, I know," replied his Latin neighbor. "We have slow trains in Mexico, too."

922   A passenger on a train visited the dining car and ordered a bowl of soup. When the soup arrived, it had a fly in it.

After his trip, the outraged passenger wrote a letter to the president of the railroad, expressing his dismay and vowing never to ride that railroad again.

He soon received a letter from the president, apologizing profusely, vowing that this was an unprecedented occurrence and explaining the steps that had been taken to ensure that it never happened again.

The passenger was almost persuaded until he discovered that the envelope also contained a small paper with his name and address and a handwritten notation: "Send this guy the bug letter."

923   Mr. Singh was traveling on a train. He felt sleepy so he gave the guy opposite his seat 50 rupees and asked him to wake him up when they arrived at the station. This guy was a barber, and he felt that for 50 rupees, Mr. Singh deserved more service. So when Mr. Singh was sleeping, he shaved off his beard. After the train arrived and Mr. Singh was at home, he went to wash his face, and suddenly screamed when he saw the mirror. His wife asked, "What is the matter?" Mr. Singh replied, "That cheat on the train took my 50 rupees and woke up someone else."

924   A suburbanite made a mad dash to catch his commuter train, but he just missed it. A bystander remarked, "If you had just run a little faster, you would have made it."

"No", the suburbanite replied, "It was not a case of running faster, but of starting sooner."

925   "Help! The ship is sinking."

Italian: "How far is the land from here?"

Mr. Singh: "Two miles."

Italian: "Why are these people making so much noise? I am an experienced swimmer."

The Italian jumps off the ship into the sea, then comes up to ask, "Which direction is the land?"

Mr. Singh: "Downwards."

926   A guy went to his travel agent and tried to book a two-week cruise for him and his lady friend. The travel agent said that all the ships were booked up but that he would see what he could do. A couple of days later, the travel agent phoned and said he could get them onto a three-day cruise. The guy was disappointed that it was such a short cruise, but booked it. He went to the drugstore to buy some Dramamine and three condoms. The next day, the agent called back and reported that he now could book a five-day cruise. The guy said, "Great, I'll take it!" and returned to the same pharmacy to buy more Dramamine and two more condoms. The following day, the travel agent called yet again, and said he was delighted that he could offer them an eight-day cruise. The guy was elated and went back to the drugstore. He asked for more Dramamine and three more condoms.

The pharmacist looked sympathetically at him and said, "Look, I'm not trying to pry but, if it makes you sick, why do you keep doing it?"

927   Three Indians and three Pakistanis are traveling by train to a Cricket match at the World Cup.

At the station, the three Pakistanis each buy a ticket and watch as the three Indians buy just one ticket for them all. "How are the three of you going to travel on only one ticket?" asks one of the Pakistanis. "Watch and learn," answers one of the Indians.

They all board the train. The Pakistanis take their respective seats and the three Indians cram into the bathroom and close the door behind them.

Shortly after the train departs, the conductor comes around collecting tickets. He knocks on the bathroom door and says, "Ticket please." The door opens just a crack and a single arm emerges with a ticket in hand. The conductor takes it and moves on. The Pakistanis see this and agree it was quite a clever idea.

So after the game, they decide to copy the Indian style on the return trip and save some money. When they get to the station, they buy one ticket for three on the return trip. To their astonishment, the Indians don't buy a ticket at all.

"How are you going to travel without a ticket?" says one perplexed Pakistani. "Watch and learn," answers an Indian. When they board the train, the three Pakistanis cram into one bathroom and soon after, the three Indians cram into another nearby bathroom. The train departs. Shortly afterwards, one of the Indian leaves the toilet and walks over to the toilet where the Pakistanis are hiding. He knocks on the door and says, "Ticket please." The door opens just a crack and a single arm emerges with a ticket in hand.

928   Three people were flying in an airplane. The American said, "We are flying over New York City because I saw the Statue of Liberty." The Arabian said, "We are flying over Kuwait because I smell oil." And an Indian said, "We are flying over Bombay because I lost my watch."

929 A girl's frock went up after a motorcycle accident. Mr. Singh comes to help her and puts his turban on her exposed female parts. His friend passes by and says, "Oh my God, my friend was trying to help this girl and got stuck inside and his turban is hanging out."

930 An international conference was held to rename the penis. The English man said we should call it gentleman, because it gets up when ladies come around. The New Yorker suggested that they call it curtain, because it drops when the act is over. The San Franciscan suggested that they call it a sword, because it stabs him in the back.

931 A visitor in a zoo accidentally touched the giraffe's testicles, which made him run very fast. The visitor was then asked by the zookeeper to touch his testicles so that he can run very fast to catch the giraffe.

932 A man asks a genie to grant him three wishes. First, he wants a BMW. Second, he wants a jet airplane. Third, he wants to be between a pretty lady's legs. So the genie turned him into a tampon…

933 An Italian man went to a sex therapist. The doctor asked him to show his sex organs to diagnose the problem. The Italian stuck out his tongue and middle finger.

934 A panty and slip meet for breakfast. The slip says, "You look sad." The panty says, "Yes, I've been down all night." The panty says, "You look tired." The slip says, "Yes, I've been up all night."

935 Mr. Singh was having problems attracting girls so he went to the beach and put on a Speedo. Still no response. His friend suggested he put a potato in the Speedo. Still no success, so he goes to his friend. His friend says, "You stupid, why did you put the potato in the back?"

936 A mother and son are walking in the park. The son kills a butterfly and the mother says, "No more butter for you." After a while, the son kills a honey bee. The mother says, "No more honey for you." Later, the mother accidentally steps on a cockroach. The son says, "No more cock for you!"

937 Mr. Singh saw a little girl swinging without any panties. He gave her $5 to buy a pair of panties. An old lady saw this and copied the girl. Mr. Singh noticed her and gave her $1 and asked her to buy a blade.

938 While watching a movie, a sailor is shaking his head from side to side. The prostitute sitting behind him tells him to stop shaking his head. He says that because he spent so much time on a ship, it happens automatically. The prostitute says, "So what? You don't see me thrusting my hips, do you?"

939 An alien couple traveling from the moon sees an Earth couple breathing fast and having sex.
The alien couple asks the couple "How do you produce babies on Earth?"
They say, "It will take nine months for the baby to come."
"Then what's the hurry?"

940 Did you hear about the patriotic impotent man? He always plays the National Anthem before sex so that his penis can stand up.

941 A lady fell down and her skirt flew up. She speedily got up, pulled her skirt down and asked her helper, "Did you see my speed?" "Yes, I saw your vagina but I didn't know its name."

942 Fashion show – A lady dresses up like a radio with 2 knobs. The judge says that the radio is not working. She replies that the plug is not in.

943 There are three types of bras: The Dictator for the masses, The Salvation Army for the fallen and the Civil Servant for making a mountain out of a mole hill.

944 Question on a T.V. program: Who was the first man in this world? Reply: Adam.
Who was the first woman in the world? Reply: Eve.
What were Eve's first words? Reply: It is hard.

945 A young girl asks the meaning of the Virgin Mary. Reply by her older sister, "A girl that does not have sex." The innocent young girl does not understand and tells her mother. "Mom, I am not a virgin." The mom is in shock and asks why. The girl replies, "Because I do have sense."

946 What is long and hard going in and soggy when it comes out? Chewing gum.

947 Girlfriends are like appetizers; they create excitement but don't satisfy the need. A wife is like dinner; they don't create excitement but satisfy the need.

948 Mr. Singh asked a woman for some milk for his tea. To his surprise, she gave natural milk from her breasts. Mr. Singh thought to himself, "I am lucky that I did not ask for lemonade."

949 A lady enters a country club wearing a two-piece bikini. The club staff informed her that only a one-piece suit is allowed. "OK. Which piece should I remove?" she asked.

950 In a nudist colony, a child asks his dad why do some men have a longer penis and others have a shorter penis. The dad replies, "Those who have a longer penis are smart and those who have a short penis are dumb." The child tells his dad that "Well, I just saw mom behind the bushes with a dumb man who is getting smarter by the minute."

951 There was a survey for men of girl's legs: 5% like thin legs, 5% like long legs and 90% like in-between legs.

952 Mr. Singh describes his experience of a trade show due to his thick accent - "His goods were selling like hot cocks."

953 Sign on the Statue of Liberty: "No cost to see lady but please pay $1 to enter lady."

954 A man had a tattoo of a dollar sign on his penis. When asked why, he gave three reasons: Men like to play with money, husbands like to see it grow and wives like to blow it.

955 A man lands on an island with 6 girls. He makes love with them Monday through Saturday. Then a homosexual man is there and he says,"I can make love only on Sunday."

956 A guy asked a bartender, "Do you serve women in your bar?" "No you have to bring your own."

957 A girl asks her boyfriend, "If I didn't wear a low-cut top and tight jeans, would you still find me attractive?" "I don't know. Let's find out."

958 A lady tells a thief she has no money. He starts touching her body to find money. She gets excited and tells him to keep on touching her and she will write him a check.

959 A policeman has a flashlight and sees a boy and a girl in a car. The boy says, "Sir, I did not do anything with her." The cop says, "OK, you hold the flashlight."

960 A man who had been walking around with his fly open asked his girlfriend, "Why didn't you tell me you could see my Cadillac in my garage?" "I only saw a Schwinn with 2 flat tires."

961 A white man asked his black friend why his penis is so long. The black man said, "My wife massages it with butter." The white man couldn't find any butter so he used Crisco and his penis became shorter. He went back to his friend and explained what happened. "Well, what do you expect? Crisco has shortening in it."

962 Three men are captured in the jungle and are about to be sacrificed. The tribe chief says that if their penis lengths add up to 18" they will be saved. The first man's penis is 9" long, the second man's penis is 6" long and third man's is 3". Each is bragging about the length of his penis. The third guy says, "thank God I had an erection."

963 A man sees a sign advertising cheap prostitution. He goes there and is asked to give $50 but does not receive any services. He complains and asks why. Reply: You have already been screwed and now you may go.

964 A father is having the birds and bees talk to his son and daughter. His daughter asks why she does not have a penis like her brother. Reply: if you have good behavior you will get a penis when you grow up and if you are naughty you will get many penises.

965 What do women and airplanes have in common? They both have a cockpit.

966 A bunch of prostitutes are standing outside the police station in a long queue. An old lady asked one prostitute what the line was for. She said the police were distributing candies. The old lady also stood in the line. The police asked the old lady, "What are you doing here? You don't even have teeth." She replied: "I don't have teeth but I can suck."

967 A lioness was raped in jungle. The lion called a meeting of all the animals. One mouse was dancing and very happy because the lion suspected him of raping his wife.

968 One day, a man visited an art museum. He was mesmerized by a painting of a woman wearing nothing but a few leaves over her private parts. After staring at it for hours, the docent approached him and said, "Why have you been fixated on this one painting?" He replied, "I'm just waiting for autumn to arrive so the leaves can fall."

969 Three men go to a night club. The first puts a $5 bill in a belly dancer's panties. The second one puts a $50 bill and the third one takes out his ATM debit card, swipes it through the dancer's crack and takes out $55 from her panties.

970 She: I did not know you had such a small organ.
He: I did not know I would have to play in such a large cathedral.

971 Two cowboys are out on the range one starry night talking about their favorite sex positions.
One says, "Ever have rodeo sex?"
"Ain't heard of that one," says the second cowboy, "What is it?"
"Well you get the girl down on all fours and you mount her from behind. Then you reach for her breasts, whisper in her ear, "Boy, these feel like your sister's" and see how long you can hang on."

972 Brian invited his mother over for dinner. During the course of the meal, Brian's mother could not help but notice how beautiful Brian's roommate, Stephanie, was. She had long been suspicious of a relationship between Brian and Stephanie and this had only made her more curious. Over the course of the evening, while watching the two react, she started to wonder if there was more between Brian and Stephanie than meets the eye. Reading his mom's thoughts, Brian volunteered, "I know what you must be thinking, but I assure you Stephanie and I are just roommates."
About a week later Stephanie came to Brian saying, "Ever since your mother came to dinner, I have been unable to find the beautiful silver gravy ladle. You don't suppose she took it, do you?"
Brian said, "Well I doubt it but I'll send her an e-mail just to be sure." So he sat down and wrote: "Dear mother, I am not saying that you did take the gravy ladle from the house. I am not saying you did not take the gravy ladle. But the fact remains that one has been missing ever since you were here for dinner. Love, Brian."
Several days later, Brian received an email from his mother that read, "Dear Son, I am not saying that you do sleep with Stephanie and I am not saying that you do not sleep with Stephanie. But the fact remains that if she were sleeping in her own bed, she would have found the gravy ladle by now. Love, Mom."

973 A female reporter was interviewing a farmer regarding mad cow disease.
Reporter: Sir, would you like to comment on mad cow disease?
Farmer: Lady, do you know that a bull and a cow only have sex once in a year?
Reporter: Sir, I respect your comments but we are asking about mad cow disease…
Farmer: Lady, and do you know that we squeeze a cow's breasts for milk four times a day? That equals 1,460 times a year.
Reporter: Sir, but what has it got to do with mad cow disease?
Farmer: Lady, if I were to squeeze your breasts four times a day for a year but you get SEX once a year, wouldn't you be mad?

974 Ever wonder why ABCDEF are used to define bra sizes?
A: Almost boobs. B: Barely there. C: Can do. D: Damn good. E: Enormous. F: Fake.

975 A man was complaining, "I hate sex in the movies. The seat never stays down, and the drink always spills, pouring ice everywhere, and the floor is always sticky."

976 A Japanese girl accidentally lets out a big fart after making love. She says, "Aww, so sorry. Exkooz me pleaso. Front hole so happy, back hole laugh out loud."

977 What is common between a swimming pool and a wife? For both we pay high maintenance for the little time we spend in them.

978 Love is like a complex machine. Sometimes all you need is a good screw.

979 Sex is like a card game. If you don't have a good partner, you better have a good hand.

980 Why is breast milk good for health? Because it is great for circulation, provides heat, is refreshing and comes in attractive containers.

981 Why was the two-piece bikini invented? To separate the meat section from the dairy section.

982 All men are terrorists. They always attack women on their twin towers and destroy their Pentagon.

983 Little Johnny greeted his mother at the door after she had been out of town all week and said, "Mummy, guess what? Yesterday, I was playing in the closet in your bedroom and daddy came into the room with the lady from next door and they got undressed and they got into bed and then daddy got on top of her and…" The mother held up her hand and said, "Not another word! Wait until your father gets home and then I want you to tell him exactly what you've just told me." The father came home and the wife told him that she was leaving him. "But why?" croaked the husband. "Go ahead Johnny, tell your Daddy just what you told me." "Well," said little Johnny, "I was playing in your closet and daddy came upstairs with the lady next door and they got undressed and they got into bed and daddy got on top of her and they did just what you did, mommy, with Uncle Bob when daddy was away last summer!"

984 A husband and wife are on a nudist beach when suddenly a wasp buzzes into the wife's private parts. Naturally enough, she panics. The husband is also quite shaken but manages to put a coat on her, pull up his shorts and carries her to the car. Then he makes a mad dash to the gynecologist.

The doctor, after examining her, says that the wasp is too far in to remove with forceps so he says to the husband that he will have to try and entice it out by putting honey on his penis and withdrawing as soon as he feels the wasp. And so the honey is smeared, but because of his wife's screaming and his frantic dash to the doctor and the general panic, he just can't rise to the occasion. So the doctor says he will perform the deed if the husband and wife don't object. Naturally both agree for fear that wasp will do any damage, so the doctor quickly undresses, smears the honey on and instantly gets an erection, at which time he begins to plug the wife. Only he does not stop and withdraw, but continues plugging her with vigor. As the doctor rapidly pounds the wife, the husband asks in shock, "What the hell are you doing?"

To which the doctor replies, "There has been a change in plans. I have decided to drown the little bastard."

985   Women and Geography:

Between the ages of 15 and 18 a woman is like China or Iran. Developing at a sizzling rate with a lot of potential but as yet still not free or open.

Between the ages of 18 and 21 a woman is like Africa or Australia. She is half discovered, half wild and naturally beautiful with bush land around the fertile deltas.

Between the ages of 21 and 30 a woman is like America or Japan. Completely discovered, very well developed and open to trade, especially with countries with cash or cars.

Between the ages of 30 and 35, a woman is like India or Spain. Very hot, relaxed and convinced of her own beauty.

Between the ages of 35 and 40 a woman is like France or Argentina. She may have been half destroyed during the war but can still be a warm and desirable place to visit.

Between the ages of 40 and 50 she is like Yugoslavia or Iraq. She lost the war and is haunted by the past mistakes. Massive reconstruction is now necessary.

Between the ages of 50 and 60, she is like Russia or Canada. Very wide, quiet, and the borders are practically unpatrolled, but the frigid climate keeps people away.

Between the ages of 60 and 70 a woman is like England or Mongolia. A glorious and all conquering past but alas, no future.

After 70 they become Afghanistan or Pakistan. Everyone knows where it is, but no one wants to go there.

986 A lot of people name their dogs Rover or Fido. I named mine Sex. He's a great pal, but he has caused me a great deal of embarrassment.

When I went to city hall to renew his dog license, I told the clerk, "I would like a license for Sex." The clerk said, "I would like one, too." Then I said, "But this is a dog." He said he did not care what she looked like. Then I said, "You don't understand I have had Sex since I was 9 years old." He winked and said, "You must have been quite a kid."

When I got married and went on my honeymoon, I took the dog with me. I told the motel clerk that I wanted a room for my wife and me and a special room for Sex.

He said, "You don't need a special room. As long as you pay your bill we don't care what you do." I said, "Look, you don't seem to understand. Sex keeps me awake at night." The clerk said, "Funny – I have the same problem."

One day I entered Sex in a contest, but before the competition began, the dog ran away. Another contestant asked me why I was standing there looking disappointed. I told him I had planned to have Sex in the contest. He told me I should have sold my own tickets.

"But you don't understand," I said, "I had hoped to have Sex on TV." He said, "Now that cable is all over the place, it's no big deal anymore."

When my wife and I separated, we went to court to fight for custody of the dog. I said, "Your honor, I had Sex before I was married," The judge said, "This courtroom is not for confession. Stick to the case, please."

Then I told him that after I was married, Sex left me. He said, "That is not unusual. It happens to a lot of people."

Last night Sex ran off again. I spent hours looking around town. A cop came over to me and asked, "What are you doing in this alley at 4 a.m.?" I told him that I was looking for Sex. My case comes up Friday.

987 The Grievance

I, the Penis, hereby request a raise in salary for the following reasons:

I do physical labor.

I work at great depths.

I plunge head first into everything I do.

I do not get weekends or public holidays off.

I work in a damp environment.

I work in a dark workplace that has poor ventilation.

I work in high temperatures.

My work exposes me to contagious diseases.

The Response:

Dear Penis,

After assessing your request, and considering the arguments you have raised, the administration rejects your request for the following reasons:

You do not work 8 hours straight.

You fall asleep after brief work periods.

You do not always follow the orders of the management team. You do not stay in your designated area and are often seen visiting other locations. You do not take initiative and need to be pressured and stimulated to start working. You leave the workplace rather messy at the end of your shift. You don't always observe necessary safety regulations, such as wearing the correct protective clothing. You will fully retire well before you are 65. You are unable to work double shifts. You sometimes leave your designated work area before completing your assigned task. And if that were not enough, you have been seen constantly entering and exiting the workplace carrying two suspicious-looking bags.

Sincerely,

The Management

988   A middle-aged woman decides to have a face lift for her birthday.

She spends $5,000 and feels pretty good about the results. On her way home, she stops at a newsstand to buy a newspaper. Before leaving she says to the clerk, "I hope you don't mind my asking, but how old do you think I am?"

"About 32," was the reply.

"I'm exactly 47," the woman says happily.

A little while later she goes into McDonald's and asks the counter girl the very same question. She replies, "I guess about 29."

The woman says, "Nope, I'm 47."

Now she's feeling really good about herself. She stops in a drugstore on her way down the street. She goes up to the counter to get some mints and asks the clerk this burning question. The clerk responds, "Oh, I'd say 30."

Again she proudly responds, "I am 47, but thank you."

While waiting for the bus to go home, she asks an old man the same question.

He replies, "Lady, I'm 78 and my eyesight is going. Although, when I was young, there was a sure way to tell how old a woman was. It sounds very

forward, but it requires you to let me put my hands under your bra. Then I can tell you exactly how old you are."

They waited in silence on the empty street until curiosity got the best of her. She finally blurts out, "What the hell, go ahead." He slips both of his hands under her blouse and under her bra and begins to feel around very slowly and carefully.

After a couple of minutes of this, she says, "OK, OK. How old am I?"

He completes one last squeeze of her breasts and removes his hands and says, "Madam, you are 47."

Stunned and amazed, the woman says, "That was incredible, how did you know?"

He says, "I was behind you in McDonald's."

989   A boy tells his father that he wants to learn to ride a horse. So, the father takes the boy to a stable that sells horses. The father inspects the horses, touching them from top to bottom to make sure he gets a good quality horse. On the way home, the son asks his father the reason for touching the horse from top to bottom. The father replies, "Before you buy anything, you should touch and feel it to make sure it's strong." The son replies, "Do you think the postman is trying to buy mom?"

990   Pussy or Bitch

After playing on the playground at school, Tommy came home with some new words in his vocabulary. Puzzled at what they meant, he went to his mother. "Mom, what's a pussy? " Not at all shocked by the question, she opened up an encyclopedia and showed him a picture of a cat. He then asked "What's a bitch?" Once again, not at all disturbed, she opened the encyclopedia and showed him a picture of a female dog.

Still confused, little Tommy then went to his father. "Dad, what's a pussy?" He felt that it was time for his son to learn about life and opened up a porno and circled the area between a woman's legs. Enlightened, he then asked him, "Then what's a bitch?" His father replied, 'Everything outside of the circle."

991   This Indian boy goes to his mother one day with a puzzled look.

"Mom, why is my bigger brother named Thunderstorm?"

She told him, "Because he was conceived during a mighty storm."

Then he asked, "Why is my sister named Cornflower?"

She replied, "Well, your father and I were in a cornfield when we made her."

"And why is my other sister called Moonchild?"

"Because we were watching the moon landing while she was conceived."

Thoughtfully, the mother paused and asked her son, "Tell me, Broken Rubber, why are you so curious?"

992   Men are like laxatives: They irritate the crap out of you.

Men are like bananas: The older they get, the less firm they are.

Men are like the weather: Nothing can be done to change them.

Men are like blenders: You need one, but you're not quite sure why.

Men are like chocolate bars: Sweet, smooth, and they usually head right for your hips.

Men are like commercials: You can't believe a word they say.

Men are like department stores: Their clothes are always 1/2 off.

Men are like government bonds: They take soooooooo long to mature.

Men are like mascara: They usually run at the first sign of emotion.

Men are like popcorn: They satisfy you, but only for a little while.

Men are like snowstorms: You never know when they're coming, how many inches you'll get or how long it will last.

Men are like lava lamps: Fun to look at, but not very bright.

Men are like parking spots: The good ones are taken, the rest are handicapped.

993 Joe and John were identical twins. Joe owned an old dilapidated boat and kept pretty much to himself. One day he rented out his boat to a group of out-of-staters who ended up sinking it. He spent all day trying to salvage as much stuff as he could from the sunken vessel. Unknown to him, his brother John's wife had died suddenly in his absence. When he got back on shore he went into town to pick up a few things at the grocery store. A kind old woman there mistook him for John and said, "I'm so sorry for your loss. You must feel terrible. Joe, thinking she was talking about his boat said, "Hell no! I'm sort of glad to be rid of her. She was a rotten old thing from the beginning. Her bottom was all shriveled up and she smelled like old dead fish. She had a bad crack in the back and a pretty big hole that leaked like crazy. I guess what finally finished her off was when I rented her to those four guys looking for a good time. I warned them that she wasn't very good and that she smelled bad. But they wanted her anyway. The darn fools tried to get in her all at one time and she split right up the middle."

The old woman fainted.

994 Two little boys go into the grocery store. One is 9 years old and the other one is 4 years old. The 9-year-old grabs a box of tampons from the shelf and carries it to the register for checkout.

The cashier asks, "Oh, these must be for your mom, huh?"

The 9-year-old replies, "Nope, not for my mom."

Without thinking, the cashier responds "Well, they must be for your sister then?"

The 9-year-old quips, "Nope, not for my sister either."

The cashier has now become curious "Oh. Not for your mom and not for your sister? Who are they for?"

The 9-year-old says, "They're for my 4-year-old little brother."

The cashier is surprised. "Your 4-year-old little brother?"

The 9-year-old explains: "Well yeah, they say on TV if you wear one of these, you can swim or ride a bike and my little brother can't do either of them!"

995   What are the three biggest tragedies in a man's life?
Life sucks, job sucks and the wife doesn't.

996   Four types of women having sex.
Asthmatic: ah…aahh…ah…ahh…
Obedient: yes…oh…yes…ah…yes.
Greedy: more…more…please.
Religious: oh God…oh…oh…

997   Mr. Singh wanted to have sex with a girl in his office, but she was seeing someone else.
One day, Mr. Singh got so frustrated that he went up to her and said, I'll give you a $100 if you let me shag you.
But the girl said no.
Mr. Singh said, "I'll be fast. I'll throw the money on the floor, you bend down, and I'll be finished by the time you pick it up."
She thought for a moment and said that she would have to consult her boyfriend.
So she called her boyfriend and told him the story.
Her boyfriend said, "Ask him for $200, pick up the money very fast, he won't even be able to get his pants down."
So she agreed and accepted the proposal.
Half an hour went by, and the boyfriend was waiting for his girlfriend to call.
Finally, after 45 minutes, the boyfriend called and asked what happened.
She responded, "The bastard used coins."

998   24 Reasons Why a Beer is Better Than a Woman

1. You can enjoy beer all month long.

2. Beer stains wash out.

3. You don't have to wine and dine a beer.

4. Your beer will always wait patiently for you and when a beer goes flat, you toss it.

5. Beer is never late.

6. Hangovers go away.

7. A beer doesn't get jealous when you grab another beer.

8. Beer never has a headache.

9. What you go to a bar, you know you can always pick up a beer.

10. After a beer, the bottle is still worth a nickel.

11. A beer won't get upset when you come home with beer on your breath.

12. If you pour a beer right, you know you'll always get good head.

13. You can have more than one beer a night and not feel guilty.

14. You can share a beer with your friend.

15. A beer always goes down easy.

16. You always know you're the first one to pop a beer.

17. A beer is always wet.

18. You can have a beer in public.

19. A beer doesn't care when you come.

20. A frigid beer is a good beer.

21. You don't have to wash a beer before it tastes good.

22. It's good to get a case of beer.

23. Aging is good for beer.

24. Having a beer with nuts is all right.

999   The Zipper

A man walked into a supermarket with his zipper down.

A lady cashier walked up to him and said, "Your barracks door is open."

Not a phrase that men normally use, he went on his way looking a bit puzzled. When he was about done shopping, a man came up and said, "Your fly is open."

He zipped up and finished his shopping.

At the checkout, he intentionally got in the line where the lady was that told him about his "barracks door." He was planning to have a little fun with her, so when he reached the counter he said, "When you saw my barracks door open, did you see a Marine standing in there at attention?"

The lady (naturally smarter than the man) thought for a moment and said, "No, no I didn't. All I saw was a disabled veteran sitting on a couple of old duffel bags."

1000   The Smiths were unable to conceive a child and decided to use a surrogate father to start their family. On the day the proxy father was to arrive, Mr. Smith kissed his wife goodbye and said, "Well, I'm off now. The man should be here soon."

Half an hour later, just by chance, a door-to-door baby photographer happened to ring the doorbell, hoping to make a sale.

Good morning. Ma'am, he said, "I've come to…"

"Oh, no need to explain," Mrs. Smith cut in, embarrassed, "I've been expecting you."

"Have you really?" said the photographer. "Well, that's good. Did you know babies are my specialty?"

"Well that's what my husband and I had hoped. Please come in and have a seat."

After a moment she asked, blushing, "Well, where do we start?"

"Leave everything to me. I usually try two in the bathtub, one on the couch, and perhaps a couple on the bed. And sometimes the living room floor is fun. You can really spread out there."

"Bathtub, living room floor? No wonder it didn't work out for Harry and me!"

"Well, Ma'am, none of us can guarantee a good one every time. But if we try several different positions and I shoot from six or seven angles, I'm sure you'll be pleased with the results."

"My, that's a lot!" gasped Mrs. Smith.

"Ma'am, in my line of work, a man has to take his time. I'd love to be in and out in five minutes, but I'm sure you'd be disappointed with that."

"Don't I know it," said Mrs. Smith quietly.

The photographer opened his briefcase and pulled out a portfolio of his baby pictures.

"This was done on the top of a bus," he said.

"Oh my God!" Mrs. Smith exclaimed, grasping her throat.

"And these twins turned out exceptionally well – when you consider their mother was so difficult to work with."

"She was difficult?" asked Mrs. Smith.

"Yes, I'm afraid so. I finally had to take her to the park to get the job done right. People were crowding around four and five deep to get a good look."

"Four and five deep?" said Mrs. Smith, her eyes wide with amazement.

"Yes," the photographer replied. "And for more than three hours, too. The mother was constantly squealing and yelling – I could hardly concentrate, and when darkness approached I had to rush my shots. Finally, when the squirrels began nibbling on my equipment, I just had to pack it all in."

Mrs. Smith leaned forward. "Do you mean they actually chewed on your, uh…equipment?"

"It's true, Ma'am, yes. Well, if you're ready, I'll set-up my tripod and we can get to work right away."

"Tripod?"

"Oh yes, Ma'am. I need to use a tripod to rest my Canon on. It's much too big to be held in the hand very long."

Mrs. Smith fainted.

LAUGHTER IS THE BEST THERAPY

For orders in the USA, please contact:
Singhvi Publications
4843 Preserve Parkway
Long Grove, IL USA 60047

Phone: 847-877-9682
Email: laughteristhebesttherapy@gmail.com
Price: U.S. $14.95 + shipping

For orders in India, please contact:
Dr. Jaichand and Santosh Baid
11 Rainwool Road (in front of Ram Bhavan)
Ajmer, Rajasthan INDIA

Phone: 145-2427111
Email: laughteristhebesttherapy@gmail.com
Price: India: Rs. 495 + shipping

Quantity discounts are available.

FEEDBACK
I hope you enjoyed the "Laughter is the Best Therapy" book and that it has helped you improve your mental health. We would be delighted to hear about your story and particular situation, as well as any feedback to improve future editions. If you have any new favorite jokes that should be included, please send those to us as well at the email address: ssinghvi@yahoo.com.

Dr. Surendra Singh Singhvi is a management consultant, former professor of finance at Miami University and University of New Hampshire and a senior finance executive at Armco Steel Corporation and Edison Brother Stores, Inc. He has published more than 100 articles and books in the United States, Canada, Europe, and India. He has a PhD in Management from Columbia University, an MBA from Atlanta University and a Bachelor of Commerce from Rajasthan University, Jaipur, India. He is a member of the Rotary Club of Dayton, Ohio, and a founder Trustee of Jain Center of Dayton and Cincinnati.

Mr. Sunit K. Jain is a senior level IT and sales executive at a Chicago based strategy and consulting firm. He received his MBA from Northwestern University, a Master's in Engineering from Cornell University, and a Bachelor's in Engineering from Rutgers University.

Mrs. Sushila Singhvi is a business associate. She received her Master of Arts in Psychology from the University of New Hampshire and a Bachelor of Arts from St. Xavier's College in Bombay, India. She is also involved in managing the family hotel business.